Interactive Reader and Study Guide

with Answer Key

HOLT McDOUGAL

United States Government
Principles in Practice

HOLT McDOUGAL
a division of Houghton Mifflin Harcourt

ISBN-13: 978-0-55-400813-4
ISBN-10: 0-55-400813-0

6 7 8 9 10   0982   16 15 14   4500467915

Contents

How to Use this Book

The *Interactive Reader and Study Guide* was developed to help you get the most from your United States Government course. Using this book will help you master the content of the course while developing your reading and vocabulary skills. Reviewing the next few pages before getting started will make you aware of the many useful features in this book.

Chapter Summary pages help you connect with the big picture. Studying them will keep you focused on the information you will need to be successful on your exams.

The Chapter Summary graphic organizers help you to summarize each chapter. They are a valuable study tool to help you prepare for important tests.

Answering each question will help you to understand the graphic organizer and ensure that you fully comprehend the content from the chapter.

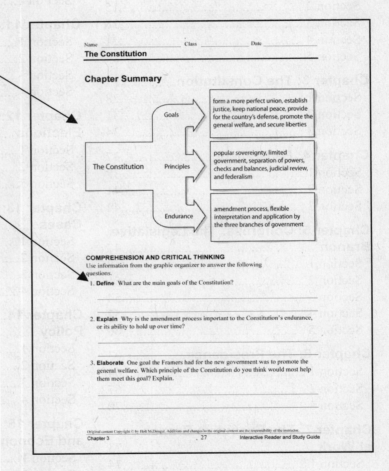

Name _____ Class _____ Date _____

The Constitution

Chapter Summary

The Constitution
- Goals → form a more perfect union, establish justice, keep national peace, provide for the country's defense, promote the general welfare, and secure liberties
- Principles → popular sovereignty, limited government, separation of powers, checks and balances, judicial review, and federalism
- Endurance → amendment process, flexible interpretation and application by the three branches of government

COMPREHENSION AND CRITICAL THINKING
Use information from the graphic organizer to answer the following questions.

1. **Define** What are the main goals of the Constitution?

2. **Explain** Why is the amendment process important to the Constitution's endurance, or its ability to hold up over time?

3. **Elaborate** One goal the Framers had for the new government was to promote the general welfare. Which principle of the Constitution do you think would most help them meet this goal? Explain.

Original content Copyright © by Holt McDougal. Additions and changes to the original content are the responsibility of the instructor.
Chapter 3   27   Interactive Reader and Study Guide

Section Summary pages allow you to interact easily with the content and key terms from each section.

Clearly labeled page headers make navigating the book very simple.

The Main Idea statement from your textbook focuses your attention as you read the summaries.

The Key Terms and People from your textbook are provided with their definitions, making studying them easier.

The Taking Notes graphic organizers will help you to summarize the important points of each section.

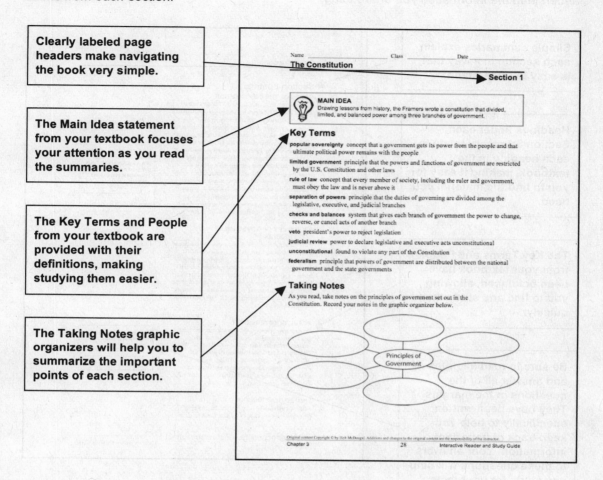

Name _____ Class _____ Date _____

The Constitution

Section 1

MAIN IDEA
Drawing lessons from history, the Framers wrote a constitution that divided, limited, and balanced power among three branches of government.

Key Terms

popular sovereignty concept that a government gets its power from the people and that ultimate political power remains with the people

limited government principle that the powers and functions of government are restricted by the U.S. Constitution and other laws

rule of law concept that every member of society, including the ruler and government, must obey the law and is never above it

separation of powers principle that the duties of governing are divided among the legislative, executive, and judicial branches

checks and balances system that gives each branch of government the power to change, reverse, or cancel acts of another branch

veto president's power to reject legislation

judicial review power to declare legislative and executive acts unconstitutional

unconstitutional found to violate any part of the Constitution

federalism principle that powers of government are distributed between the national government and the state governments

Taking Notes

As you read, take notes on the principles of government set out in the Constitution. Record your notes in the graphic organizer below.

Principles of Government

Chapter 3   28   Interactive Reader and Study Guide

Notes throughout the margins help you to interact with the content and understand the information you are reading.

Simple summaries explain each section in a way that is easy to understand.

Headings under each Section Summary relate to each heading in the textbook, making it easy for you to find the material you need.

The Key Terms and People from your textbook have been boldfaced, allowing you to find and study them quickly.

Be sure to read all notes and answer all of the questions in the margins. They have been written specifically to help you keep track of important information. Your answers to these questions will help you study for your tests.

Name _____ Class _____ Date _____
Section 1 *continued*

Section Summary

GOALS OF THE CONSTITUTION

As they wrote the Constitution, the Framers had six definite goals for the new national government: form a more perfect union; establish justice, or laws; insure domestic tranquility, or national peace; provide for the common defense of the country; promote the general welfare of states and citizens; and secure the blessings of liberties won by fighting the American Revolution.

Although they knew what the government had to do, the Framers were at first uncertain of how to create the government itself. They knew from recent experience what could happen when a government suppressed the natural rights of its citizens. But the Framers also knew that citizens needed certain laws for the new nation to survive. A strong national government would be able to enforce these laws.

> What were the Framers afraid would happen if they designed a national government that was too powerful?
> _____
> _____

PRINCIPLES OF GOVERNMENT IN THE CONSTITUTION

The Framers solved their dilemma over the balance of power by drawing upon six basic principles of governing: popular sovereignty, limited government, separation of powers, checks and balances, judicial review, and federalism. These principles ensure that the government's powers are subject to the will of the people and are presented in general terms throughout the Preamble, seven Articles, and 27 Amendments of the Constitution.

POPULAR SOVEREIGNTY

Popular sovereignty is the idea that a government gets it powers from the people it governs. The Framers began the Constitution with this idea: "We the People of the United States…do ordain and establish this Constitution…" Today, people participate in popular sovereignty in every election, when they choose and vote for the citizens they wish to lead their community, state, or country.

> How is voting a good example of popular sovereignty?
> _____
> _____

LIMITED GOVERNMENT

Limited government is the idea that the powers of government are restricted by the U.S. Constitution and

Chapter 3   29   Interactive Reader and Study Guide

Name _____ Class _____ Date _____

Foundations of Government

Chapter Summary

Around the world, governments have different purposes. These purposes vary according to the theory on which a government is based and how power is organized.	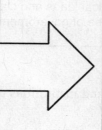	American democracy is built around the ideals of liberty, equality, and self-government, as well as a free-enterprise economic system.

COMPREHENSION AND CRITICAL THINKING

Use information from the graphic organizer to answer the following questions.

1. **Identify** What ideals characterize the U.S. government?

_____

_____

2. **Compare** Why do the purposes of governments differ?

_____

_____

3. **Develop** Judging from the core ideals of American democracy, what do you think are some of purposes of the U.S. government?

_____

_____

Foundations of Government

MAIN IDEA
Understanding major political ideas and classic forms of government will help you understand the purpose of government.

Key Terms

government the formal structures and institutions through which decisions are made for a body of people

power the government's authority and ability to get things done

policy any decision made by government in pursuit of a particular goal

state a political community made up by a group of people that lives within a clearly defined territory

sovereignty the supreme power of the state to act within its territory

politics the process by which government makes and carries out decisions as to whose interests will be served in society

legitimacy when rulers are seen as right and proper by important segments of a nation's population

divine right of kings a theory put forth by Jacques-Bénigne Bossuet that the king is answerable only to God, not the people he ruled

social contract theory theory of rule that says the first governments formed as a result of people agreeing among themselves to submit to the authority of a state, which in turn would protect and support them

Taking Notes

As you read, take notes on the purposes of government. Record your notes in a graphic organizer like this one.

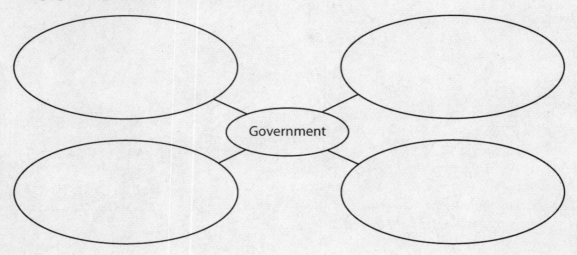

Government

Section Summary

WHAT IS GOVERNMENT?

Government is the formal structures and institutions through which decisions are made for a body of people. A government is a typically composed of three things: people, powers, and policies. The people of government include everyone from elected officials to public servants who carry out local, state, and national government business. A government's **power** is its authority and ability to get things done. In American government, this includes legislative, executive, and judicial powers. The **policies** of a government are any decisions it makes in pursuit of a goal, ranging from specific laws to general programs or actions.

CHARACTERISTICS OF A STATE

Most modern governments are run within a **state**, a political community made up by a group of people that lives within a clearly defined territory. A state is typically defined by four characteristics. First, a state is made up of territory, land whose formal borders are recognized by other states. Second, a state has a population. Third, a state has a government, recognized by its people, which creates and enforces laws. Finally, a state has **sovereignty**, or the supreme power to act within its own territory. Although this power does mean the government is the highest authority in the state, the government remains subject to the same laws as its people.

> **Give an example of a government decision that classifies as a policy.**
>
> _____
>
> _____
>
> _____

FUNCTIONS OF GOVERNMENT

Today, the majority of governments share five important functions. First, a government must ensure national security, often by both funding defense forces and by fostering international diplomacy.

Second, a government must maintain order. This function consists of establishing laws in order to protect people and property. The government is responsible both for enforcing these laws and for punishing those persons who refuse to follow them.

Third, a government needs to resolve conflict. It does this through **politics**, the process by which government makes and carries out decisions as to

> **The government is responsible for creating laws. What else is it expected to do with these laws?**
>
> _____
>
> _____

whose interests will be served in society. These decisions are made by officials elected by the state's people, many of whose wants and needs are very different. The government must therefore make compromises within the political process before creating new laws and enacting new programs.

Fourth, a government must provide the services its citizens need. These services are paid for with taxes, which are used to build roads, fund education, provide public housing, and much more.

Finally, the government must provide for the public good, or the needs and interests of the people as a whole. One example of government fulfilling this purpose is regulating food safety, an action that protects all Americans. As American society and culture has changed over the centuries, citizens and government have needed to reevaluate what defines "public good" and even "public."

> **Name another way the government provides for the public good.**
>
> _____
>
> _____

THEORIES OF RULE

There are various political philosophies as to why people allow governments to rule them. At the heart of these philosophies is the notion of **legitimacy**, the idea that rulers are seen as right and proper by important segments of a nation's population. People, therefore, will voluntarily accept governance.

In the past, European kings attempted to claim their legitimacy was a result of the **divine right of kings**, declaring that they received the right to rule from God directly. Yet many philosophers who came both before and after these claims did not agree. As far back as ancient Greece, philosophers wrote of natural law, a system of rules derived from the natural world that includes the idea that individuals possess natural rights. In the 1600s, **social contract theory**, which states that the first governments formed as a result of people agreeing among themselves to submit to the authority of the state, surfaced. Philosophers Thomas Hobbes, John Locke, and Jean-Jacques Rousseau built upon this theory, proposing ideas of government that depended on cooperation among citizens, consent of the governed in exchange for protection of natural rights, and a combination of a social contract and responsiveness to the "general will" of citizens.

> **Under the social contract theory, how were the first governments created?**
>
> _____
>
> _____
>
> _____

MAIN IDEA
Different forms of government are categorized based on who exercises authority and how power is organized.

Key Terms

monarchy a system of government headed by one person, such as a king or queen, who exercises absolute authority

dictatorship a system of rule in which one person, a dictator, or a small group of people can hold unlimited power over government

oligarchy a dictatorship led by a small group of people; means "rule by a few"

direct democracy a system of government in which citizens meet regularly in a popular assembly to discuss issues and vote for leaders

republic an indirect form of democracy that places political decision making at least one step away from the people; instead, people elect representatives to make decisions on their behalf

unitary system a system of government in which sovereignty, or ultimate authority, rests in a single national government

federal system a system of government in which power over people and territory is divided between a national government and smaller, regional levels of government

confederal system a system of government in which a confederation of independent states form a central government to pursue common interests

presidential system a system of government distinguished by having a president who is elected by the people for a limited term of office

parliamentary system a system of government in which the legislative and executive branches are combined

Taking Notes

As you read, takes notes on different types of government systems. Record your notes in a chart like this one.

Form	Details

Section Summary

THE CLASSIC FORMS

The most common form of government in world history has been the **monarchy**, a system of government headed by one person who inherits power, such as a king or queen. In an absolute monarchy, the monarch's power is unlimited, but in the more common constitutional monarchy, the monarch is a ceremonial figure, less powerful than other parts of the government.

In a **dictatorship**, one person—called a dictator—or a group of people—called an **oligarchy**—hold unlimited power over government. The strength of dictators, who have usually taken over the former government by force, varies. Some are independent of religion; others, called theocracies, are linked closely to religion. The most powerful are totalitarian governments, which attempt to dominate all aspects of society, including religion and the economy.

Democracy, literally meaning "rule by the people," is a much different form of government. In a **direct democracy**, citizens meet regularly to discuss and address issues and vote directly for leaders. Since this system is hard to accomplish in large nations, many countries, including the United States, choose to be **republics** (sometimes called representative democracies). In a republic, the people elect representatives to make decisions for them.

> Is a monarch more powerful in a constitutional monarchy or an absolute monarchy?
>
> _____
>
> _____

> What is the difference between a direct democracy and a republic?
>
> _____
>
> _____
>
> _____

ORGANIZING NATIONAL POWER

There are a variety of ways in which countries govern their smaller administrative units, such as states, cities, and provinces. Most countries employ the **unitary system**, through which ultimate authority, or sovereignty, rests in a single national government. While local governments can still exist in the unitary system, the national government can overrule their decisions and even abolish them completely.

In a **federal system**, invented by the Framers of the U.S. Constitution, power over people and land is divided between the national government and regional levels of government, such as state governments. Unlike a unitary system, in a federal system neither level of government can abolish the other nor can each operate completely independently of the other.

The third organizational form of national power, the **confederal system**, is uncommon today. Under this system, independent states govern their own people and land while still maintaining a weak central government. This central government is only responsible for functions important to the group of states, or confederation, such as defense and trade.

What is the difference between regional levels of government in a federal system and those in a confederal system?

_____

_____

_____

PRESIDENTS AND PARLIAMENTS

Democracies, though they can vary somewhat in structure, follow either a presidential political system or a parliamentary political system. The United States' government is an example of a **presidential system**. In this system, besides acting as the head of state, the president is also the head of the executive branch. His or her duties as chief executive range from setting foreign policy to appointing cabinet members to introducing legislation.

Since the U.S. government structure includes separation of powers, the president's authority is balanced by the way the legislature can check his or her actions. The president and Congress must work together to make sure the daily business of government gets done. Unfortunately, this system of divided government can sometimes result in political gridlock; when the president and Congress disagree, the political process can come to a halt.

Gridlock is less of a problem in **parliamentary systems** since the executive and legislative branches are one entity. Members of the legislature, called parliament, are elected by the people. These officials in turn choose the prime minister, who is both the head of state and the leader of the majority party in parliament. If the prime minister loses support of his or her party, he or she must resign, at which points parliament chooses another head of state.

Why is gridlock less of a problem in parliamentary systems?

_____

_____

_____

Critics of the parliamentary system feel that it is wrong that the voting public cannot directly elect a prime minister and that the prime minister is too much under the control of parliament. But supporters believe that it is easier to pass laws in this kind of united system than in the presidential system.

Foundations of Government

MAIN IDEA
American democracy is characterized by core democratic ideals and principles, as well as by the free enterprise system.

Key Terms

ideal a conception of something in its most perfect form

liberty the ability of people to act and think as they choose, as long as their choices do no harm to the liberty or well-being of others

equality the principle that all people possess a fundamental, moral worth that entitles them to fair treatment under the law and equal opportunity in all aspects of life

self-government the belief that ordinary people could aspire to rule themselves and do so as political equals

majority rule a decision-making system in which the candidate who receives more than half the votes cast, or more votes than any other candidate, wins the election

minority rights the political rights held by groups who make up less than half of the population

liberal democracy a form of democracy that protects the rights of the minority

free enterprise an economic system in which people and businesses make their own choices about how best to produce, distribute, and exchange goods and services, with limited interference from the government

Taking Notes

As you read, take notes on democracy in the United States. Record your notes in a graphic organizer like this one.

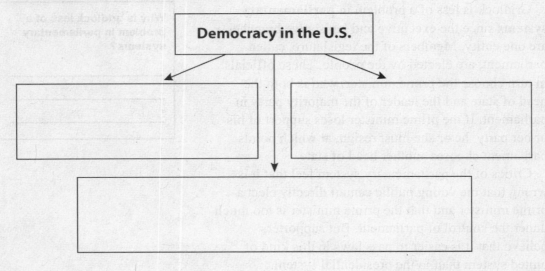

Section Summary

IDEALS OF AMERICAN DEMOCRACY

American democracy is centered around three **ideals**, or conceptions of something in its most perfect form: liberty, equality, and self-government. Over the centuries, these ideals have been applied to more and more of the American population—an excellent example of how American democracy is constantly evolving.

Liberty, also called freedom, is the ability of people to think and act as they choose, so long as their choices do not harm the liberty or well-being of other people. The Framers designed the Constitution and the Bill of Rights to specifically protect this ideal. For example, Americans' basic rights are protected from government interference by the First Amendment, which protects free speech, assembly, the press, and religion. The Framers also ensured that Americans would be able to exercise these protected rights, such as exercising their right to counsel or to vote.

Equality, the second ideal, is the principle that all people possess a fundamental, moral worth that entitles them to fair treatment under the law and equal opportunity. Yet some groups of Americans, including Native Americans and enslaved African Americans, were not always treated with equality. The American people and their government have had to make changes to guarantee that equality in its fullest form does indeed exist and is adequately balanced with the ideal of liberty.

Self-government is the third ideal at the heart of American democracy. This ideal is the belief that ordinary people can aspire to rule themselves and can do so as political equals. The Declaration of Independence proclaimed the importance of self-government to the American colonists, and the American Revolution was fought to make self-government possible. Under self-government, the power of the government lies primarily with the people, who have the right to keep or abolish the government as they see fit.

> How is Americans' freedom of speech an example of liberty?
> _____
> _____

> Explain equality in your own words.
> _____
> _____
> _____
> _____

PRINCIPLES OF AMERICAN DEMOCRACY

Five key principles underlie the success and continuity of American democracy. First, the worth of the individual is held in high esteem. If a person is allowed to pursue his or her own individual freedoms and ambitions, the Framers believed, he or she is more likely to reach their highest potential.

Second, American democracy depends on the rule of law. According to this principle, no government official is above the law.

Third, both **majority rule**, the idea that the candidate with more than half of votes cast or more votes than any other candidate wins, and **minority rights**, the political rights of those who make up less than half of the population, are respected. This mutual protection of rights is an example of how American democracy is also a **liberal democracy**, a form of democracy that protects the rights of the minority.

Fourth, compromise is key to the success of democracy. Faced with the diverse needs and wants of Americans, opposing groups in government must compromise in order to continue the political process.

Finally, American democracy depends on the participation of citizens. People must educate themselves on issues in order to vote wisely, hold their leaders accountable, protest what they consider wrongful government actions, and generally be as involved as possible in the political process.

> **Why is liberal democracy necessary to American democracy?**
> _____
> _____
> _____

FREE ENTERPRISE

Economic freedom is the basis of the American **free enterprise** system, which allows people and businesses to make their own economic choices about how best to produce, distribute, and exchange goods and services. Furthermore, free enterprise protects the products and services a person produces and his or her other private property.

In this kind of free market, the government is largely uninvolved. The theory behind this design is that with little government interference, people and businesses will compete to offer better products at lower prices. As the American economy has evolved, some government intervention has become necessary; however, the national economy remains mainly open.

> **Why is it important that government plays only a minor role in a free market?**
> _____
> _____
> _____

Origins of American Government

Chapter Summary

```
┌─────────────────────┐     ┌─────────────────────┐     ┌─────────────────────┐
│ American colonists  │     │ New British policies│     │ The U.S. government │
│ were inspired by    │ ──▶ │ led to colonial     │ ──▶ │ under the Articles  │
│ their political     │     │ rebellion and       │     │ of Confederation    │
│ heritage and        │     │ eventually war.     │     │ was ineffective.    │
│ intellectual        │     │                     │     │                     │
│ influences.         │     │                     │     │                     │
└─────────────────────┘     └─────────────────────┘     └─────────────────────┘
```

```
┌─────────────────────┐     ┌─────────────────────┐
│ Delegates at the    │     │ Supporters and      │
│ Constitutional      │     │ opponents of the    │
│ Convention          │ ──▶ │ Constitution        │
│ compromised to      │     │ debated its         │
│ create a new system │     │ ratification in     │
│ of government.      │     │ all the states.     │
└─────────────────────┘     └─────────────────────┘
```

COMPREHENSION AND CRITICAL THINKING

Use information from the graphic organizer to answer the following questions.

1. **Describe** What prompted colonists to rebel in the mid-1700s?

   _____

   _____

2. **Analyze** Were you surprised to learn that the Constitution was heavily debated before it was ratified? Explain.

   _____

   _____

3. **Elaborate** After the country's experience with the Articles of Confederation, why do you think the compromises made at the Constitutional Convention were so important?

   _____

   _____

Origins of American Government

 MAIN IDEA
American democracy was shaped by our English political heritage, colonial experiments in self-government, as well as a range of intellectual influences.

Key Terms

bicameral two-chamber

Magna Carta an English document signed by King John in 1215 that instituted that "rule of law" and protected certain individual rights

Petition of Right an English document signed by King Charles in 1628 that required monarchs to obtain Parliament's approval before levying new taxes and said that monarchs could not unlawfully imprison people, force citizens to house soldiers, or establish military rule during times of peace

English Bill of Rights an English document passed by Parliament in 1689 that limited monarchs' power to enact laws, raise taxes, or keep an army without Parliament's consent; guaranteed Parliament the privilege of free speech; and gave all people protection from cruel and unusual punishment

Fundamental Orders of Connecticut a 1639 set of laws that limited the power of the government and gave all free men the right to choose the people to serve as judges

proprietary colony a colony based on a grant of land by the English monarch to a proprietor

royal colonies colonies directly controlled by the king through an appointed governor

charter colonies colonies operated under charters agreed to by the colony and the king

Taking Notes

As you read, take notes on the political ideas and historical events that shaped government in the English colonies. Record your notes in the graphic organizer below.

Ideas	Events

Section Summary
ENGLISH POLITICAL HERITAGE

When the first English settlers arrived in North America, they brought their political heritage with them, ready to adjust it as necessary for their new home. This heritage included the idea of representative government, which in England had evolved from a king's advisory council to a **bicameral**, or two-house, legislature called Parliament. This legislature was made up of the noble-dominated House of Lords and the less prestigious House of Commons who worked to limit the power of English monarchs. One of the first efforts toward limited government was **Magna Carta**. This English document signed by King John in 1215 instituted the "rule of law" and eventually protected the individual rights of most citizens.

England's focus on protecting individual rights further developed with the creation of the 1628 **Petition of Right**. This document, which was signed by King Charles, required monarchs to obtain Parliament's approval before levying new taxes and banned monarchs from unlawfully imprisoning people, forcing citizens to house soldiers, or establishing military rule during times of peace. In the years that followed, Parliament's power grew and the monarchy's authority weakened, circumstances that eventually led to a constitutional monarchy. The **English Bill of Rights** greatly contributed to this, forbidding monarchs to enact laws, raise taxes, or keep an army without Parliament's consent; guaranteeing Parliament the privilege of free speech; and giving all people protection from cruel and unusual punishment.

THE ENGLISH COLONIES

As they settled the colonies, the English settlers drew on their political heritage to establish societies and laws. The Jamestown House of Burgesses, established in 1619, was an experiment in representative democracy, and the Mayflower Compact was an agreement to govern according to majority rule and the consent of the people. In 1639 the **Fundamental Orders of Connecticut**, a set of laws that limited the

> What ideas of government did settlers bring with them from England?
>
> _____
> _____
> _____
> _____

power of the government and gave all free men the right to choose the people to serve as judges, was approved by Connecticut colonists. Laws adopted within the Massachusetts Bay Colony also protected several individual rights.

However, all of these laws and practices were created within colonies that existed under charters, or agreements by which the English king gave settlers the right to establish a colony and promised them "the rights of Englishmen." There were three types of colonies. A **proprietary colony** was based on a grant of land by the English monarch to a proprietor, who could appoint all officials and make all laws. A **royal colony** was directly controlled by the king through an appointed governor. Royal colonies had two-house legislatures, in which members of the lower house were elected but members of the upper house were appointed by the king. Finally, a **charter colony** operated under charters agreed to by the colony and the king and therefore had the most independence. Colonists elected a legislature that made laws and appointed a governor. By the time the American Revolution began, there were only two charter colonies, and the king's attempts to control royal colonies—which most other colonies were at that time—greatly angered colonists.

How did royal colonies differ from charter colonies?
_____
_____
_____

INTELLECTUAL INFLUENCES

The developing American democracy also drew on intellectual influences outside of Great Britain. The Framers of the U.S. Constitution would turn to ancient Greek and Roman scholars, Renaissance scholar Niccolò Machiavelli, and French philosopher Charles de Montesquieu for ideas about republicanism, or representative government, and the role the people should play within a republic. The Framers would also incorporate Judeo-Christian beliefs in human equality and the divine origin of rights into their design for a new American government. Finally, the Framers reviewed the thoughts of Enlightenment thinkers like John Locke and Jean-Jacques Rousseau in order to best understand ideas such as natural rights and economic and civil liberties.

What ideas did the Framers borrow from Enlightenment thinkers?
_____
_____
_____
_____

Origins of American Government

MAIN IDEA
The British imposed new policies on the American colonies, sparking rebellion, and in time, the American Revolution.

Key Terms

New England Confederation confederation formed between the Plymouth, Connecticut, Massachusetts Bay, and New Haven colonies to defend against Native Americans and nearby Dutch colonies

Iroquois Confederation a powerful alliance of six Native American nations—the Mohawk, Oneida, Onondaga, Cayuga, Seneca, and Tuscarora

Albany Plan of Union a plan proposed by Benjamin Franklin that called for a council of representatives appointed by the colonial assemblies and a president general appointed by the king

Stamp Act Parliament's first attempt to tax American colonists directly, which required a government tax stamp on paper goods and all legal documents

First Continental Congress first general meeting of the colonies in Philadelphia, Pennsylvania, called by the Virginia and Massachusetts assemblies at which delegates sent King George III the Declaration of Resolves

Second Continental Congress second general meeting of the colonies in Philadelphia, Pennsylvania, at which delegates took strong measures against the Crown

Virginia Declaration of Rights declaration issued by the Virginia House of Burgesses that proclaimed "all men are by nature equally free and independent and have certain inherent rights" and that likely inspired parts of the Declaration of Independence

Taking Notes

As you read, take notes on the causes and effects of the American Revolution. Record your notes in the graphic organizer below.

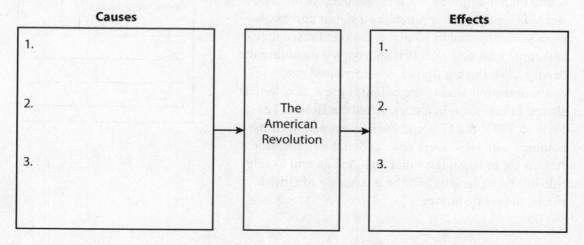

Causes

1.

2.

3.

The American Revolution

Effects

1.

2.

3.

Section Summary

THE ROAD TO INDEPENDENCE

The American colonies first took steps toward unity in 1643, with the creation of the New **England** **Confederation**, formed between the Plymouth, Connecticut, Massachusetts Bay, and New Haven colonies to defend themselves against Native Americans and nearby Dutch colonies. Later, in 1754 and during the French and Indian War, the British government asked the colonies to sign a treaty with the **Iroquois Confederation**, a powerful alliance of six Native American nations—the Mohawk, Oneida, Onondaga, Cayuga, Seneca, and Tuscarora—whose support would help the British defeat the French. Not long after, Benjamin Franklin, inspired by what he had learned about Iroquois government, proposed the **Albany Plan of Union**, which called for a council of representatives appointed by the colonial assemblies and a president general appointed by the king. While both the colonial assemblies and the British government rejected Franklin's proposal, it would eventually inspire the U.S. Constitution.

By the mid-1700s, there were more reasons for colonial unifications. Beginning with 1764's Sugar Act, Great Britain began imposing new trade restrictions and taxes on the colonists. The colonists had no representation in Parliament and felt that taxes imposed by anyone outside of colonial assemblies were unfair, especially after the passage of the 1765 **Stamp Act**, Parliament's first attempt to tax American colonists directly that required a government tax stamp on paper goods and all legal documents. The Act was repealed after much protest, but new taxes were soon imposed in its place. Colonial resistance and confrontations with British troops—including the deadly 1770 Boston Massacre—increased, and communication among the colonies grew as colonists shared information in letters. After the Boston Tea Party in 1773, the king and Parliament punished the colonies with what were soon called the Intolerable Acts, a set of harsh laws that included an end to self-rule in Massachusetts and the quartering of British troops in private homes.

> **What was the purpose of the New England Confederation?**
> _____
> _____
> _____

> **Why did the American colonists feel that the new taxes were unfair?**
> _____
> _____
> _____
> _____

THE CONTINENTAL CONGRESSES

Despite the Intolerable Acts, most colonists hoped a compromise could be reached that would lead to a removal of the taxes. To this end, the **First Continental Congress**, the first general meeting of the colonies in Philadelphia, Pennsylvania, met in fall of 1774. Delegates issued a Declaration of Resolves, which included a call for a repeal of the Intolerable Acts. After their demands were rejected, the colonies met in the **Second Continental Congress**, a second general meeting where delegates organized the Continental Army. Once a last petition to the king was rejected, the Congress organized as a government and prepared for war—and independence. Thomas Paine's bestselling political pamphlet *Common Sense* supported the Congress's decisions, declaring that independence was now a "common sense" action and inspiring hundreds of thousands of colonists.

> **What did the Second Continental Congress prepare for once the king rejected their last petition?**
>
> _____
> _____
> _____

THE DECLARATION OF INDEPENDENCE

On July 2, 1776, delegates at the Continental Congress passed a resolution to declare independence from Great Britain. Virginia delegate Thomas Jefferson wrote most of the resolution's formal statement within a two-week period in June, probably drawing heavily on the **Virginia Declaration of Rights**, a declaration issued by the Virginia House of Burgesses that proclaimed "all men are by nature equally free and independent and have certain inherent rights." The resulting Declaration of Independence, adopted on July 4, reflected the philosophy of John Locke, discussing people's "unalienable" natural rights and the need for the "consent of the governed." A new nation had been formed.

THE STATE CONSTITUTIONS

By 1780 all 13 colonies had adopted written constitutions, which included ideas about republicanism that would soon influence the U.S. Constitution. While voting rights varied, all of the constitutions established legislatures of elected representatives, as well as judicial and executive branches, and limited the powers of the legislative and executive branches. Many also included bills of rights.

> **What did the state constitutions have in common?**
>
> _____
> _____

Section 3

MAIN IDEA
The states' first attempts to build a national government, the Articles of Confederation, proved too weak to last.

Key Terms

Articles of Confederation the first constitution of the United States

ratify formally approve

Northwest Ordinance 1787 legislation that established a plan for settling the Northwest Territory

Shays's Rebellion a rebellion of Massachusetts farmers who were angry at the prospect of losing their land

Taking Notes

As you read, take notes on the advantages and disadvantages of the Articles of Confederation. Record your notes in the graphic organizer below.

The Articles of Confederation	
Advantages	Disadvantages

Section Summary

FIRST NATIONAL GOVERNMENT

In anticipation of declaring independence, the Second Continental Congress began designing a plan for a national government in June 1776. By June 12, 1777, the Congress adopted the first constitution of the United States, the **Articles of Confederation**, a name reflective of the friendly confederation the delegates wished the former colonies to become.

However, not all of the states were ready to **ratify**, or formally approve, the Articles. In particular, small states were afraid that large states with claims to western lands would become too powerful. Once the Congress agreed that the entire Confederation would control the Western lands, ratification was completed in 1781.

The Articles left most power to the states, creating only a weak federal government with no executive or judicial branches. While a one-house legislature called Congress was created—in which each state had one vote—at least nine states would have to approve legislation in order to pass it, and the approval of all 13 was needed to approve any changes to the Articles themselves. Congress was given the power to act on matters of common interest to the states, admit new states and organize western lands, organize a postal service, coin and borrow money, appoint military officers and raise an army, declare war, make peace, and conduct foreign policy. The states retained all other powers, including those to collect taxes, enforce national laws, and contribute funds to the national government as they deemed necessary.

> **How would legislation pass in the new Congress, according to the Articles of Confederation?**
>
> _____
> _____
> _____

WEAKNESSES OF THE ARTICLES

There were many problems with the Articles of Confederation, including the lack of a federal executive branch to carry out laws and a federal court system to apply them. Also, since the Articles did not allow Congress to tax the states, it had no formal way of raising money—and the states chose not to contribute much. Furthermore, Congress could not regulate commerce between states, even when interstate tax laws were unfair, and its power to coin money conflicted with the states' same power,

> **Did the new national government successfully raise money? Explain.**
>
> _____
> _____

resulting in several different currencies in circulation.
Finally, very rarely did 9 of the 13 states agree to pass
legislation, making it difficult for Congress to act
decisively.

PRESSURES FOR STRONGER GOVERNMENT

It gradually became obvious to Americans and their
new government that the Articles of Confederation
would not work as a constitution. While in 1787
Congress did manage to pass the **Northwest
Ordinance**—legislation that established a plan for
settling the Northwest Territory, banned slavery in the
territory, created a system for admitting new states,
and guaranteed certain rights to settlers—it met little
success in other areas, especially when it came to
raising money to pay national war debts. Events such
as **Shays's Rebellion**, a rebellion by thousands of
Massachusetts farmers angry at the prospect of losing
their land, highlighted Congress's military and
economic weaknesses.

In March 1785, George Washington and
representatives from Virginia and Maryland met at
Washington's Mount Vernon home to discuss how to
resolve a trade dispute between the states. When the
talks were successful, certain state officials were
inspired to ask Congress to call a meeting of all the
states to revise the Articles of Confederation. The
meeting was scheduled for May, 1787 in Philadelphia.

> **What happened in
> Massachusetts that further
> highlighted Congress's
> weaknesses?**
> _____
> _____

> **MAIN IDEA**
> Delegates at the Constitutional Convention compromised on key issues to create a plan for a strong national government.

Key Terms

Framers the delegates to the Constitutional Convention

Virginia Plan a proposed plan for government that called for a strong central government divided into three branches—legislative, executive, and judicial—each with the power to check the others; included a bicameral legislature in which membership would be based on a state's population

New Jersey Plan another proposed plan for government that called for a strong central government divided into three branches; included a unicameral legislature in which each state would get one vote

Great Compromise plan of government that combined elements of the Virginia and New Jersey plans; included a bicameral legislature in which membership in one house would be based on state population and membership in the other would be limited to two members per state

Three-Fifths Compromise the resolution to a dispute over how enslaved people should be counted within a population; provided that three-fifths of the enslaved people in a state would be counted when determining a state's population

Taking Notes

As you read, take notes on the writing of the U.S. Constitution. Record your notes in the graphic organizer below.

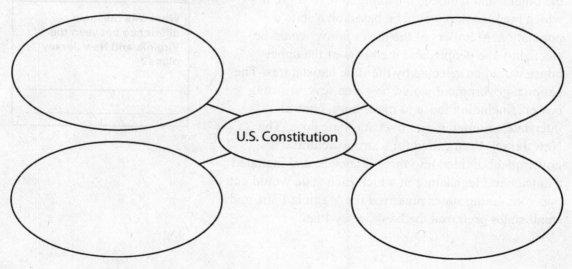

Section Summary

DRAFTING A NEW CONSTITUTION

On May 25, 1787, 12 of the 13 states—Rhode Island chose not to participate—met in Philadelphia to revise the Articles of Confederation—a task that would soon change to designing an entirely new government. Delegates kept all meeting proceedings confidential. Each state received one vote and only a simple majority was required for any decisions. Almost all of the attendees had some form of government experience, and many had served in the Continental Army. George Washington served as president of the convention. James Madison—now known as Father of the Constitution—played a key role in planning the convention and calling for a new government. Today, all delegates at the convention are called **Framers** of the Constitution.

> **Did large states have more voting power than small states at the convention? Explain.**
> _____
> _____
> _____

RIVAL PLANS

Only days into the convention, it became clear to delegates that the Articles of Confederation would need to be replaced with a plan for a stronger government. Two plans were proposed shortly thereafter.

The **Virginia Plan** called for a strong central government divided into three branches—legislative, executive, and judicial—each with the power to check the others, and included a bicameral legislature in which membership would be based on a state's population. Members of the lower house would be elected by the people, and members of the upper house would be selected by the state legislatures. The national government would be given several strong powers, including those to make laws, control interstate commerce, and override state laws. The **New Jersey Plan** called for a strong central government divided into three branches, and included a unicameral legislature in which each state would get one vote. Large states preferred the Virginia Plan, and small states preferred the New Jersey Plan.

> **What was the main difference between the Virginia and New Jersey plans?**
> _____
> _____

CONFLICT AND COMPROMISE

After a long period of deadlock, delegates finally agreed to an alternate plan on July 16, 1787. The **Great Compromise**, as it became known, combined elements of the Virginia and New Jersey plans. It included a bicameral legislature in which membership in the lower house, the House of Representatives, would be based on state population and membership in the upper house, the Senate, would be limited to two members per state. House members would be elected by the people and Senate members would be selected by the state legislatures.

With a decision on the design of government finalized, delegates next needed to compromise on issues surrounding slavery. The first issue involved how enslaved people should be counted as part of a state's population. The **Three-Fifths Compromise** eventually settled this dispute between northern and southern delegates by providing that three-fifths of the enslaved people in a state would be counted when determining a state's population. Delegates also reached a compromise on the future importation of slaves, which the northern delegates resisted but southern delegates supported. It was agreed that the Atlantic slave trade would be protected from interference by Congress until 1808—in exchange for the agreement that only a simple majority would be needed in each house of Congress to regulate commerce.

Delegates also compromised on how the president should be elected. The president would be chosen by state electors—who themselves could be elected by the people—unless no one candidate received a majority of votes, in which case the House of Representatives would choose the president.

By September 1787, a constitution reflecting the delegates' decisions and compromises was complete. Thirty-nine delegates from 12 states signed the document—three delegates abstained because of the absence of a Bill of Rights—and the convention adjourned on September 17. The American people would now need to ratify the new U.S. Constitution.

> **How were enslaved people counted as part of the population under the Three-Fifths Compromise?**
>
> _____
> _____
> _____

> **Why did a few delegates choose not to sign the Constitution?**
>
> _____
> _____
> _____

Origins of American Government

Section 5

MAIN IDEA
Before the Constitution could take effect, a heated debate between those in favor
of the Constitution and those who opposed it took place in all the states.

Key Terms

Federalists supporters of the Constitution

Antifederalists opponents of the Constitution

Publius the pen name used by Alexander Hamilton, James Madison, and John Jay in a
series of articles defending the Constitution

Federalist Papers essays written by Alexander Hamilton, James Madison, and John Jay
to defend the Constitution

Bill of Rights a series of 10 amendments to the Constitution ratified by the states that
protect such rights as freedom of speech, press, and religion, as well as due process
protections

Taking Notes

As you read, take notes on the ratification debate. Record your notes in the
graphic organizer below.

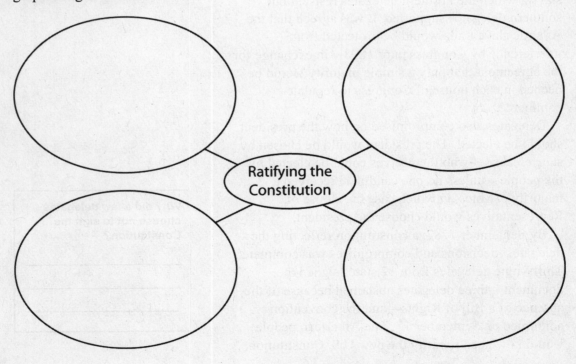

Ratifying the
Constitution

Section Summary

ANTIFEDERALISTS VERSUS FEDERALISTS

The Framers were aware that the existing Congress and state legislatures would not be happy with the new, stronger national government they were proposing. Therefore, they had included a process for ratifying the Constitution that would bypass both groups, instead calling for voters to elect representatives to a state ratifying convention. The Constitution would become law once 9 of the 13 states ratified it.

The battle for ratification involved the **Antifederalists**, the opponents of the Constitution, and **Federalists**, the supporters of the Constitution. Antifederalists claimed that the national government proposed by the Constitution would become too strong and threaten republicanism and state sovereignty. They also criticized the absence of a bill of rights, without which they feared the new national government could violate personal civil liberties with no fear of punishment. Federalists countered that a sufficiently powerful national government would strengthen the union of the states and have the power to defend the nation against foreign enemies, regulate trade, and control internal disturbances like the earlier Shays's Rebellion. Federalists also highlighted how the separation of powers officially limited federal power.

> **What arguments did Antifederalists make against ratifying the Constitution?**
> _____
> _____

THE FEDERALIST PAPERS

In order to summon more support for ratification, prominent Federalists James Madison, Alexander Hamilton, and John Jay, under the pen name **Publius**, wrote the *Federalist Papers*, a series of articles defending the Constitution for New York newspapers. The 85 articles—each of which discussed principles underlying the Constitution, such as checks and balances—were collected into a single volume of essays and widely circulated, strongly influencing the ratification debate. Antifederalists responded with essays of their own that frequently addressed the importance of liberty and the guarantee of "unalienable and fundamental rights."

> **What was the point of the *Federalist Papers*?**
> _____
> _____

THE FIGHT FOR RATIFICATION

The Federalists had been better prepared for the fight over ratification than the Antifederalists, quickly pointing out to small states that they would have equal representation in the Senate, despite their small populations. Yet Federalists found the largest and most powerful states difficult to persuade. Federalists finally agreed to the Antifederalists' demand for a bill of rights. This change had a remarkable effect on ratification. On June 21, 1788, the ninth state ratified the Constitution, and the remaining 4 states ratified it shortly thereafter.

Once the first Congress met, James Madison emphasized that the promised bill of rights should be proposed and ratified quickly. Madison suggested a number of amendments, or changes to the Constitution, that reflected earlier declarations of rights, including the English Bill of Rights and the Declaration of Independence. In September 1789, Congress sent 12 amendments to the states for ratification. By December 1791, the states had ratified 10 of the amendments. Traditionally called the **Bill of Rights**, these 10 amendments protect a number of civil liberties and civil rights, including the freedom of speech, press, and religion.

> **How was the Bill of Rights added to the Constitution?**
>
> _____
> _____

Chapter Summary

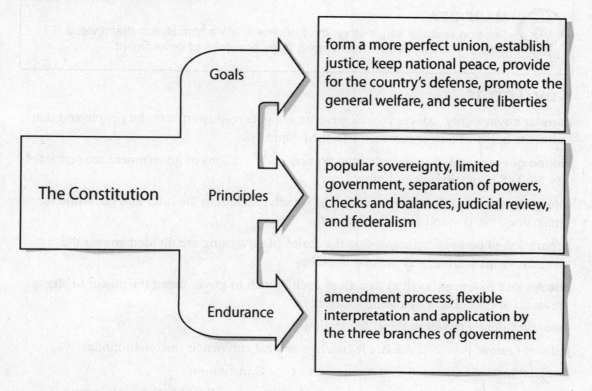

The Constitution

Goals → form a more perfect union, establish justice, keep national peace, provide for the country's defense, promote the general welfare, and secure liberties

Principles → popular sovereignty, limited government, separation of powers, checks and balances, judicial review, and federalism

Endurance → amendment process, flexible interpretation and application by the three branches of government

COMPREHENSION AND CRITICAL THINKING

Use information from the graphic organizer to answer the following questions.

1. **Define** What are the main goals of the Constitution?

_____

_____

2. **Explain** Why is the amendment process important to the Constitution's endurance, or its ability to hold up over time?

_____

_____

3. **Elaborate** One goal the Framers had for the new government was to promote the general welfare. Which principle of the Constitution do you think would most help them meet this goal? Explain.

_____

_____

The Constitution

 MAIN IDEA
Drawing lessons from history, the Framers wrote a constitution that divided, limited, and balanced power among three branches of government.

Key Terms

popular sovereignty concept that a government gets its power from the people and that ultimate political power remains with the people

limited government principle that the powers and functions of government are restricted by the U.S. Constitution and other laws

rule of law concept that every member of society, including the ruler and government, must obey the law and is never above it

separation of powers principle that the duties of governing are divided among the legislative, executive, and judicial branches

checks and balances system that gives each branch of government the power to change, reverse, or cancel acts of another branch

veto president's power to reject legislation

judicial review power to declare legislative and executive acts unconstitutional

unconstitutional found to violate any part of the Constitution

federalism principle that powers of government are distributed between the national government and the state governments

Taking Notes

As you read, take notes on the principles of government set out in the Constitution. Record your notes in the graphic organizer below.

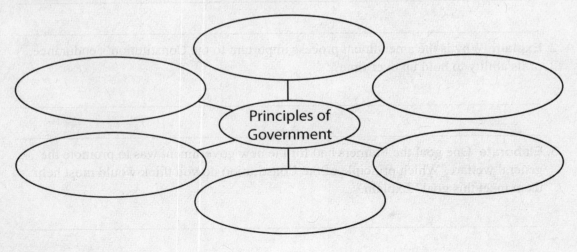

Section Summary

GOALS OF THE CONSTITUTION

As they wrote the Constitution, the Framers had six definite goals for the new national government: form a more perfect union; establish justice, or laws; insure domestic tranquility, or national peace; provide for the common defense of the country; promote the general welfare of states and citizens; and secure the blessings of liberties won by fighting the American Revolution.

Although they knew what the government had to do, the Framers were at first uncertain of how to create the government itself. They knew from recent experience what could happen when a government suppressed the natural rights of its citizens. But the Framers also knew that citizens needed certain laws for the new nation to survive. A strong national government would be able to enforce these laws.

> **What were the Framers afraid would happen if they designed a national government that was too powerful?**
>
> _____
>
> _____

PRINCIPLES OF GOVERNMENT IN THE CONSTITUTION

The Framers solved their dilemma over the balance of power by drawing upon six basic principles of governing: popular sovereignty, limited government, separation of powers, checks and balances, judicial review, and federalism. These principles ensure that the government's powers are subject to the will of the people and are presented in general terms throughout the Preamble, seven Articles, and 27 Amendments of the Constitution.

POPULAR SOVEREIGNTY

Popular sovereignty is the idea that a government gets it powers from the people it governs. The Framers began the Constitution with this idea: "We the People of the United States…do ordain and establish this Constitution…" Today, people participate in popular sovereignty in every election, when they choose and vote for the citizens they wish to lead their community, state, or country.

> **How is voting a good example of popular sovereignty?**
>
> _____
>
> _____

LIMITED GOVERNMENT

Limited government is the idea that the powers of government are restricted by the U.S. Constitution and

other laws. This idea follows the concept of the
rule of law, which means that everyone in the country,
from everyday citizens to the president, is subject to the
same laws. Although you will find many examples of
the government's powers throughout the Constitution,
such as the power to declare war or collect taxes, you
will also find examples of how these powers are limited.

> **Why was it important to the Framers that government officials follow the same laws as all other Americans?**
>
> _____
> _____

SEPARATION OF POWERS

The Framers included the **separation of powers**
within the Constitution by assigning specific
responsibilities to the three branches of government:
legislative (Congress), executive (president), and
judicial (Supreme Court).

CHECKS AND BALANCES

By separating powers, the Framers also guaranteed a
system of **checks and balances** that applies to all
three branches. For example, by giving the president
the power to **veto** legislation passed by Congress, the
Framers made it possible for the executive branch to
check the power of Congress. Yet, Congress can
override a veto if it has enough votes, checking one of
the executive branch's powers. Likewise, the Supreme
Court and other federal courts can declare legislation
unconstitutional—but the president gets to nominate
and Congress gets to approve all judges.

> **What is one way the judicial branch can check the legislative branch? What is one way the legislative branch can check the executive branch?**
>
> _____
> _____

JUDICIAL REVIEW

The federal courts have the very important power of
judicial review, although that power is only implied
in the Constitution. This power allows the courts to
determine if a law or other government action is
unconstitutional, or violates the Constitution.

FEDERALISM

The final principle the Framers built the Constitution
upon is **federalism**, or a system in which a
government's power is divided between the national
government and state governments. The Tenth
Amendment to the Constitution was passed in order to
clarify those powers that belong to the federal
government and those that belong to the states.

> **Why was the Tenth Amendment necessary?**
>
> _____
> _____

MAIN IDEA
The Constitution is both a product of its time and a document for all time. It can be changed as society's needs change.

Key Terms

supermajority any majority that is larger than a simple majority, such as three-fifths, two-thirds, or three-fourths

repeal cancel or revoke a law by a legislative act

Taking Notes

As you read, take notes on the amendment process. Record your notes in the chart below.

Proposing	Ratifying
1.	1.
2.	2.

Section Summary

JEFFERSON AND MADISON ON AMENDING THE CONSTITUTION

Thomas Jefferson and James Madison had different views on whether it should be possible to amend the Constitution. Jefferson believed that an amendment process was necessary, since future generations would need to modify laws as society changed. Madison argued that the ability to change the Constitution would take away its authority. Madison also was worried that, if the process for changing the Constitution was made too easy, political groups would change the document to meet their own needs.

> **What adjective could you use to describe Jefferson's view on amending the Constitution? What about Madison's view?**
>
> _____
>
> _____

A DOCUMENT FOR ALL TIME

The Constitution the Framers wrote has needed to be amended over the years—but only a few times. Many of these amendments have corrected injustices in the original document. For example, original compromises allowing slavery and prohibitions on who was permitted to vote were some of the first sections of the Constitution to be amended. Americans' ability to amend their Constitution helps the document remain relevant for each generation.

THE AMENDMENT PROCESS

Article V describes the amendment process. The Framers purposely designed this process so that it would be complicated enough to discourage factions from making changes that did not represent the needs of most Americans.

Every amendment must first be proposed, in one of two ways. Either a **supermajority**—a majority larger than a simple majority—of Congress (at least two-thirds of the House and two-thirds of the Senate) or a national convention called by at least two-thirds of the state legislatures may propose the amendment. Due to uncertainty over the wording of Article V, all existing amendments have been proposed by Congress

The amendment then needs to be ratified. This can also happen in one of two ways. Three-fourths of state legislatures can vote to ratify, sometimes after first calling citizens to cast an advisory vote. Alternatively,

> **Explain two different ways an amendment could be proposed and ratified.**
>
> _____
>
> _____

elected delegates at state conventions called by at least three-fourths of the states can vote to ratify the proposed amendment.

Amendments, like other sections of the Constitution, can also be amended. To **repeal**, or revoke, an amendment, another amendment must be proposed and ratified. One example of this is the Twenty-First Amendment, which was ratified in order to repeal the Eighteenth Amendment of the Constitution.

> Why is it logical that a new amendment is needed to repeal an earlier amendment?
>
> _____
> _____

MORE THAN 200 YEARS OF AMENDMENTS

Twenty-seven amendments have been added to the Constitution. The first 10 comprise the Bill of Rights, which was added almost immediately after the Constitution itself was ratified. These amendments protect Americans' personal freedoms and liberties, including freedom of speech and religion, the right to bear arms, and the right to a speedy trial. The later amendments in the Bill of Rights further protect individual rights by preventing the government from taking away any of them—or those belonging to the individual states.

The 17 other amendments were added over the next 200 years and reflected changes in American society. Among these are a series of amendments banning slavery and recognizing the rights of African Americans—passed shortly after the end of the Civil War—as well as amendments that allow the popular election of senators and give women the right to vote. Every amendment is proof of how the Constitution makes it possible for Americans to have a flexible government.

> How does an amendment that changes voting laws reflect changes in American society?
>
> _____
> _____
> _____

The Constitution

MAIN IDEA
The scope and impact of the Constitution have expanded as it has been put into practice, interpreted, and applied to new or changing social and political challenges.

Key Terms

executive agreements arrangements or compacts with foreign leaders or foreign governments

political party an organized group that seeks to win elections in order to influence the activities of government

cabinet a group of advisers consisting of the heads of the executive departments

gridlock inability to govern effectively due to separation of powers

electoral college body of 538 people elected from the 50 states and the District of Columbia who elect the president and vice president

Taking Notes

As you read, take notes on how the reach of the Constitution has expanded. Record your notes in the graphic organizer below.

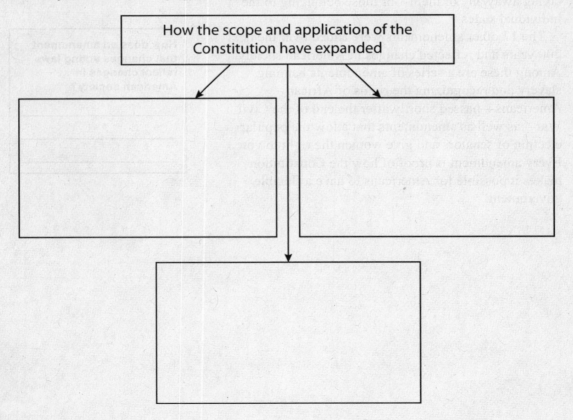

Section Summary

THE FEDERAL GOVERNMENT APPLIES THE CONSTITUTION

Over the years, each branch of government has applied and thereby expanded the meaning of the Constitution—and the scope of government itself. The legislative branch, using powers it has interpreted in the Constitution, has increased the lower level of the judicial branch, created various executive departments and agencies, and passed legislation that often requires a new way of looking at old laws. The executive branch has interpreted the Constitution in other ways to make **executive agreements**—arrangements with foreign countries—and adopt rules for its departments and agencies.

The judicial branch's interpretation has resulted in court rulings that apply laws to modern-day situations. This power of judicial review is often the subject of the debate over "loose" versus "strict" construction of the Constitution. Some Americans believe that it is possible to infer other concepts beyond what the actual words in the document say—this is loose construction. Other Americans believe that the powers of the Constitution lie in the literal meaning of its words—this is strict construction.

> **Give two examples of how the legislative branch has interpreted the Constitution.**
>
> _____
>
> _____
>
> _____
>
> _____

> **Why do you think judicial review is often a controversial subject in politics?**
>
> _____
>
> _____

POLITICAL PARTIES, CUSTOMS, AND TRADITIONS

In addition to the three branches, other groups also influence how the Constitution is interpreted. For example, **political parties**, or groups who wish to win elections in order to influence government, can have a great effect on candidates, the kind of legislation Congress passes, and who a president nominates to become federal judges. Other groups, including political action committees and political bloggers, also affect legislation by making their voices heard—sometimes with the help of a political party and sometimes without.

Customs and traditions also play a role in how government is carried out. For example, George Washington created his **cabinet**—a group of advisers consisting of the heads of the executive departments—through an interpretation of Article II of the

> **What do you think the relationship is between a political party and its candidates? Underline evidence for your answer in the paragraph at left.**
>
> _____
>
> _____

Constitution. Since then, every U.S. president has created a cabinet. Other traditions have become formal law, as in the case of the Twenty-second Amendment. Although earlier presidents had all served a maximum of two terms in office, President Franklin D. Roosevelt served four terms. In response to this break from tradition, Congress passed the Twenty-second Amendment, which limited presidents to two terms.

CRITICISMS OF THE CONSTITUTION

While the U.S. Constitution is one of the most respected documents in the world, it is criticized for various reasons. Some criticize the **gridlock,** or inability to govern, that can take place due to separation of powers. These critics feel that it is too easy for one branch to blame another when certain policy-making cannot be accomplished. Others believe that the Constitution does not allow for fair representation in Congress, arguing that states with much larger populations should be given more senators.

Additional criticisms involve the effectiveness of the **electoral college**—the body of people from the 50 states and the District of Columbia who elect the president and vice president—and winner-take-all elections. In both cases, critics worry that large portions of the popular vote do not hold enough value.

> **Why do some people criticize how states are represented in the Senate?**
> _____
> _____

Federalism

Chapter Summary

Past

- Supreme Court acts as a referee between the nation and the states.
- Dual federalism begins.
- National power grows with cooperative and creative federalism.
- New federalism returns power to states.

The federal system developed by the Framers divides powers between the national government and the state governments.

Present

- National government influences state government through fiscal federalism.
- Grants and federal mandates shape state policies.
- Debate remains over which level of government can best deal with certain issues.

COMPREHENSION AND CRITICAL THINKING

Use information from the graphic organizer to answer the following questions.

1. **Identify** How does the national government influence state policy today?

_____

_____

2. **Analyze** What type of national event might have inspired the shift from dual federalism to a system in which the national government grew more powerful?

_____

_____

3. **Develop** Why do you think some policymakers wished to return authority to the state governments during the period of new federalism? What might they have been hoping to change?

_____

_____

_____

Federalism

MAIN IDEA
The Framers of the Constitution established a federal system that divides powers and responsibility between the national and state governments.

Key Terms

expressed powers powers granted to the national government by the Constitution

implied powers powers that are not specifically listed in the Constitution but are logical extensions of expressed powers

inherent powers powers that historically have been recognized as naturally belonging to all governments that conduct the business of a sovereign nation

reserved powers powers that belong to the states because the Constitution neither delegates these powers to the national government nor prohibits them to the states

concurrent powers powers held by the national government and the state governments at the same time

full faith and credit clause Article IV of the Constitution, which requires that states give "full faith and credit" to the public acts, official records, and judicial proceedings of every other state

Taking Notes

As you read, take notes on the powers of the national, state, and shared powers. Record your notes in the graphic organizer below.

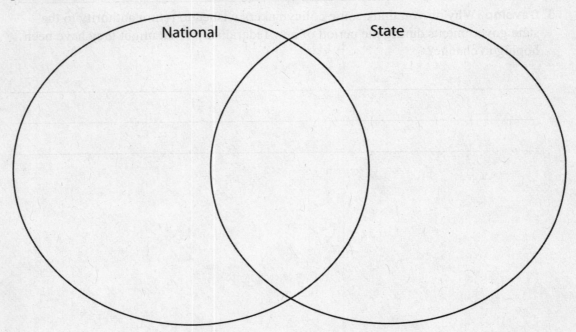

National   State

Section Summary

WHY FEDERALISM?

When the Framers met at the Constitutional Convention, they knew they needed to design a stronger national government, yet avoid the dangers of a unitary system. The biggest challenge was to balance this powerful national government with states' rights and still ensure a republican government. The Framers met this challenge in the Constitution, which divides powers between two levels of government: state and national. In this federal-style government, the national government was granted all powers having to do with the states' best interests and the state governments were granted all other powers.

> **How did the Framers decide which powers to give the states?**
> _____
> _____

NATIONAL POWERS

The Constitution grants the national government and each of its branches specific powers, known as **expressed powers** or enumerated powers. The national government also has **implied powers**, or powers that are not specifically listed in the Constitution but are logical extensions of expressed powers. Finally, the national government possesses **inherent powers**—powers that historically have been recognized as naturally belonging to all governments that conduct the business of a sovereign nation.

> **What is the difference between expressed powers and implied and inherent powers?**
> _____
> _____
> _____

STATE POWERS

Per a clause in the Bill of Rights, states have **reserved powers**—powers that belong to the states because the Constitution neither delegates those powers to the national government nor denies them to the states. States use this authority to regulate health, public safety, and general welfare, from controlling public school systems to enforcing criminal laws.

SHARED POWERS

Powers held by the national government and the state governments at the same time are called **concurrent powers**. Although Article VI of the Constitution—known as the supremacy clause—states that the Constitution and national laws and treaties are the supreme law of the land, states may also exercise any

power not given *exclusively* to the national
government, such as the power to collect taxes.

THE LIMITS OF POWER

The Constitution denies certain powers to both the
national and state governments. Among other limits
on its power, the national government cannot tax
exports between states, spend money unless
authorized by Congress, exercise powers reserved to
the states, or interfere with basic liberties. The states
are also denied specific powers, including the power
to coin money or enter into treaties. Both levels of
government are denied some of the same powers, such
as denying a citizen the right to a trial by jury or
passing ex post facto laws.

> **Give an example of one power denied to the national government. Then give one example of a power denied to the states.**
>
> _____
>
> _____
>
> _____

NATION AND STATE RELATIONS

The Constitution also sets guidelines for relationships
between states and between states and the national
government. The national government may only
recognize representative or republican state
governments, and is responsible for protecting the
states from foreign invasions and domestic uprisings.
Additionally, the national government must grant
states equal representation in the Senate and levy
taxes equally across states, and is prohibited from
splitting up states or changing state boundaries.

The Constitution encourages cooperation among
states, and although state laws vary, it requires states
to extradite a person charged with a crime to the state
in which the crime occurred for prosecution. To ease
extradition and other processes, the **full faith and
credit clause**, or Article IV, requires that states give
"full faith and credit" to the public acts, official
records, and judicial proceedings of every other state.
Also, the privileges and immunity clause prevents
most circumstances in which a person from one state
may be discriminated against by another state.

> **What does the privileges and immunity clause prohibit?**
>
> _____
>
> _____

The Constitution says nothing about local
governments, and so those are created and reorganized
by the state government. The only provision, which
concerns Native American nations, simply authorizes
the national government to make treaties with these
nations.

Name _____ Class _____ Date _____

Federalism

MAIN IDEA
Over the past 200 years, conflicts over the balance of power between the
national and state governments have led to different trends in federalism.

Key Terms

dual federalism a system of federalism in which both state and national governments
were equal authorities operating within their own spheres of influence, as defined by a
strict reading of the Constitution

doctrine of nullification the idea that states had the right to cancel national laws that they
believed contradicted or clashed with state interests

doctrine of secession the idea that states had the right to separate themselves from the
Union

cooperative federalism a system of federalism under the New Deal in which the national
and state governments worked together to meet a crisis

creative federalism a system of federalism under President Lyndon Johnson in which the
national government released grants to state and local communities to achieve national
goals

new federalism a system of federalism in which authority is returned to the state
governments

devolution the idea of returning power to states

Taking Notes

As you read, take notes on the people and events that led to changes in
American federalism. Record your notes in the graphic organizer below.

```
┌─────────────────────────────┐
│                             │
│                             │
│                             │
└─────────────────────────────┘
              │
              ▼
┌─────────────────────────────┐
│                             │
│                             │
│                             │
└─────────────────────────────┘
              │
              ▼
┌─────────────────────────────┐
│                             │
│                             │
│                             │
└─────────────────────────────┘
```

Section Summary

ROLE OF THE SUPREME COURT

The Framers of the Constitution were aware that the system of federalism would eventually lead to conflicts between the national and state governments. They disagreed over which level of government should have more power and so addressed that decision indirectly. In Article III of the Constitution, the Supreme Court is given the power to act as referee by hearing cases involving the Constitution, U.S. laws, and disputes between states. The Framers also included Article VI, or the supremacy clause, which states that the Constitution and national laws and treaties are "the supreme law of the land."

> Who referees disputes between states?
>
> _____

DUAL FEDERALISM

The United States first followed a system of **dual federalism**, under which both state and national governments were equal authorities operating within their own spheres of influence. The national government used the powers assigned to it in the Constitution and the states exercised all other powers, per the Tenth Amendment. This form of federalism lasted from about 1789 to the 1930s, first coming into national debate in a dispute over whether the national government had the authority to establish a national bank. In *McCulloch* v. *Maryland* (1819), the Supreme Court ruled that the Constitution's necessary and proper clause gave the national government the power to take actions necessary and proper to carrying out its expressed powers, in this case starting a national bank to regulate commerce and currency.

> In *McCulloch* v. *Maryland*, why did the Supreme Court rule that the government had the power to establish a national bank?
>
> _____
> _____
> _____
> _____

In the tense years leading up to and during the Civil War, the struggle between states' rights and national power intensified. Southern states proclaimed their belief in the **doctrine of nullification**, the idea that states had the right to nullify, or cancel, national laws that they believed contradicted or clashed with state interests. Under the doctrine, if a state did vote to nullify a law, three-quarters of the other states would then have to ratify an amendment to enact the law; the original state could then follow the law or secede. This latter action fell under the **doctrine of secession**, the idea that states had the right to separate themselves from the Union. South Carolina did nullify a law in 1832, and 11 southern states seceded from the Union at the start of the Civil War in 1861. Yet the outcome of the war resolved that states could *not* secede from the Union when they disagreed with its policies, as well as broadened the national government's power, exemplified by the passage of the Reconstruction Amendments.

EXPANDING NATIONAL POWER

The national government's power continued to increase into the twentieth century, as states became unable to handle all of the social and economic issues that accompanied a huge influx of immigrants and technology. Congress passed several pieces of important legislation, including bills to regulate the now-mammoth railroad industry's rates and to prevent monopolies and encourage competition.

During the Great Depression, national power expanded yet again under President Franklin Roosevelt's New Deal programs, although the states worked hand-in-hand with federal policymakers to address the crisis—a form of federalism called **cooperative federalism**. In the 1960s, under President Lyndon Johnson, this system transformed into **creative federalism**—a system of federalism in which the national government released grants to state and local communities to achieve national goals. Johnson's Great Society plan convinced states to address poverty and social inequality by withholding funding if states did not cooperate.

> **Explain creative federalism in your own words.**
>
> _____
>
> _____
>
> _____
>
> _____

NEW FEDERALISM

President Ronald Reagan took office at the beginning of the 1980s and immediately carried through on a promise to return authority to the state governments, a system now known as **new federalism**. President Reagan believed that the states were better equipped to deal with citizens' needs than the national government and adjusted federal grants accordingly. In the 1990s, the Republican Party also promised to scale down federal spending and return power to the states, a concept known as **devolution**.

> **What was the purpose of new federalism?**
>
> _____
>
> _____

Federalism

Section 3

MAIN IDEA
Today, the balance of power between the states and the national government is characterized by a system of grants and mandates, as well as by a number of key policy areas.

Key Terms

fiscal federalism a system of spending, taxing, and providing aid in the federal system

grants-in-aid money and other resources that the national government provides to pay for state and local activities

categorical grant a federal grant that can only be used for a specific purpose, or category, of state and local spending

block grant a federal grant that is given for general purposes or for broad policy areas

federal mandates demands on a state to carry out certain policies as a condition of receiving grant money

Taking Notes

As you read, take notes on the features of present-day federalism. Record your notes in the graphic organizer below.

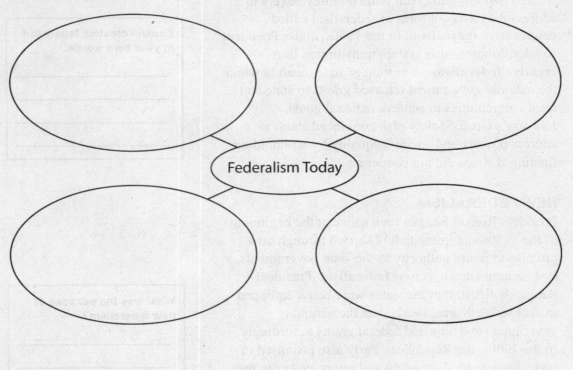

Federalism Today

Section Summary

FISCAL FEDERALISM

Today the national government influences state policies—and its own priorities—through **fiscal federalism**, a system of spending, taxing, and providing aid in the federal system. The national government has been assisting states as far back as the Articles of Confederation, often giving states grants of land to sell or do with as they like. In the twentieth century, the national government's power increased with the use of **grants-in-aid**—money and other resources that the national government provides to pay for state and local activities, ranging from low-income housing to disaster preparedness programs. These grants are funded by federal income taxes.

What makes up the system of fiscal federalism?

_____

_____

_____

GRANTS AND MANDATES

The national government frequently uses **categorical grants**, or federal grants that can only be used for a specific purpose, or category, of state and local spending, to give aid to states. These kinds of grants can fund a variety of programs, from the construction of a new airport to relief efforts in a region affected by a natural disaster. States are often expected to also contribute money toward the project being funded, and the quantity of the categorical grant may depend on the state's population.

Block grants are federal grants that are given for more general purposes than a categorical grant or for broad policy areas, such as welfare or education. States can spend the money as they see fit. When the era of new federalism began in the 1980s, many categorical grants were changed to block grants.

Federal mandates are the third way the national government gives monetary aid to states. Leaving much less spending control to the states than categorical or block grants do, **federal mandates** are demands to carry out certain policies as a condition of receiving grant money. In the past, the mandates have been applied—and justified by the equal protection clause of the Fourteenth Amendment—to establish affirmative action and certain environmental regulations, including the Clean Air Act of 1970. States who do not meet the demands of a mandate

What is the main difference between block grants and federal mandates?

_____

_____

_____

_____

may lose the funding. Additionally, some federal mandates are unfunded—a source of contention between the two levels of government.

ISSUES IN FEDERALISM TODAY

Federalism is at the center of many national debates today. One such debate involves welfare systems, over which the states have had control through federal block grants since 1996. Although the number of people on welfare has decreased since this shift in authority, some critics argue that the decrease is simply the result of a strong economy and contend that the states will not always be able to handle the responsibility of a welfare system. Also the recent establishment of the Department of Homeland Security—which involves federal, state, and local governments—has raised questions over how different levels of government can better work together.

The environment is another source of conflict between the national and state governments. While protecting the environment has traditionally been the responsibility of the national government, many Americans believe that state and local governments are better be able to address environmental issues, as they are familiar with regional needs and threats.

Immigration and health care are two more issues that continue to challenge all levels of government. While states have assumed many costs of immigration-related issues, such as health and social services, Congress has yet to pass major reforms at the national level. Additionally, neither Congress nor the state governments have resolved how to address the rising costs of medical services and the millions of Americans who do not have health insurance.

> **According to supporters, why would it be better to address environmental issues at the state level?**
>
> _____
> _____
> _____
> _____

Congress: The Legislative Branch

Chapter Summary

The Constitution both defines and limits the powers of Congress.

In the Senate, each state is represented equally. Today's Senate has 100 members—two senators from each of the 50 states.

Congress is the branch of government that makes laws. It is divided into two houses, the House of Representatives and the Senate.

The House of Representatives is the more representative house of Congress. Representation in the House is based on a state's population.

The main job of Congress is to make laws. To become a law, a bill goes through a multistage process involving both houses of Congress and approval by the president.

COMPREHENSION AND CRITICAL THINKING

Use information from the graphic organizer to answer the following questions.

1. **Describe** What is the source of Congress's power?

   _____

   _____

2. **Compare** How does representation in the House of Representatives compare to representation in the Senate?

   _____

   _____

3. **Evaluate** What is your opinion about the Framers' decision to limit the powers of Congress?

   _____

   _____

Congress: The Legislative Branch

MAIN IDEA
The voters elect members of Congress to represent them and to enact laws in their name. Congress plays a vital role in our government's system of checks and balances

Key Terms

constituents the people who live within the particular geographic area a member of Congress represents

apportionment the distribution of House seats among the states based on population

appropriation a bill that sets aside funds for a specific purpose

impeachment when Congress charges an official in the executive or judicial branch with wrongdoing and brings them to trial

oversight when Congress uses its broad powers to review how the executive branch is operating and to make sure it is following the laws Congress has passed

Taking Notes

As you read, take notes on the powers and features of Congress. Record your notes in the graphic organizer below.

Representing the People	Structure	Checks and Balances

Section Summary

CONGRESS AND THE PEOPLE

Although the people hold sovereign power in the system of American government, they elect representatives to make and carry out laws. Therefore, Congress is the body through which the will of the people becomes law.

Members of Congress represent the people in different ways. First, each member is responsible for representing the often conflicting needs and interests of his or her **constituents**—the people who live within the particular geographic area he or she represents. Second, a member of Congress must balance the demands of various interest groups—organized groups of like-minded people who join together to influence government and its policies—with the need to represent everyone fairly, even though interest groups typically include only a small number of the member's constituents. Finally, a member of Congress must consider the needs of the country as a whole. To do this, the member may sometimes need to serve his or her constituents directly and sometimes need to vote for legislation that benefits the country at large, not just his or her constituency.

Members of Congress share some personal characteristics. The average age of members is mid- to upper fifties. Most members are wealthier than the general population. Also, most members are white men, although gender and racial diversity has increased in recent years.

> **What different groups does a member of Congress represent?**
> _____
> _____

THE STRUCTURE OF CONGRESS

Congress is a bicameral legislature whose two houses are the House of Representatives and the Senate.

In the House, the process of **apportionment** is how seats are distributed among the states based on population. Each House seat is meant to represent about the same number of people; therefore, larger states have more representatives. The total number of House seats is fixed by law at 435, and all members serve two-year terms that are contested at the same time.

In the Senate, there are two members per state, for a total of 100 senators. While the Constitution originally

> **What is the purpose of apportionment?**
> _____
> _____

gave the state legislatures the power to elect senators, members of the Senate are now elected by the people for six-year terms. The terms are staggered so that every two years one-third of senators are up for election.

The delegates at the Constitutional Convention chose a bicameral design for Congress as part of the Great Compromise—an agreement to settle the fierce debate over how state population should affect representation. A bicameral legislature allowed one house in which small and large states had equal representation and one house in which representation was based on population. The final design also settled a debate over which members of Congress should be directly elected: Until 1913, members of the House were popularly elected, but senators were not.

Which house of Congress gives small and large states equal representation?
_____

CONGRESS AND CHECKS AND BALANCES

There are several ways Congress can check the other two branches. With few limits, Congress can deny federal spending with which it disagrees by refusing to enact an **appropriation**—a bill that sets aside funds for a specific purpose. Congress can also refuse to approve treaties the president has made with foreign governments and reject presidential appointees, such as potential Supreme Court justices.

Congress also has the power to impeach officials in both other branches. **Impeachment** involves charging an official with wrongdoing and bringing them to trial, where, if convicted, they can be removed from office. The House of Representatives begins the process by drawing up and voting to approve charges. The Senate then holds a trial, at which the vice president—or in some cases, the Chief Justice of the Supreme Court—serves as judge. A two-thirds vote by the Senate is required to remove a person from office.

Why is impeachment an important power?
_____
_____

Congress can further check the judicial branch by starting the process of amending the Constitution, possibly limiting the courts' power to declare certain legislation unconstitutional. Additional checks on the executive branch include voting to override a veto and conducting congressional **oversight**, or checking up on how the executive branch is operating and whether it is following laws Congress has passed.

Congress: The Legislative Branch

MAIN IDEA
The Constitution gives Congress many expressed powers, and it implies some others. The Constitution also places limits on the powers of Congress.

Key Terms

necessary and proper clause Article I, Section 8, Clause 18 of the Constitution, which states Congress's implied powers; also called the elastic clause

indirect tax a tax levied on one person but passed on to another for payment to the government

direct tax a tax an individual pays directly to the government

deficit when the federal government is not generating enough income to meet its expenses

commerce clause Article I, Section 8, Clause 3 of the Constitution, which states that the federal government has the right to regulate interstate commerce

subpoenas legal documents that require a person to testify in a certain matter

writ of habeas corpus a court order that forces the police to present a person in court to face charges, except in cases of rebellion or invasion

bill of attainder a law that punishes a person without a trial

ex post facto laws laws that criminalize an action that took place in the past and was legal at the time

Taking Notes

As you read, take notes on the powers of Congress. Record your notes in the graphic organizer below.

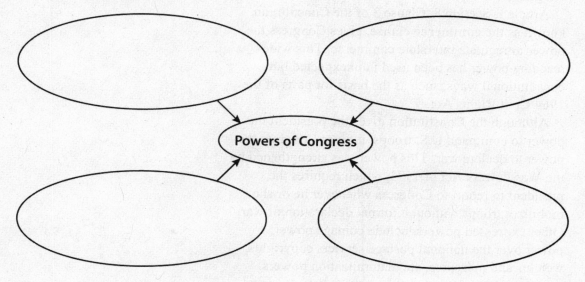

Section Summary

DEFINING THE POWERS OF CONGRESS

Article I, Section 8, lists specific, or expressed, powers, of Congress. Clause 18 of the same section, known as the **necessary and proper clause** or the elastic clause, suggests that Congress also has implied powers to "make all laws that are necessary and proper" for executing government. Additionally, Americans assume that Congress—and the other branches—have inherent powers, or those that all governments of independent nations possess. Finally, there are some powers explicitly denied Congress.

> **How are Congress's implied powers different from its expressed powers?**
>
> _____
>
> _____

EXPRESSED POWERS OF CONGRESS

The expressed powers of Congress mainly fall into three categories: financing, commerce, and defense.

Congress's financial powers involve the power to levy taxes and borrow money. Until the Sixteenth Amendment gave Congress the power to levy an income tax, most revenue was collected through **indirect taxes**, or taxes levied on one person but passed on to another for payment to the government. Today, revenue from income taxes—an example of a **direct tax**, or a tax an individual pays directly to the government—far exceeds that of indirect taxes. Congress also borrows money to allow the government to function even when there is not enough revenue to cover spending—a situation known as a budget **deficit**.

> **How does Congress collect most revenue today: direct taxes or indirect taxes?**
>
> _____

Article I, Section 8, Clause 3 of the Constitution, known as the **commerce clause**, gives Congress the power to regulate interstate commerce. This wide-reaching power has been used in unexpected but constitutional ways, such as the basis for parts of the 1964 Civil Rights Act.

Although the Constitution gives the president the power to command U.S. troops, it gives Congress the power to declare war. This power was strengthened by the War Powers Act of 1973, which requires the president to report to Congress whenever he or she mobilizes troops without a formal declaration of war. Other expressed powers include coinage power; power over the national postage service, copyrights, weights and measures; and naturalization powers.

IMPLIED POWERS OF CONGRESS

The necessary and proper clause gives Congress implied powers it may need to carry out its expressed powers. For years, politicians have debated how loosely or strictly this part of the Constitution should be applied, and how extensively congress should be able to apply the clause to expand its national power.

NONLEGISLATIVE POWERS

Congress has some nonlegislative powers. Both houses can propose amendments to the Constitution, conduct investigations—sometimes issuing **subpoenas**, legal documents that require a person to testify in a certain matter—contribute to impeachments, and confirm replacements if the vice presidency is vacant. The House alone can choose a president or vice president if no candidate receives a majority of votes in the electoral college. The Senate alone can choose a vice president in the same situation, as well as advise on and approve presidential appointees and treaties.

> If you receive a subpoena, what must you do?
> _____

LIMITS ON THE POWERS OF CONGRESS

Congress's powers are limited by the system of checks and balances. Article I, Section 9 also denies Congress specific powers, such as the power to suspend the **writ of habeas corpus**, a court order that forces the police to present a person in court to face charges, except in cases of rebellion or invasion. Furthermore, Congress cannot pass **bills of attainder**, laws that punish a person without a trial, or **ex post facto laws**, laws that criminalize an action that took place in the past and was legal at the time.

> Name two things Congress cannot do.
> _____
> _____

THE CHANGING POWER OF CONGRESS

The power of Congress has grown steadily, especially during periods of national crisis or outcry, including the Great Depression and the Civil Rights Era. The relationship between Congress and the president varies, with some presidents allowing Congress to be more aggressive than others.

MAIN IDEA
The House of Representatives, with its frequent elections and regular reapportionment, is the more representative chamber of Congress. Its members carry out much of their work in committees.

Key Terms

reapportionment the process in which seats are redistributed among states based on the results of the census

gerrymandering the practice of drawing district boundaries for political advantage

Speaker of the House the most powerful member and the presiding office of the House of Representatives

bills proposed laws

floor leader elected member of the majority or minority party who helps manage the actions and strategy of the party in the House of Representatives

whips elected members of the majority or minority party who encourage fellow party members to vote as the party leadership wants

party caucus a meeting of all the House of Representatives members from a particular party

standing committees permanent committees in the House of Representatives

select committees committees, typically temporary, that carry out specific tasks not already covered by existing committees

joint committees committees formed with Senate members that address broad issues affecting both chambers

Taking Notes

As you read, take notes on the features of the House of Representatives. Record your notes in the graphic organizer below.

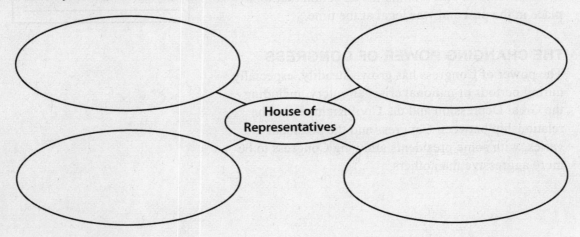

House of Representatives

Section Summary

MEMBERSHIP IN THE HOUSE

When writing the Constitution, the Framers designed the House of Representatives to be the chamber of Congress more representative of the people. To that end, the Constitution requires slightly less of House members than senators. Representatives in the House must be at least 25 years old, have been a U.S. citizen for at least seven years, and live in the state—and customarily the district—he or she represents. Informally, members typically require an appealing personality to win election in the first place, as well as the means to raise money for expensive campaigns.

There are very few situations in which the House can exclude an elected representative. However, it can expel a sitting member by a two-thirds vote.

> **What three requirements does the Constitution include for members of the House?**
>
> _____
>
> _____

REAPPORTIONMENT AND REDISTRICTING

The 435 members of Congress represent an average of approximately 690,000 Americans, with a minimum of one representative per state. The process of **reapportionment** ensures that seats are redistributed every 10 years based on census results. In this process, some states may lose seats and others may gain them.

Although Congress is given the responsibility of reapportionment, the state governments control redistricting, or the process of creating district boundaries. Often, the party in power in a state legislature will redraw boundaries for political purposes, a process known as **gerrymandering**. Over the years, the Supreme Court has placed some limits on gerrymandering, ruling the practice of creating districts that include many more people than other districts, or districts drawn to disenfranchise or benefit racial minorities, unconstitutional.

> **How and when does Congress decide to redistribute seats?**
>
> _____
>
> _____

LEADERSHIP IN THE HOUSE

The Constitution grants the House of Representatives the power to choose its own leaders. The presiding officer of the House and its most powerful member is the **Speaker of the House**. This official is second in the line of succession for the presidency and is elected by the other members, always originating with the majority party. House rules and years of tradition have granted the Speaker the power to preside over debates; give members the authority to speak on the House floor; assign **bills**, or proposed laws to specific committees; schedule if and when a measure comes up for debate and how it is debated; and assign members to different House committees.

Other House officials include elected floor leaders and party whips. Each of the two major parties has a **floor leader**, who helps manage the actions and strategy of the party in the house. The majority party's floor leader assists the Speaker. The minority party's floor leader acts as chief House spokesperson for the party and tries to unify fellow party members on issues. Each party also has a **whip**, whose job it is to encourage fellow party members to vote as the party leadership wishes. The election of floor leaders and whips—as well as the Speaker—take place during **party caucuses**, meetings of all the House members from a particular party.

Under rules it created, the House can vote to issue a reprimand or a censure against a member. Also, the Rules Committee sets rules for when, how, and under what conditions debate on a bill will take place.

Describe a whip's role in your own words.

_____
_____

THE ROLE OF COMMITTEES

The House of Representatives depends on its many committees to gather knowledge on specific issues. There are 20 **standing committees**, or permanent committees, in which there are several more focused subcommittees. The House Committee on Ways and Means is one of the most powerful standing committees, dealing with taxes and other revenue-raising measures. There are also **select committees**, which are typically temporary and carry out tasks not covered by existing committees. **Joint committees** are those that the House forms with the Senate when an issue affects both chambers. Conference committees are the fourth type of committee.

With some exceptions, House members can serve on up to two standing committees and four subcommittees. Each committee is headed by a chair, who is elected—partially on the basis of seniority—with a six-year term limit.

What is the difference between standing and select committees?

_____
_____

MAIN IDEA
Senators represent entire states, have longer terms, and follow different rules of debate. These features help give the Senate its reputation as a more weighty and careful body than the House.

Key Terms

president of the Senate position assigned to the vice president of the United States by the Constitution that allows the vice president to preside over debates and break tie votes

president pro tempore the person who presides over the Senate in the absence of the president of the Senate

Senate majority leader the most powerful position in the Senate, elected by the majority's party caucus

seniority rule tradition that says the most senior majority senator on a committee becomes committee chair

filibuster when opponents of a measure take control of the Senate floor and refuse to stop talking in an effort to prevent the measure from coming up for a vote

cloture an end to debate

Taking Notes

As you read, take notes on the features of the Senate. Record your notes in the graphic organizer below.

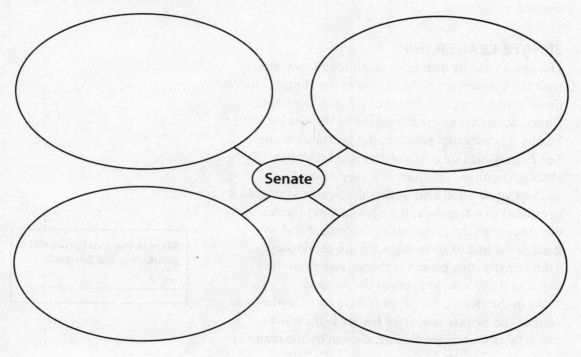

Section Summary

THE SENATE AND ITS MEMBERSHIP

The Senate is also known as the upper house, an alternate name that indicates the prestige of the chamber and its special powers. Senators are typically national figures, since there are so few of them and each must win statewide, as opposed to district-wide, election.

The constitutional requirements for senators are somewhat more stringent than those for members of the House of Representatives. A senator must be at least 30 years old, have been a U.S. citizen for at least nine years, and live in the state he or she represents. Informally, most senators are white men, older and wealthier than their colleagues in the House.

Senators serve a six-year term—four years longer than that of any member of the House—and their election is staggered so that only one-third of the seats are contested at one time. Senatorial elections were designed this way so that members could presumably focus more on serving the nation than worrying about re-election. Elections were initially open only to the state legislatures, but after years of indecisive legislators and corrupt elections, the Seventeenth Amendment was passed in 1913 to establish popular election of senators.

> **When do senatorial elections take place and who votes in them?**
> _____
> _____

SENATE LEADERSHIP

The Senate has its own leaders, although they are typically less powerful than those in the House. The Constitution mandates that the vice president of the United States act as the **president of the Senate**. Mostly a ceremonial position, the president of the Senate may preside over debates and break ties, although neither event happens very often.

The Constitution also directs the Senate to choose a **president pro tempore**, the person who presides in the absence of the president of the Senate and who is third in the line of succession for the presidency. Traditionally, this person is the senator from the majority party who has served the longest.

As in the House, the Senate elects party leaders and whips. The **Senate majority leader** is the most powerful person in the Senate, chosen by the majority

> **What is the most powerful position in the Senate?**
> _____

party during its caucus. As the party's Senate spokesperson and chief strategist, the Senate majority leader helps fellow party members with committee assignments and other issues—in return for their cooperation and support on legislation.

COMMITTEES IN THE SENATE

Much of the work of senators is done in committee. The Senate has 16 standing committees—which include many subcommittees—and several select and special committees, whose job it is to examine a specific issue, advise the Senate as a whole, or provide oversight of government agencies. Senators also participate in joint and conference committees.

Senators are typically limited to sitting on no more than three committees and five subcommittees. The number of seats each party has on a committee reflects its numbers in the Senate, and assignments are made at the beginning of a congressional session, in a party conference or caucus. For the most part, priority is given according to seniority. The tradition of **seniority rule** also dictates that the most senior senator on a committee become chair. In the past, there have sometimes been term limits on chairs.

Some committees have roles related to powers specific to the Senate. For example, the Judiciary Committee conducts hearings on nominees for federal judges before the Senate votes to confirm. Likewise, the Foreign Relations Committee has great influence on the Senate's role in ratifying treaties.

> **Explain seniority rule.**
> _____
> _____
> _____

RULES AND TRADITIONS

The Senate has several rules and tradition. It can expel or censure its members, although both practices are rare. Another rule involves filling vacancies, as directed by the Seventeenth Amendment: When a member dies or retires while in office, his or her state's governor appoints a replacement until a special election can be held. Perhaps the most well-known tradition is the **filibuster**, a Senate practice during which opponents of a measure take the floor and refuse to stop talking to prevent a vote from occurring. Only a two-thirds vote for **cloture**—an end to debate—can stop a filibuster.

> **What is the purpose of a filibuster?**
> _____

Congress: The Legislative Branch

Section 5

MAIN IDEA
The main job of Congress is to make laws. The process of making laws is well established and orderly.

Key Terms

rider a provision attached to a bill that bears little relationship to the bill's main topic

joint resolution Congressional action used in certain unusual circumstances that follows the same procedures as a bill and has the force of law if passed by both houses and signed by the president

concurrent resolutions Congressional actions without the force of law that are passed by both houses to address matters that affect the operations of both chambers

discharge petition a document that a majority of House members sign to force a bill out of committee

Committee of the Whole when all House members become members of a single committee to allow the House to function when many members are at hearings or are otherwise absent

quorum the number needed to legally conduct business

roll-call vote a vote in which each member is required to publicly state his or her vote, also known as a record vote

conference committee a committee formed when the House and Senate must reconcile different versions of the same bill

pocket veto an indirect veto that takes place when the president does not sign a bill within 10 days, during which time Congress adjourns

Taking Notes

As you read, take notes on the process of making law in Congress. Record your notes in the graphic organizer below.

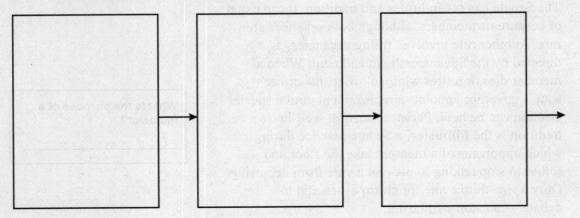

Section Summary

BILLS IN CONGRESS

Congress makes the nation's laws, which start out as bills. Only a member of Congress can submit a bill, but the idea behind a bill can come from Congress, constituents, interest groups, or the president. Private bills affect only a person or a small group; public bills affect all of society. Also, bills can involve a single subject or many. Many bills include **riders**, or attached provisions that have little to do with the rest of the bill but would otherwise be impossible to pass as legislation.

Besides bills, Congress also passes resolutions. **Joint resolutions** follow the same process as and sometimes have the same force as a bill, unlike other resolutions; they are used in specific, unusual situations. Both chambers pass **concurrent resolutions** when they need to address operations in both the House and Senate. Each chamber can also pass simple resolutions for its own individual operational issues. Finally, nonbinding resolutions give Congress an opportunity to express its opinion on an issue without legal impact.

> **Why would a member of Congress add a rider to a bill?**
>
> _____
>
> _____

BILLS IN COMMITTEE

Most work on bills happens in committee. First, a bill is referred, either by the Speaker of the House or the Senate majority leader, to one or more committees, and then to a subcommittee. Next, the committee holds hearings, at which witnesses make statements on the bill. The subcommittee then votes to report a bill favorably, unfavorably, or no comment, and recommends whether the larger committee should take further action. In the House, subcommittees may amend a bill; in the Senate, the full committee amends bills.

After the subcommittee report, the full committee holds a meeting called a markup to discuss the report, examine the bill closely, and decide whether to report the bill as favorable, unfavorable, or without recommendation to the entire chamber. The committee can alternatively decide to take no further action, although in the House a majority of members can sign a **discharge petition** to force the bill out of

> **How does a subcommittee learn more about a bill and its potential impact?**
>
> _____
>
> _____

committee. Another House-specific step in the process involves the powerful Rules Committee, which almost always assigns rules for amending the bill and time limits on debate.

THE BILL ON THE FLOOR

Once a bill leaves committee in the House of Representatives, it is assigned rules by the Rules Committee, upon which the entire House votes. The Constitution dictates that the House can only conduct business when half its members are present—a number known as the **quorum**, currently at 218 members. When many members are at hearings or absent, the remaining members can form a **Committee of the Whole** and become members of one committee whose quorum is only 100. The committee then debates the bill and amends it as necessary, submitting its changes for a full House vote. Very important votes often require record votes, or **roll-call votes**, in which each member is required to publicly state his or her vote.

In the Senate, there is no Rules Committee, although a senator can request limits on a bill. These requests require a unanimous vote, which sometimes inspires a filibuster. After debating the bill, senators vote on the bill and any amendments, often by roll-call vote.

> **Why does the Senate sometimes need to form a Committee of the Whole?**
> _____
> _____

THE CONFERENCE COMMITTEE

If majorly different versions of a bill pass in the House and Senate, a **conference committee** is formed to reconcile the differences. Once committee members from both chambers reach an agreement on a final bill, they issue a conference report. Both chambers must then vote to accept the report before the bill is sent to the president.

> **Why are conference committees formed?**
> _____

PRESIDENTIAL ACTION ON A BILL

Once the president receives a bill, he or she can sign it, thereby making it law, or veto it. The president can also choose not to sign the bill, in which case it either becomes law after 10 days or is considered the victim of a **pocket veto** if Congress adjourns during that 10-day period.

The Presidency

Chapter Summary

The President	
Roles	chief executive, chief administrator, commander in chief, foreign policy leader, chief agenda setter, and unofficial roles
Qualifications	at least 35 years old, have lived in country at least 14 years, natural-born citizen, and unofficial qualifications
Powers	executive, diplomatic, military, judicial, and legislative powers
Administration	Executive Office of the President, vice president, cabinet

COMPREHENSION AND CRITICAL THINKING

Use information from the graphic organizer to answer the following questions.

1. **Identify** What types of powers do presidents have today?

_____

2. **Explain** Does it surprise you that the president has both official and unofficial roles?

_____

_____

3. **Develop** The vice president's and the cabinet's powers have expanded as the role of the president has increased over time. Why does this make sense?

_____

_____

MAIN IDEA
The Constitution gives only a brief description of the president's qualifications and powers. Yet the job is vast and complex, as the president must fulfill many roles.

Key Terms and People

chief executive the role the president plays when executing, or carrying out, the nation's laws

commander in chief the role the president plays when ordering troops into action and calling them back home

foreign policy a nation's plans and procedures for dealing with other countries

diplomacy the art of negotiating with foreign governments

chief of state the role the president plays when acting as the symbolic figurehead of the United States

succession the process of succeeding, or coming after someone

Taking Notes

As you read, take notes on the duties and qualifications of the president. Record your notes in the graphic organizer below.

The President	
Formal	Informal

Section Summary

ROLES OF THE PRESIDENT

Article II of the Constitution outlines five official roles for the president. First, the president is **chief executive**, meaning he or she has the power to execute, or carry out, the nation's laws, both by running government programs and implementing laws passed by Congress. Next, the president is chief administrator, managing the executive departments that advise him or her. Third, the president acts as **commander in chief** of the military, holding the power to send troops into action and call them back home. Fourth, the president is the country's foreign policy leader. In this role, the president negotiates treaties, receives foreign ambassadors, and directs all efforts toward **diplomacy**—the art of negotiating with foreign governments. Through each of these activities, the president shapes the country's **foreign policy**, the United States' plans and procedures for dealing with other countries. Finally, the president acts as chief agenda setter when giving the annual State of the Union address and helping Congress with the budget.

Unofficially, the president is the **chief of state** when playing the role of symbolic figurehead of the United States. Although not stated in the Constitution, the president is also considered the head of his or her political party and, along with the vice president, the chief citizen—a representative of all American people.

> **Name the president's five official roles.**
> _____
> _____
> _____

FORMAL CHARACTERISTICS OF THE PRESIDENCY

Article II of the Constitution also briefly outlines qualifications, terms of office, election, succession, and benefits. There are three formal qualifications. The president must be at least 35 years old, have lived in the country for 14 years, and be a natural-born citizen, meaning he or she was born a U.S. citizen. In recent years, this third qualification has come under much scrutiny, with critics claiming that it may block qualified candidates.

As for terms of office, the Constitution originally only stated that the president would serve a four-year term with the opportunity for re-election. After first president George Washington chose to serve two

> **Could a 45-year old woman who was born a French citizen become president? Explain.**
> _____
> _____
> _____

terms, a pattern was established and no president served more than two terms until the 1940s, when Franklin D. Roosevelt was elected to a third and then a fourth term. Partially in response to this break in tradition, the Twenty-second Amendment was added to the Constitution in 1951, limiting the president to two full terms and no more than 10 years in office.

As described in Chapter 3, the president and vice-president are chosen by the electoral college. The Constitution gives states the power to decide how to pick these electors. The electoral college remains the focus of much criticism, since states only receive the same number of electors as it has members of Congress. Therefore, small states receive disproportionate representation in the election process.

Article II is unclear as to who formally succeeds the president. For years, it was assumed that the vice president would be next in the line of **succession**, the process of succeeding or coming after someone. This tradition became law when the Twenty-fifth Amendment was passed in 1967. The Presidential Succession Act of 1947 further extended the line of succession, naming the Speaker of the House next in line after the vice president.

The Constitution also prevents Congress from changing a president's salary while he or she is in office. The president also has a personal staff, access to air and ground transportation, health and retirement benefits, tax deductions, and permission to live in the White House for the duration of his or her term.

> **Why were the Twenty-fifth Amendment and the Presidential Succession Act necessary?**
>
> _____
>
> _____
>
> _____

INFORMAL QUALIFICATIONS FOR THE PRESIDENCY

Some qualifications for the presidency are not listed within the Constitution but still play a major role in the selection of the president. Although people of both genders and many different ethnic and religious backgrounds have run for president, as of 2007, every president has been a well-educated white male belonging to a Christian denomination. Most have had some military experience. Personality traits are also important to voters. For example, most Americans want a likeable, dignified, organized president who communicates well and remains calm in a crisis.

> **What have most past presidents had in common?**
>
> _____
>
> _____

MAIN IDEA
The powers of the presidency, outlined in Article II of the Constitution, are vast and have grown throughout the history of the United States. They are, however, checked by the other branches of government.

Key Terms and People

executive orders a formal rule or regulation instructing executive branch officials on how to carry out their jobs

executive privilege the power of the president to refuse to release information to Congress or a court

diplomatic recognition the president's power to formally recognize the legitimacy of a foreign government

reprieve an act of clemency that postpones the carrying out of a sentence

pardon an act of clemency that releases a convicted criminal from having to fulfill a sentence

amnesty an act of clemency that grants a group of offenders a general pardon for offenses committed

commute the president's power to reduce a person's sentence

Taking Notes

As you read, take notes on the powers of the presidency. Record your notes in the graphic organizer below.

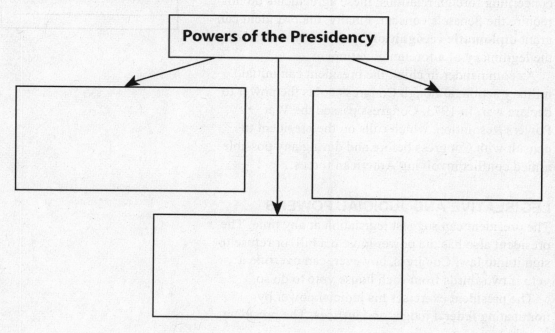

Section Summary

EXECUTIVE POWERS

The Constitution gives the president specific powers.
First, the president directly appoints about 3,000
positions in the executive branch, a third of which
need to be confirmed by the Senate. The president can
use this power however he or she sees fit. With some
exceptions, the president can remove appointees at
any time.

Through interpretation of Article II, Section 3 of
the Constitution, presidents also have the power to
issue **executive orders**, formal, signed statements that
instruct or guide executive officials and have the force
of law. These are different than signing statements,
which make modifications to existing laws.
Constitutional interpretation also grants the president
the right of **executive privilege**, which allows a
president to refuse to release information to Congress
or a court.

DIPLOMATIC AND MILITARY POWERS

As foreign policy leader, the president can negotiate
treaties, although the Senate needs to approve and can
override them. Presidents can also make executive
agreements with the heads of other countries
concerning foreign relations; these agreements do not
require the Senate's consent. Finally, the president can
grant **diplomatic recognition** by formally recognizing
the legitimacy of a foreign government.

As commander in chief, the president can initiate
military action, although Congress holds the power to
declare war. In 1973, Congress passed the War
Powers Resolution, which calls on the president to
consult with Congress before and during any possible
armed conflict involving American forces.

> **What is one way that treaties and executive agreements differ?**
> _____
> _____

LEGISLATIVE AND JUDICIAL POWERS

The president can suggest legislation at any time. The
president also has the power to veto a bill, or refuse to
sign it into law. Congress, however, can override a
veto if two-thirds from each house vote to do so.

The president exercises his judicial power by
nominating federal judges and justices. The president

can also give **reprieves**, which postpone jail time, or **pardons**, which release a convicted criminal from a sentence; offer **amnesty**, which grants a group of offenders a general pardon; and **commute**, or reduce, sentences. These four powers of clemency, or mercy, only apply to federal cases and cannot be used in impeachment cases.

> **What are the president's four powers of clemency?**
>
> _____
> _____
> _____
> _____

INFORMAL POWERS

The president's informal powers stem from access to the media and his or her position as party leader. With constant media coverage, the president can reach out to the public for support at any time. As party leader, the president typically has the support of fellow party members in Congress.

CHECKS ON THE PRESIDENT'S POWERS

The president's powers can be formally checked by judicial review, blocked nominations, and veto overrides. The media and public approval are sources of informal checks on the president's power.

CHANGES IN PRESIDENTIAL POWER

Until the late nineteenth century, the executive branch played a much less powerful role than the legislative branch. However, as the United States entered world wars and became a major player in international politics, Americans began to expect more of the men representing it. Presidents like Lyndon B. Johnson initiated social problems that strengthened the connection between presidents and the people. As mass media further developed, from print to radio to television to the Internet, presidents found an expanded outlet for reaching out to the public for support. Today's presidents maintain this relationship by fully taking advantage of the exposure the media gives them, ensuring that they and their policies remain prominent in the public eye.

> **How can a president use the media to his or her advantage?**
>
> _____
> _____

The Presidency

Section 3

MAIN IDEA
The president leads a large team of people who help carry out the duties of the office. This team includes a staff of advisers, the vice president, and members of the cabinet.

Key Terms

administration the group of people who work for the executive branch under a specific president

Executive Office of the President the organizational structure that helps manages the executive programs and agencies

White House Office a central office of the Executive Office of the President in which many key assistants and deputy assistants to the president work

chief of staff the person who manages the White House Office

National Security Council an executive office that brings together the top military, foreign affairs, and intelligence officials to coordinate U.S. national security

Council of Economic Advisers an executive office that provides the president with expert analysis of the economy

Office of Management and Budget an executive office that helps develop and implement the federal budget and to oversee its execution by the agencies in the executive branch

executive departments departments within the president's administration that are responsible for carrying out laws, administering programs, and making regulations in their particular area of responsibility

Taking Notes

As you read, take notes on the president's administration. Record your notes in the graphic organizer below.

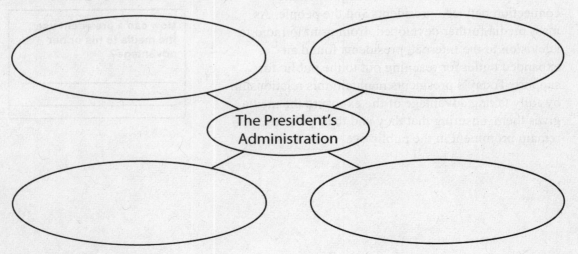

The President's Administration

Section Summary
EXECUTIVE OFFICE OF THE PRESIDENT

The group of people who work for the executive branch under a president are known as the president's **administration**. Up until the twentieth century, presidents had a relatively small number of staff. Beginning with Theodore Roosevelt, the number of executive programs and agencies began to increase, making it necessary to better manage these many offices. In 1939 Congress authorized the creation of the **Executive Office of the President** (EOP), an organizational structure under which the president's many advisers and assistants fall. Almost all members are appointed by the president and confirmed by the Senate.

> **Why was the Executive Office of the President created?**
> _____
> _____

Several important offices fall under the EOP. The **White House Office** includes many key assistants and advisers to the president. Within this office is the president's **chief of staff**. This position consists of different responsibilities depending on the president in office, but can include managing everyday office operations, mapping political strategy, and handling relations with Congress and the cabinet. The chief of staff also manages the people responsible for delivering the president's message, including speechwriters and the White House press secretary.

Formed during the Cold War to combat the influence of the nation's enemies, the **National Security Council** (NSC) is chaired by the president, with the presidentially-appointed national security adviser working as his or her second in command. The Council meets regularly to coordinate issues of U.S. national security. These meetings are also attended by the vice president, several cabinet members, and the chairman of the Joint Chiefs of Staff, a group made up of the heads of each major branch of the armed forces.

> **What is the purpose of the National Security Council?**
> _____
> _____
> _____

The **Council of Economic Advisers** (CEA) has been part of the EOP since 1946. This office consists of three nominated and confirmed members, as well as a staff of assistants and advisers. The CEA advises the president on his or her economic policy and U.S. economic performance. Members also help the president prepare the detailed annual *Economic Report*.

The **Office of Management and Budget** (OMB) is the largest office within the EOP, headed by a nominated and confirmed director. Its purpose is to help develop and implement the federal budget, legislation, and government regulations, as well as set policies on government finance and purchases. Members work with both the executive and legislative branches.

THE VICE PRESIDENT

The vice presidency is the only administrative office besides the president that is an elected position. The vice president is assigned three responsibilities by the Constitution: preside over the Senate, open and count the electoral votes in a presidential election, and serve as president if the president is unable. Until recently, most vice presidents did very little else, with the exception of helping to get the president elected or re-elected. Starting in the 1970s, presidents began to rely more heavily on their vice presidents for advice and to manage certain executive projects.

How has the role of the vice president changed in recent decades?
_____
_____
_____

THE CABINET

The cabinet is an organization made up of the heads, or secretaries, of the **executive departments**. These departments carry out laws, administer programs, and create regulations in their area of responsibility. Each secretary is nominated by the president and confirmed by the Senate. Secretaries both advise the president and run their own department. There are 16 official cabinet positions, including the vice president. Presidents can also invite other people to sit on the cabinet if necessary.

The power to create and expand the cabinet comes from an interpretation of the Constitution, which says that the president "may require the opinion, in writing, of the principal officer of each of the executive departments." The experience and background of cabinet members vary from president to president, as does the degree to which the president depends upon members' advice.

Where does the president's power to create a cabinet come from?
_____
_____

The Executive Branch at Work

Chapter Summary

Many executive organizations and agencies make up the federal bureaucracy. Civilians are hired according to merit, unlike in the past.	
The executive departments and independent agencies administer specific areas of government responsibility.	→ Executive Branch
The government raises funds through taxes and borrowing. The federal budget outlines which programs receive these funds.	

COMPREHENSION AND CRITICAL THINKING

Use information from the graphic organizer to answer the following questions.

1. **Recall** What is the role of the executive departments and independent agencies?

   _____

   _____

2. **Summarize** How does the government raise funds?

   _____

   _____

3. **Draw Conclusions** Why is the executive branch divided into so many smaller agencies?

   _____

   _____

The Executive Branch at Work

MAIN IDEA
The federal bureaucracy includes all the organizations and agencies of the executive branch. The civil service system is used to place qualified civilians into positions within the agencies of the federal bureaucracy.

Key Terms

bureaucracy any government or private-sector organization that has a clear formal structure, a division of labor, and a set of rules and procedures by which it operates

bureaucrats the administrators and skilled, expert workers who carry out many specific tasks of the bureaucracy

civil service the civilian workers who carry out the work of the federal government

spoils system the practice by which government jobs were given out by the president as political rewards to people who supported that president's policies or election campaign

Taking Notes

As you read, take notes on what makes up the federal bureaucracy. Record your notes in the graphic organizer below.

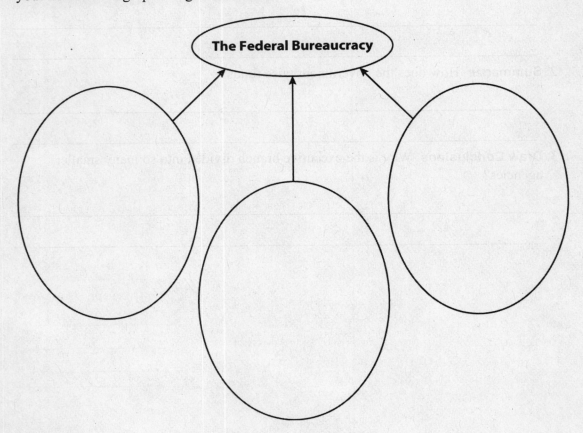

The Federal Bureaucracy

Section Summary

WHAT IS THE FEDERAL BUREAUCRACY?

A **bureaucracy** is a government or private-sector organization that has a clear, formal structure; a division of labor; and a set of rules and procedures by which it operates. The federal bureaucracy is the overarching organization that includes all of the executive branch's agencies and departments. Contained within the federal bureaucracy are the office of the vice president and the Executive Office of the President, the executive departments, and the three types of independent agencies: independent executive agencies, independent regulatory commissions, and government corporations.

There are currently about 2.7 million people working within the federal bureaucracy. The top administrators are either appointed by the president or nominated by the president and then approved by the Senate. These political appointees usually leave when a president's term of office is complete. However, **bureaucrats**, or the administrators and skilled workers who carry out many specific tasks of the federal bureaucracy, typically keep their jobs regardless of who is in office. Bureaucrats get their jobs through a competitive hiring process and are experts who help the bureaucracy implement legislation and executive orders.

What is a bureaucracy?
_____
_____
_____

THE CIVIL SERVICE

The **civil service** is the name given to the group of civilians who carry out the work of the federal government. Any nonmilitary government worker is considered a member of the civil service. The people who work in the civil service are hired through a competitive selection process.

Job placement within the civil service did not always follow this competitive process. Up until the late 1800s, the president usually gave out government jobs as rewards to people who supported his campaign or the president's policies while in office—a practice called the **spoils system**. Many Americans grew tired of the spoils system by the late 1800s, criticizing the government corruption, with political appointees rewarding supporters with contracts for work on

Describe the spoils system.
_____
_____
_____

federal projects. In addition, each time a new president came to office, existing workers were fired and new employees hired. Most workers had little time to build skills, making the federal bureaucracy inconsistent and difficult to stabilize.

Early attempts to reform the civil-service system were largely unsuccessful. The Civil Service Commission, created by Congress in 1871, had too little funding to change hiring and placement practices. However, after the assassination of President James Garfield by a disappointed office seeker, the legislative and executive branches began to take more action. In 1883 the Pendleton Civil Service Act became law. The act directed all hiring and promotions to be based on merit, not party affiliation. The Pendleton Act also created a new Civil Service Commission, whose job it was to administer objective exams to potential employees and hire only those whose test scores proved them to be qualified.

Today, the reach of the Pendleton Civil Service Act encompasses even more workers, due partly to additional legislation. The Civil Service Reform Act of 1978 established new agencies whose job it is to manage the civil service. The Office of Personnel Management runs the civil-service system, testing and placing job applicants, and manages the administrative functions of the civil service. The Federal Labor Relations Authority handles and attempts to resolve complaints about unfair labor practices. The United States Merit Systems Protection Board protects civil-service employees from politically-motivated hiring practices and other abuses. More than 90 percent of government jobs are now protected by civil-service legislation.

> **How did the Pendleton Act prevent the spoils system from returning?**
>
> _____
>
> _____
>
> _____

The Executive Branch at Work

MAIN IDEA
Executive departments and independent agencies provide key services and regulate important industries for the American people.

Key Terms

independent agencies government agencies that operate separately from the executive departments

independent executive agencies independent agencies whose purpose is to oversee and manage a specific aspect of the federal government

independent regulatory commissions independent agencies whose purpose is to regulate some aspect of the economy

bipartisan including members from both major political parties

government corporations independent agencies that are organized and run like businesses but are owned in whole or in part by the federal government

Taking Notes

As you read, take notes on the executive departments and independent agencies. Record your notes in the graphic organizer below.

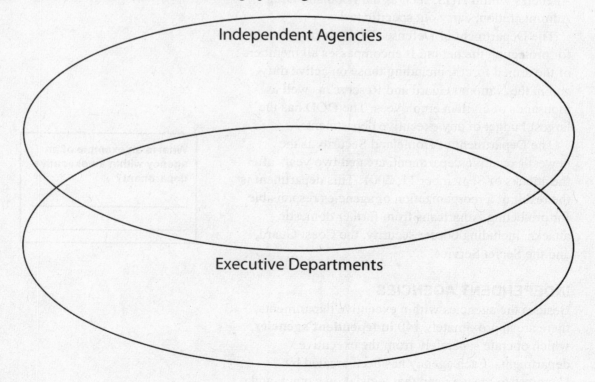

Section Summary

EXECUTIVE DEPARTMENTS

The 15 executive departments, which are headed by members of the cabinet, employ about 60 percent of all federal government employees. They are the primary units of both administration and policy-making in the executive branch. Every department focuses on its own general area of responsibility, and smaller agencies within each department focus on more specific issues. While the president has the power to nominate high-level positions in these departments, the Senate must confirm these nominations. Congress also controls the departments' duties, powers, and budgets.

> How is Congress involved with the executive departments?
>
> _____
> _____
> _____

THE DEPARTMENTS TODAY

Today, there are 15 executive departments. Each has important goals and functions.

The goal of the Department of Health and Human Services (HHS) is to protect Americans' health. It administers Social Security, Medicare, and Medicaid. Agencies within HHS, such as the Food and Drug Administration, carry out specific tasks.

The Department of Defense (DOD) is responsible for protecting the nation. It encompasses all members of the armed forces, including those on active duty and in the National Guard and Reserve, as well as thousands of civilian employees. The DOD has the largest budget of any executive department.

The Department of Homeland Security is the newest executive department, created two years after the attacks of September 11, 2001. This department is the result of a reorganization of agencies responsible for protecting Americans from further domestic attacks, including border security, the Coast Guard, and the Secret Service.

> What is an example of an agency within an executive department?
>
> _____
> _____

INDEPENDENT AGENCIES

Besides the agencies within executive departments, there are approximately 140 **independent agencies**, which operate separately from the executive departments. Each agency has been created by Congress to meet a need that legislation cannot, and ultimately remains under the control of Congress.

Independent executive agencies oversee and manage a specific aspect of the federal government. Similar in power and sometimes in organization to executive departments, these agencies often fulfill a president's strategic vision, as the Peace Corps did for President John F. Kennedy. The National Aeronautics and Space Administration (NASA) is another example of an independent executive agency.

Independent regulatory commissions regulate some aspect of the economy. They are run by three- to seven-person boards whose members are nominated by the president and confirmed by the Senate. Boards must be **bipartisan**, or include members from both major political parties. The commissions can create, implement, and enforce its own laws, although Congress can override them if necessary.

Government corporations are the third type of independent agency, organized and run like businesses but partially or fully owned by the federal government. They are created when the government recognizes that a private corporation cannot meet a specific national need for a sufficient profit. The U.S. Postal Service and AMTRAK are both government corporations that were established when Congress realized that geography was preventing private mail and rail companies from offering affordable service to all Americans.

> **How does Congress decide when to create a government corporation?**
> _____
> _____
> _____
> _____

POWER AND ACCOUNTABILITY IN THE FEDERAL BUREAUCRACY

The Constitution provides tools for ensuring the accountability of the federal bureaucracy. The president and Congress both exercise checks on the federal bureaucracy. Over the years, Congress has passed legislation to check agencies, including setting guidelines for agency rules and making information available to the public. However, sometimes agencies, congressional committees, and interest groups form alliances in which each group benefits from the actions of the others. These relationships are labeled *iron triangles* because outsiders, including the president, cannot seem to penetrate it.

> **How has Congress checked the power of the independent agencies?**
> _____
> _____

The Executive Branch at Work

Section 3

MAIN IDEA
By collecting taxes and borrowing money, the federal government is able to generate the funds it needs to run the nation. The government then assigns these funds to create a federal budget for the upcoming year.

Key Terms

income tax a tax on a person's or corporation's income

progressive tax a tax whose rates increase as the amount subject to taxation increases

payroll tax a tax that is withheld from a person's paycheck by his or her employer to help pay for forms of social insurance

regressive tax a tax that has a greater impact on lower-income earners than on upper-income earners

proportional tax a tax that is applied at the same rate against all income

bond a financial instrument by which a borrower agrees to pay back borrowed money, plus interest, at a future date

federal debt the total amount of money that the government has borrowed and not repaid

mandatory spending a type of government spending that is mandated by federal laws and is not subject to the annual budget process

discretionary spending a type of government spending that is subject to the annual budget process

fiscal policy a financial policy that involves creating the federal budget and taxation laws

monetary policy a financial policy that involves altering the amount of money in circulation and the interest rates at which money is borrowed

Taking Notes

As you read, take notes on financing the federal government. Record your notes in a graphic organizer like the one below.

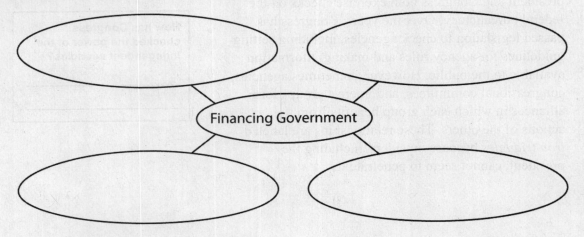

Financing Government

Section Summary

PAYING FOR GOVERNMENT

The federal government pays for its programs and services by collecting revenue and by borrowing.

The largest percentage of the federal government's revenue—around 59 percent—comes from **income taxes**, which are taxes on a person's or corporation's income. The income tax is an example of a **progressive tax**—a tax whose rates increase as the amount that is subject to taxation increases. **Payroll taxes**, money withheld from a person's paycheck that helps pay for Social Security, Medicare, and other forms of social insurance, are examples of a **regressive tax**. This kind of tax only applies to income up to a certain amount and therefore impacts lower-income earners more than upper-income earners. The Social Security tax is a regressive tax. The Medicare tax is both a regressive and a **proportional tax**, a tax that is applied at the same rate against all income.

The government collects a much smaller amount of its revenue—about six percent—from excise taxes; tariffs, or taxes on imported goods; estate taxes, or taxes on money and property passed on to heirs when someone dies; gift taxes, or taxes on money or property given to one living person from another; and non-tax sources, such as entrance fees to national parks.

Additionally, the government borrows money by selling **bonds**, financial instruments by which the government agrees to pay back the borrowed money, plus interest, at a future date. In the past, the government only sold bonds in emergencies. However, in recent decades, economic depressions have led to almost continuous budget deficits, which occur when a government's revenues are lower than its expenses. Bond sales have therefore increased. The total amount of borrowed money yet to be repaid is called the **federal debt**. As long as the government is operating under a deficit, it will pay only the interest on the debt.

Why is a proportional tax also a regressive tax?
_____
_____
_____
_____

How does the government borrow money?
_____
_____

GOVERNMENT SPENDING

There are two types of government spending. **Mandatory spending** is spending mandated by laws and not subject to the annual budget process. **Discretionary spending** is spending that is subject to the annual budget process. The president and Congress most work together closely to decide how and where to use these discretionary funds.

THE BUDGET PROCESS

The federal budget is first prepared by the president, who is assisted by the Office of Management and Budget. The president presents the budget to Congress by the first Monday in February. Next, Congress and the nonpartisan Congressional Budget Office review and modify the budget. Then the House and Senate Budget Committees hold hearings on and eventually pass a concurrent resolution that includes the year's grand totals for revenue and spending. Once the resolution is in place, the House and Senate Appropriations Committees assign discretionary funding to programs and write appropriations bills that reflect these spending decisions. The bills are then sent to the president to sign, ideally by October 1, the beginning of the government's fiscal year.

> **Who decides which programs will receive discretionary funding?**
>
> _____
>
> _____

FISCAL AND MONETARY POLICY

Government spending and borrowing affects the economy enormously. When they create the budget and tax laws, the president and Congress are making a **fiscal policy**. This kind of policy can be used to stimulate the economy by spending money in specific areas or by cutting taxes. When the government changes the amount of money in circulation or interest rates, it is creating a **monetary policy**. An independent regulatory commission called the Federal Reserve System, or the Fed, actually controls monetary policy. It does this by raising or lowering the amount of money banks must have in reserve, raising or lowering the interest rate it charges banks, and buying or selling bonds. The government uses both fiscal and monetary policy to work toward economic growth, low unemployment, stable prices for goods and services, and a balanced budget.

> **How does fiscal policy stimulate the economy?**
>
> _____
>
> _____
>
> _____

The Federal Courts and the Judicial Branch

Chapter Summary

The Federal Court System		
The Constitution created a three-level court system, with district courts on the bottom and the Supreme Court on top.		
District Courts	**Courts of Appeals**	**Supreme Court**
Trial courts, with original jurisdiction for most federal cases	Appellate courts hear cases appealed from district courts and some federal agencies	Highest court in the nation, ruling on questions of federal law and the Constitution

COMPREHENSION AND CRITICAL THINKING

Use information from the graphic organizer to answer the following questions.

1. **Describe** What is the structure of the U.S. federal court system?

_____

_____

2. **Explain** Why do you think the courts of appeals are higher than the district courts?

_____

_____

3. **Predict** The Supreme Court's power has increased over time as the nation has turned to the Court to decide questions of federal and constitutional law. Do you think the Court's importance will continue to increase or will it decrease? Explain.

_____

_____

_____

The Federal Courts and the Judicial Branch

Section 1

MAIN IDEA
The Framers created an independent judicial branch as part of the separation of powers of the national government. At the federal level, the judicial branch consists of three tiers of courts, each performing a different function.

Key Terms

jurisdiction the authority to hear and decide a case

exclusive jurisdiction the sole right to hear a case

concurrent jurisdiction when both state courts and federal courts have the right to hear a case

plaintiff the person making a legal complaint

defendant the person against whom a legal complaint is filed

original jurisdiction a court's right to have heard a case simply because it was the first court to hear it

appellate jurisdiction a court's right to hear a case once it has been appealed from a lower court

judicial restraint the concept that a judge should interpret the Constitution according to the Framers' original intention

judicial activism the concept that judges can adapt the meaning of the Constitution to contemporary realities

precedent previous court rulings on a given legal question

senatorial courtesy tradition in which a senator from the same state as a judicial nominee and from the same political party as the president can block the nominee and expect no opposition from other senators

Taking Notes

As you read, take notes on the federal court system. Record your notes in the graphic organizer below.

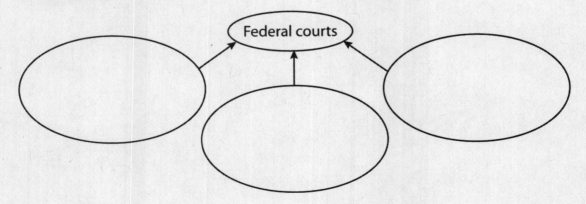

Section Summary

THE AMERICAN COURT SYSTEM

Courts perform three functions: they identify if a law has been broken and if penalties apply, they decide how to provide relief to those who have been harmed, and, if relevant, they determine the meaning of a specific law or part of the Constitution.

When the Framers wrote the Constitution, they chose to keep the existing state courts and add a federal court system. They created specific rules for **jurisdiction**, or the authority to hear and decide a case. Today, state courts, directed by state laws and constitutions, hear the majority of cases. Federal courts have **exclusive jurisdiction**, or the sole right to hear a case, in certain situations, such as when a case involves the interpretation of the Constitution or a foreign ambassador.

In some cases, courts have **concurrent jurisdiction** and the **plaintiff**, or person making the legal complaint, can file the case in either state or federal court. However, the **defendant**, or person against whom the complaint is filed, can sometimes insist that the case is heard in federal court.

The court that first hears a case is said to have **original jurisdiction**. Any court that hears the case at a higher level is said to have **appellate jurisdiction**.

What three purposes do courts fulfill?
_____
_____
_____
_____
_____

STRUCTURE OF THE FEDERAL COURT SYSTEM

Since the Constitution is vague about how the federal court system should be structured, Congress has passed laws to determine the types and purposes of federal courts. The Judiciary Act of 1789 set up a three-tiered federal court structure. The 94 district courts are on the lowest level. These trial courts have original jurisdiction over almost all federal criminal and civil cases. Courts of appeals make up the middle level of the federal court system. These 13 courts hear appeals from the lower courts and from certain federal agencies. Finally, the Supreme Court is the entire top tier of the system. Although the Court does have original jurisdiction in a few very special situations, it acts mainly as the ultimate appellate court in the United States. Each year, its chief justice and eight

Summarize the three tiers of the federal court system, including each tier's jurisdiction.
_____
_____
_____
_____
_____

associates review about 100 cases involving the
Constitution or federal law.

Since the original Judiciary Act, Congress has
added a number of other courts whose jurisdiction is
limited to cases that Congress specifies. Judges in
these special courts do not have guaranteed pay or
lifetime appointment, as do all other federal judges.

APPOINTING FEDERAL JUDGES

When nominating federal judges, presidents must
consider four factors. First, the president must
consider the person's legal expertise. Next, the
president must consider the person's party affiliation;
most presidents pick nominees from their own party.

Third, the president needs to think about whether
the person's judicial philosophy and respect for
precedent, or previous court rulings on a given legal
question, matches his or her own. Presidents typically
gauge judicial philosophy by identifying where the
prospective nominee falls along the spectrum of
judicial restraint—the concept that a judge should
interpret the Constitution according to the Framers'
original intention—and **judicial activism**—the
concept that judges can adapt the meaning of the
Constitution to contemporary realities.

Finally, the president must consider whether the
Senate will approve the person. If a district court
judge is nominated, a senator from the same state as
the nominee and the same party as the president can
block the nominee with little argument from other
senators. This practice is called **senatorial courtesy**.

> **Which end of the judicial spectrum would include a strict interpretation of the Constitution?**
>
> _____
>
> _____

CHECKS AND BALANCES

Under the system of checks and balances, the judicial
branch checks the legislative and executive branches
through the power of judicial review. In return, the
other two branches check the judicial branch through
the appointment process of judges, the amendment
process, and with the power to impeach and remove
judges. This last check is extremely difficult to
exercise, since judicial independence, or the freedom
to rule without fear of political retaliation, is carefully
guarded by American society.

> **Identify two ways that the other two branches can check the judicial branch.**
>
> _____
>
> _____
>
> _____
>
> _____

The Federal Courts and the Judicial Branch

MAIN IDEA
Congress has created a system of lower courts for the federal judicial system.
Each court has a specific role to play in the judicial branch.

Key Terms

grand juries panels of citizens that hear evidence of a possible crime and recommend whether the evidence is sufficient to file criminal charges

bankruptcy a legal process by which citizens who cannot pay money they owe others can receive court protection and assistance in settling their financial problems

magistrate judges district-court officials who are appointed for eight years and hear some of the early hearings of criminal trials as well as some misdemeanor and civil cases

misdemeanor a minor criminal case punishable by one year or less of prison time

public defenders lawyers provided to defendants who cannot afford to hire a lawyer

marshals officials who provide security and police protection at federal courthouses

appellant a person who files an appeal to have their case reviewed by a court of appeals

briefs written arguments

sovereign immunity principle that a sovereign nation is immune from being sued unless it agrees to be sued

courts-martial hearings held by the U.S. Court of Appeals for the Armed Forces to decide cases involving violation of the Uniform Code of Military Justice

Taking Notes

As you read, take notes on the federal court system. Record your notes in the graphic organizer below.

District Courts	Courts of Appeals	Other Courts

Section Summary

FEDERAL DISTRICT COURTS

The 94 district courts each have between two and 44 judges. These judges hear over 300,000 cases a year. These cases range those that are directly assigned to the federal courts by the Constitution to cases concerning a variety of criminal and civil offenses. Serious criminal cases involve a **grand jury**, a panel of 16 to 23 citizens who hear evidence of a crime and recommend whether the evidence is sufficient to file criminal charges.

Federal judges are nominated by the president, approved by the Senate, and have no set term. The exception to this involves bankruptcy judges, who serve 14-year terms and are appointed by the local circuit's Court of Appeals. These judges preside in bankruptcy court, a smaller part of a district court. They only hear cases involving **bankruptcy**, a legal process by which people who cannot pay money they owe others can receive court protection and assistance.

Judges play the most important role in a federal court, presiding over trials, ensuring proper legal procedures, and instructing juries. **Magistrate judges**, appointed by federal judges for eight-year terms, are responsible for overseeing parts of criminal trials and some civil cases and **misdemeanor** cases—minor criminal cases that have a maximum punishment of one year in prison. Each district court also has a clerk of the court, who performs administrative duties.

There are three other groups of officials who are heavily involved in the operations of a district court. The first group is the U.S. attorneys. U.S. attorneys are appointed by the president and represent the United States in federal court. For example, when a person is charged with a federal crime, the U.S. attorney acts as a prosecutor. The second group is the **public defenders**, lawyers assigned to defendants who cannot afford to hire one, are present in every federal court. The third and final group is the U.S. **marshals**, who provide security and police protection at federal courthouses. Marshals also track criminal suspects and protect witnesses.

> **What is the purpose of a grand jury?**
> _____
> _____
> _____

> **Explain the role of a U.S. attorney in a federal district court.**
> _____
> _____

FEDERAL COURTS OF APPEALS

There is one court of appeals for each of the 12 U.S. regional circuits and an additional Court of Appeals for the Federal District, which only hears cases related to specific areas of the law. Each year, the 13 courts hear about 65,000 cases on appeal from district courts and certain federal agencies, but fewer than four percent of appeals are successful. In order for an appellate court to overturn a previous ruling, the **appellant**, or person who filed the appeal, needs to show that the original ruling was affected by a legal mistake. During the appeal, a randomly chosen panel of three circuit judges examines the factual record from the first trial and reads **briefs**, or written arguments, from both sides. The panel then decides the case based on precedents from Supreme Court rulings and the circuit court's own earlier rulings.

Almost all rulings by a court of appeals are final. In rare situations, a case may be sent back to the district court for additional hearings, the original prosecutor may retry a case, or an *en banc* review may take place, during which other judges from the court examine the case. Additionally, a very small number of rulings are reviewed by the Supreme Court each year.

> **What does an appellant need to prove in order to have a successful appeal?**
>
> _____
> _____
> _____
> _____

OTHER FEDERAL COURTS

Besides the district and appellate courts, Congress has created several special federal courts with very limited jurisdictions. These include courts just for Washington, D.C. and the U.S. territories, a court to hear cases involving international trade, a tax court for federal-tax cases, and a court of appeals to hear veterans' claims. The U.S. Court of Federal Claims hears complaints against the U.S. government in cases where **sovereign immunity**, or the nation's immunity from being sued unless agreeing to it, does not apply.

In addition, the Foreign Intelligence Surveillance Court, the Alien Terrorist Removal Court, and military commissions that try people captured by U.S. armed forces all hear cases involving national security. The U.S. Court of Appeals for the Armed Forces holds hearings called **courts-martial** to decide cases involving violation of military code.

> **Name three other federal courts created by Congress.**
>
> _____
> _____
> _____

The Federal Courts and the Judicial Branch

MAIN IDEA
The Supreme Court is the highest court in the nation and the most important component of the judicial branch. It serves as the final word on questions of federal law and the Constitution.

Key Terms

writ of certiorari an order issued by the Supreme Court to review a lower court's decision

docket the list of cases to be heard

majority opinion a court opinion signed by at least five of the nine justices of the Supreme Court

concurring opinions court opinions that agree with the overall conclusion in a case but stress different or additional legal reasoning

dissenting opinions court opinions held by the minority of justices who do not agree with the ruling in a case

Taking Notes

As you read, take notes on the Supreme Court. Record your notes in the graphic organizer below.

History	Appointments	Procedures

Section Summary

HIGHLIGHTS OF SUPREME COURT HISTORY

The Supreme Court has experienced many shifts in political power since the Constitution was ratified. Alexander Hamilton was the first to really explain the Court's purpose and the importance of its judicial review of acts of Congress and the executive branch. But it was not until 1801, when John Marshall was appointed chief justice, that Court rulings began to have a major effect on Americans. Under Marshall, the judicial branch became an equal of the two other branches, issuing important rulings on the reach of judicial review, the implied powers of Congress, and interstate commerce.

In 1857 the Court's decision in *Dred Scott* v. *Sandford* threw the country into an uproar that eventually led to the Civil War. In their decision, the justices declared that a slave brought to a free territory was not actually free and could not become a citizen. Furthermore, the Court ruled that Congress did not have the power to outlaw slavery in territories.

In the years after the Civil War, the Court narrowly interpreted the Thirteenth, Fourteenth, and Fifteenth Amendments in relation to civil rights. The Court struck down the Civil Rights Act of 1875, stating that it was the responsibility of the states, not the federal government, to protect African Americans from discrimination.

Throughout the twentieth century, the Court has ruled in other landmark decisions. These decisions cover a wide-range of issues from economic regulation to desegregation to individuals' rights.

> What did the *Dred Scott* decision demonstrate about the relationship between the Supreme Court and Congress?
>
> _____
> _____
> _____

CHOOSING SUPREME COURT JUSTICES

As they do with all other federal judicial nominees, presidents must consider each Supreme Court nominee's legal expertise, party affiliation, judicial philosophy, and acceptability to the Senate. Almost all justices have had a background in law, and most have belonged to the same party and shared the same beliefs about Constitutional interpretation as the nominating president. Typically, nominees are carefully evaluated to ensure that they will not inspire strong opposition within the Senate.

> What do most Supreme Court nominees have in common?
>
> _____
> _____
> _____
> _____

Conducted by the Senate Judiciary Committee, the hearings for a Supreme Court nominee are televised and usually intense. The nominee is questioned about past writings and decisions, judicial beliefs, and even his or her personal background. Senators often try to gauge the nominee's likeliness to judge one way or the other on a major issue, but their efforts are usually unsuccessful. When the hearings are complete, the committee votes on the nominee, after which the Senate votes as a whole. Senators not on the Senate Judiciary Committee almost always follow the lead of the committee's vote.

> **What information do members of the Senate Judiciary Committee seek during a Supreme Court nominee's hearings?**
>
> _____
>
> _____
>
> _____
>
> _____

SUPREME COURT PROCEDURES

The Supreme Court is in session from early October to June or July, during which time the justices alternate between one week of hearing cases and one week of working on rulings and upcoming cases. There are three ways that a case can be placed on the Court's **docket,** or list of cases to be heard. First, the Court has original jurisdiction in select cases, such as those involving disputes between states. Second, the Court can issue a **writ of certiorari**, an order seeking review of a lower court's case. Third, a state case can arrive at the Court if it has already gone through appeals but still involves a question about the Constitution or federal law.

When the Supreme Court hears a case, it first reads briefs, or written arguments, submitted by each side and sometimes by outside parties. The Court then hears and questions 30 minutes of oral arguments from each side. Next, the justices study and discuss the case behind closed doors. They then issue their decision within an opinion, a detailed written explanation of the major issues, judicial precedents, and legal reasoning behind the decision. This entire process is called plenary review.

There is more than one type of court opinion. A **majority opinion** is signed by at least five of the nine justices and represents the actual ruling. **Concurring opinions** agree with the overall conclusion of the case but stress other legal reasoning as well. **Dissenting opinions** are issued by those justices who did not agree with the majority opinion.

> **When the Supreme Court issues a ruling, do all of the justices always agree? Explain.**
>
> _____
>
> _____
>
> _____

The Political Process

Chapter Summary

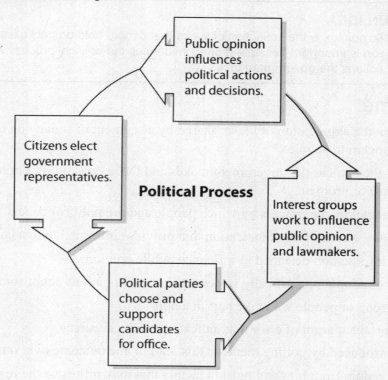

Public opinion influences political actions and decisions.

Citizens elect government representatives.

Political Process

Interest groups work to influence public opinion and lawmakers.

Political parties choose and support candidates for office.

COMPREHENSION AND CRITICAL THINKING

Use information from the graphic organizer to answer the following questions.

1. **Describe** What do interest groups do?

   _____

2. **Make Generalizations** Think of an important issue in American government today. How might public opinion influence how lawmakers address the issue?

   _____

   _____

3. **Declare** Voting behavior is mainly affected by party identification, personal views, a candidate's background, and the voter's background. How do you think political parties target these factors?

   _____

   _____

MAIN IDEA
Public opinion is the collection of views that people hold on public issues. Public opinion is important because it often influences the political process and affects the actions the government takes.

Key Terms

public opinion the aggregation of views shared by a segment of society on issues of interest or concern to people

public policy the choices the government makes and the actions it takes in response to a particular issue or problem

political socialization the process by which people acquire political beliefs

mass media any means of communication that provides information to a large audience

propaganda information designed to influence public opinion

poll a survey of people scientifically selected to provide opinions about something

sample the group of people who take part in a poll

sampling error the margin of error that indicates a poll's accuracy

bias errors introduced by polling methods that lead to one outcome over others

objectivity freedom from bias and outside factors that may influence the results of a poll

exit poll a poll that surveys a randomly selected fraction of voters after they have voted

Taking Notes

As you read, take notes on factors that shape public opinion. Record your notes in the chart below.

Factor	How it shapes public opinion

Section Summary

WHAT IS PUBLIC OPINION?

Public opinion is the group of views shared by a segment of society on issues of interest to people. Public opinion is often divided and can focus on a variety of issues, ranging from the government's foreign policy to community problems.

Public policy, the choices the government makes and the actions it takes in response to an issue or problem, is related to public opinion. On the one hand, public policy can form public opinion, as Americans react to government actions. On the other hand, public opinion can form public policy. If enough Americans decide that a certain action needs to be taken, they can often convince government officials to make policy that addresses this need.

There are many ways Americans can express their individual and collective opinions. Voting is one example. People can also protest, write letters or blogs, or testify at public hearings. Additionally, people can join and support private organizations whose missions they respect and that work to influence policymakers.

FORMING PUBLIC OPINION

A number of factors can affect a person's **political socialization**, or the way a person acquires political beliefs. Family is an important factor, since children grow up listening to family members' beliefs on a range of political issues. School and work are two other factors that help shape the way a person feels about politics. Age, race, gender, and religion can further influence a person's opinions.

MEDIA AND PUBLIC OPINION

Mass media—any means of communication that provides information to a large audience—also influences public opinion. Newspapers, online news, and television news, all report on politics and issues that are important to both politicians and the public. Through coverage of an issue—or lack thereof—mass media can help shape the public agenda. However, as critics point out, mass media can sometimes be

> Imagine that you just voted in an election for governor. How did you share your beliefs by voting?
> _____
> _____
> _____

> Name three factors that shape a person's political beliefs.
> _____
> _____
> _____

harmful, when there is bias in reporting or story selection, factual inaccuracy, or over consolidation of media outlets.

The earliest and longest-lasting form of mass media in the United States is print media, such as newspapers and magazines. Today, newspapers remain an important source of news and opinion, as do television, talk radio, and Internet news sites. It is now easier than ever to access news in very little time. Comparing information from multiple sources of news media helps people avoid **propaganda**, information purposely designed to shape public opinion.

> **Why is it important to receive news from more than one source?**
>
> _____
>
> _____
>
> _____
>
> _____

MEASURING PUBLIC OPINION

A public opinion **poll** is a survey of people scientifically selected to provide opinions about something. When a poll is designed and conducted accurately, it can be an excellent gauge of public opinion.

The first step to ensuring accuracy in a poll is to pick an appropriate **sample**, or group of people who will take part in the poll. The size of the sample must be large enough to reflect the body of people the poll is supposed to represent, such as all registered voters. Additionally, the people who make up the sample must be chosen randomly. A well-designed scientific poll will also include questions that are worded in a way that does not unduly influence the respondent's answers. If a poll includes questions without **bias**, or polling method errors that lead to one outcome over others, it is more likely that the results of the poll will be **objective**—free from bias and other outside influences.

> **Explain the role of a sample in a poll.**
>
> _____
>
> _____
>
> _____
>
> _____

There is room for error in even the best designed poll. The **sampling error**, or margin of error in a poll, indicates a poll's accuracy and is given as a percent above and below the poll's results.

Exit polls are frequently used during elections. In these polls, voters are asked who they voted for, right after they vote. While these results can sometimes predict winners before elections are over, critics argue that they may discourage those who have not voted yet from voting and alter final results.

The Political Process

MAIN IDEA
Interest groups are private organizations that try to influence public opinion and convince public officials to accept their goals and views. They give political power to segments of society that have similar views.

Key Terms

interest group a collection of people who hold similar views and goals

political action committee an organization created to raise and contribute money legally to the campaigns of political candidates

trade association a type of business group that represents certain industries or parts of industries

labor unions organizations of workers who do the same job or work in related industries

endorse to publicly declare support for a candidate

lobbying contacting public officials to persuade them to support certain interests

grass roots the name given to the lowest level of an organization or society

Taking Notes

As you read, take notes on the different types of interest groups. Record your notes in the graphic organizer below.

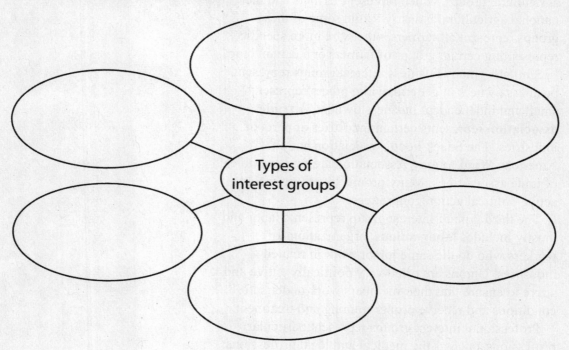

Types of interest groups

Section Summary

INTEREST GROUPS AND WHAT THEY DO

An **interest group** is a collection of people who hold similar views and goals. Interest groups have three main functions: organize people with common views, provide members with a way to participate in politics, and supply information about the group's views to policymakers and other members of the public. Interest groups often form **political action committees**, organizations whose purpose is to legally raise and contribute money to candidates whom members want to support.

For many Americans, interest groups provide a more powerful outlet for influencing public policy and the politicians behind it. While membership in interest groups has been lower in recent years, financial contributions to these groups have been higher. This monetary increase has helped interest groups extend their reach to a broad television and Internet audience.

> **How do interest groups give their members more of a political voice?**
>
> _____
>
> _____
>
> _____
>
> _____

TYPES OF INTEREST GROUPS

There are six types of interest groups. The first type are agricultural groups, which represent farmers and the national agricultural industry While some of these groups represent all farmers, others are more specific, representing certain groups of farmers or a certain crop.

Similarly, many business interest groups represent business owners in general, while others represent small and independent business owners. A **trade association** represents certain industries or parts of industries. The Snack Food Association and the American Wind Energy Association are two examples of trade associations. Many groups like these include active political action committees.

The third type of interest group represents labor and mostly includes **labor unions**, organizations of workers who do the same job or work in related industries. Unions are often very politically active and strive to ensure that their members work under safe conditions and receive proper training and treatment.

Professional interest groups represent particular professions, such as the medical and legal professions. Professional groups typically educate the public about their specific profession, monitor training and licensing within the profession, and create a set of professional standards.

The fifth type of interest group is societal groups, organizations that represent certain religious, social, racial, and ethnic segments of the population. The National Organization of Women and the American Muslim Alliance are both examples of societal groups.

The last category of interest group is made up of cause-based groups, which focus on a particular cause rather than a segment of the U.S. population. Cause-based groups include Mothers Against Drunk Driving and the Center for Civic Education.

> **How are cause-based interest groups different from other interest groups?**
>
> _____
> _____
> _____

HOW INTEREST GROUPS WORK

Interest groups work very hard to influence both public opinion and public policy. They **endorse**, or publicly declare support for, candidates who share their views and contribute to campaigns via political action committees. Interest groups also spend a great deal of time **lobbying**—contacting public officials to persuade them to support their members' interests. Providing people to testify at public hearings and summoning support at the **grass roots** level—the lowest level of an organization or society—are additional strategies. In the past, interest groups have also filed lawsuits on behalf of the population or cause they represent in order to influence public policy.

INTEREST GROUPS AND THE PUBLIC GOOD

Interest groups affect the public good in different ways. For Americans not in the majority, be it due to their background, profession, or opinion, interest groups provide a way to be heard.

While interest groups can help protect minority interests, critics believe that they can have too much influence, especially when they are well funded. Critics further argue that the groups often focus too narrowly on an issue, rely too heavily on emotional appeals, and may prevent Congress from acting swiftly on issues. Congress has placed limits on interest groups and their relationship with legislators as recently as 2007, tightening ethics rules and lobbying opportunities.

> **What is one advantage of interest groups? What is one disadvantage?**
>
> _____
> _____
> _____
> _____

MAIN IDEA
Political parties are formal organizations that work to elect candidates to public office. Our political system is dominated by two major parties, but other parties are actively involved in the system.

Key Terms

political party an organization that tries to elect its members to public office so that its views can become public policy

political spectrum the continuum of general political beliefs

nomination process naming candidates for elective office

electorate the body of people entitled to vote

one-party system a party system in which a single political party controls government

two-party system a party system in which two major parties compete to control government

multiparty system a party system in which several parties compete for control

third party any political party in a two-party system besides the two major ones

independent candidate a candidate who is not associated with any party

precinct the smallest unit for administering elections and local voting

ward a voting district made up of several precincts

Taking Notes

As you read, take notes on how political parties serve the public good. Record your notes in the graphic organizer below.

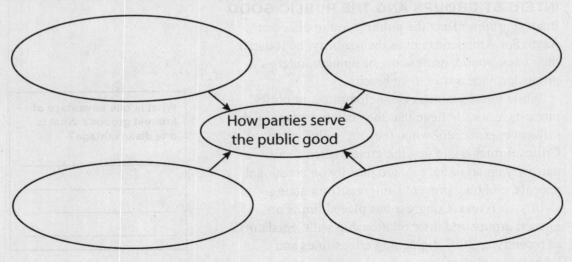

How parties serve the public good

Section Summary

THE ROLE OF POLITICAL PARTIES

A **political party** is an organization that tries to elect its members to public office in order to make its views public policy. Party members share similar ideas and views about society and government and unite these ideas in a political program called an ideology. What the ideology includes determines a party's place on the **political spectrum**, or the continuum of general political beliefs. For example, in the United States, the Democratic Party falls on the liberal end of the spectrum and the Republican Party on the conservative end.

Political parties have three roles within the political system. First, parties shape the **nomination process**, or the naming of candidates for public office, by identifying, and supporting candidates who share their views. Second, parties assist the electoral process by educating and motivating the **electorate**—the body of people entitled to vote—about issues and the voting process itself, making candidates more accessible by giving them a "brand name," and monitoring the actions of party and non-party policymakers. Finally, parties help determine the organization of government. The president typically nominates people who share his or her party's basic views, and Congress is controlled by the party that has the most members in each house.

> How are political parties involved in the political process after one of their candidates has been elected?
>
> _____
> _____
> _____
> _____

THE AMERICAN TWO-PARTY SYSTEM

There are three types of party systems: one-party, two-party, and multiparty. In a **one-party system**, a single party controls government; if other parties are permitted to operate, they typically have little power. Likewise, in a **two-party system**, as in the United States, additional parties do exist but have limited influence on the electoral process. In a **multiparty system**, several parties compete for control, sometimes forming coalitions to create a majority.

The United States' two-party system dates back to the first American political parties, the Federalists and the Democratic-Republicans. While these parties ceased to exist during the early 1800s, the parties that formed from the remains of the Democratic-

> How is the competition within a multiparty system different than that in a two-party system?
>
> _____
> _____
> _____
> _____

Republican Party continue to be the most powerful in the country: the Democrats and Republicans. While **third parties**—any political party in a two-party system besides the two major ones—and **independent candidates**—those not affiliated with a party—can affect elections, the Democratic and Republican parties continue to wield the most influence within the electoral process.

PARTY ORGANIZATION

Political parties are organized at the local, state, and national levels. At the local level, county parties identify and support local candidates, as well as organize support for candidates at higher levels. County parties are run by county committees, the members of which are elected by party members in county **precincts**—the smallest units for administering elections and local voting. Voting districts made up of several precincts are called **wards**.

At the state level, state committees composed of members of county committees work on supporting party candidates at the local, state, and national levels. A state chairperson leads these efforts.

At the national level, a committee made up of a national chairperson and members of state parties organizes major outreach and fundraising efforts for candidates at all levels. The national committee also creates and supports specific, affiliated organizations, such as the College Democrats of America or the National Teenage Republicans.

> Does support for local candidates end at the county level? Explain.
>
> _____
> _____
> _____

POLITICAL PARTIES AND THE PUBLIC GOOD

Parties can benefit the political process by filtering out extreme ideas, building inclusive support for issues, providing political and social stability, discouraging short-term shifts in power, and giving voters a "brand-name" idea of who is running. However, by reaching out to so many segments of the population at once, parties can sometimes lack unity, discipline, and loyalty. Additionally, the monetary support that parties receive from interest groups often prompts critics to question whether elected officials are always acting in the public interest.

> Explain three benefits of political parties.
>
> _____
> _____
> _____

The Political Process

MAIN IDEA
The Constitution creates a system in which citizens elect representatives to public office. Each citizen has the responsibility to help make this system work. Citizens can affect the electoral process in many ways, but the most powerful is by voting on election day.

Key Terms

hard money money donated to an individual campaign

soft money money given to a party rather than to a specific candidate

write-in candidates candidates who ask voters to write in his or her name on a ballot

caucus a meeting of party members who select the candidates to run for election

direct primary election in which a party's candidates for office are chosen directly by voters

closed primary election in which only voters registered as party members may vote for that party's candidates

open primary election in which registered voters may vote for any party's candidates, as long as they only vote for one party

plurality when a candidate receives more votes than any other candidate in that election

absentee ballot a ballot submitted on or before election day by a voter who cannot be present on election day

Taking Notes

As you read, take notes on some factors that may influence voter behavior. Record your notes in the graphic organizer below.

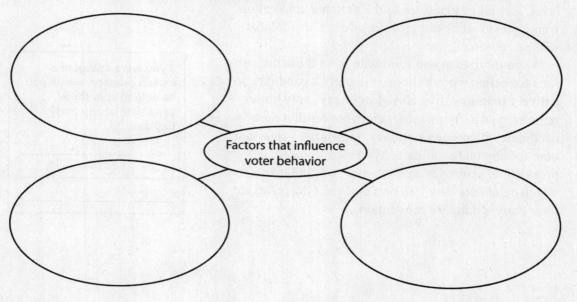

Factors that influence voter behavior

Section Summary

ORGANIZING AND FINANCING CAMPAIGNS

When running for office, candidates need to reach out to voters however possible, be it on television or by ringing doorbells. Doing all of this takes money. The candidate can raise money through his or her party, private individuals, personal or private funds, or political action committees. A **hard-money** contribution is money donated directly to a campaign. **Soft-money** contributions, created to get around the limits on hard money, are donations made to a candidate's party rather than directly to the candidate.

> What is the difference between hard and soft money?
>
> _____
>
> _____
>
> _____

CHOOSING CANDIDATES

There are several ways that a candidate can get his or her name on the ballot. He or she can seek a party's nomination or run as an independent candidate, self-nominate by collecting signatures on a petition, or simply run as a **write-in candidate** by asking voters to write in his or her name on the ballot.

Candidates can also be chosen by a party caucus or convention. A **caucus** is a meeting of elected party delegates at which candidates are selected. Caucus members are elected during lower-level precinct caucuses, which are open to all party members. Conventions are completely open to the public, with delegates representing party members not present. Local and state conventions select candidates at their level, as well as delegates to the national convention, where presidential and vice-presidential candidates will be chosen.

When more than one candidate from the same party runs for office, voters choose the party's candidate in a **direct primary**. In a **closed primary**, only voters registered as party members can vote for that party's candidate; in an **open primary**, registered voters can vote for any one candidate. Most states hold presidential primaries so that voters can indicate which candidate they like best and elect delegates to their party's national convention.

> If you were voting in a closed primary, would you be able to vote for a candidate of any party? Explain.
>
> _____
>
> _____
>
> _____

VOTING AND VOTING BEHAVIOR

Recently, voter turnout has ranged from less than two-thirds of voters in presidential elections to lower than 40 percent in state and local elections. One explanation for low turnout is that some people do not believe that their vote will make a difference. Another explanation may lie in the difficulty of registering to vote, the step one must take before actually voting.

When people do vote, there are four major factors that can influence the decisions they make: party identification, the voter's own views on issues, a candidate's personal and professional background, and the voter's background.

> **What two factors might be contributing to low voter turnout?**
>
> _____
>
> _____
>
> _____

MORE ABOUT ELECTIONS

General elections take place at the end of campaigns. In most states, the candidate who receives a **plurality**, or more votes than any other candidates, wins the election. A few states hold runoff elections if no candidate receives a majority of the vote. Special elections are held when an officeholder has died or resigned.

Regardless of the type, most elections follow standard practices and all adhere to state and federal laws. Federal elections take place on the first Tuesday following the first Monday in November in even-numbered years. Most state and many local elections also take place on this day. On election day, voters go to their precinct polling place and cast a secret ballot, sometimes on paper and sometimes on machines.

If a voter knows he or she will be unable to vote on election day, whether due to illness, travel, or another reason, he or she can cast an **absentee ballot**, or in some states, vote earlier than election day.

> **Is a plurality of votes always the same as a majority of votes? Explain.**
>
> _____
>
> _____
>
> _____
>
> _____

CAMPAIGNS AND THE PUBLIC GOOD

Political campaigns help voters become informed about both issues and candidates. However, some Americans feel that campaigns rely too heavily on short television ads, which can only share a very small amount of information and sometimes relay a distorted message to viewers. Negative ads also bother some people, who prefer candidates to explain their own views instead of attacking those of others.

Civil Liberties

Chapter Summary

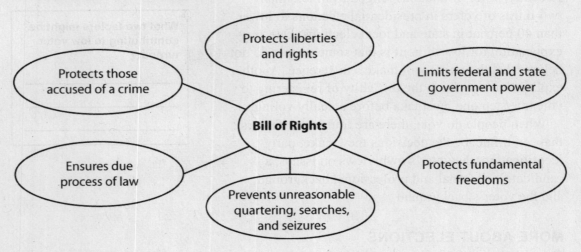

COMPREHENSION AND CRITICAL THINKING

Use information from the graphic organizer to answer the following questions.

1. **Describe** What does the Bill of Rights protect?

_____

_____

2. **Identify Cause and Effect** Due process of law ensures that the laws and procedures the government uses when prosecuting a person are fair. How do you think due process helps both accused persons and victims?

_____

_____

3. **Evaluate** The Bill of Rights protects the fundamental freedoms of religion, speech, the press, assembly, and petition. Choose one of these freedoms and explain in your own words why the adjective *fundamental* applies to it.

_____

_____

_____

Civil Liberties

MAIN IDEA
The United States was formed out of a belief that individuals had certain important liberties and rights. The Constitution's Bill of Rights protects these liberties and rights.

Key Terms

civil liberties basic freedoms to think and act that all people have and that are protected against government abuse

civil rights rights of fair and equal status and treatment and the right to participate in government

due process following established and complete legal procedures

incorporation doctrine the Supreme Court's reasoning for incorporating much of the Bill of Rights into the Fourteenth Amendment; holds that certain protections are essential to due process of the law

Taking Notes

As you read, take notes on how the Bill of Rights protects Americans' civil liberties and rights. Record your notes in the graphic organizer below.

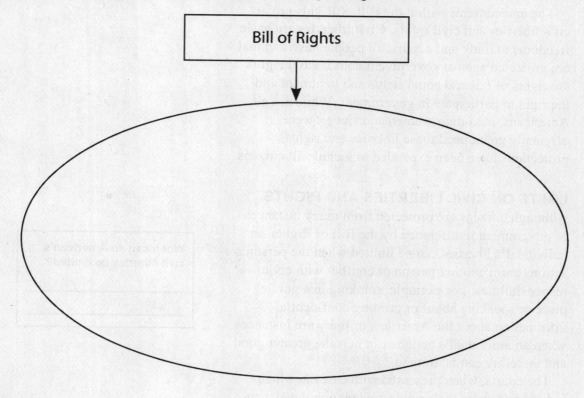

Bill of Rights

Section Summary

THE BILL OF RIGHTS

The Constitution did not originally include the Bill of
Rights. After gaining independence from Great
Britain, the states adopted their own individual
constitutions, the majority of which protected
individual freedoms and rights. Although Virginian
delegate George Mason proposed a bill of rights at the
Constitutional Convention, his idea was defeated by
others' arguments that the state constitutions and a
separation of powers were sufficient.

Yet it soon became clear that not all of the states
would ratify the Constitution without at least the
prospect of a bill of rights. Supporters of the
Constitution finally agreed to add one as soon as the
new government met, and in 1789, James Madison
drafted a number of amendments. After much debate,
Congress settled on 10 amendments—which listed
specific rights yet did not deny any other rights—that
were ratified and formally made part of the
Constitution in 1791.

The amendments within the Bill of Rights protect
civil liberties and civil rights. **Civil liberties** are basic
freedoms to think and act that all people have and that
are protected against government abuse. **Civil rights**
are rights of fair and equal status and treatment and
the right to participate in government. While not all
Americans, including women and slaves, were
originally guaranteed these liberties and rights,
protections have been expanded to include all citizens.

> **Does the Bill of Rights limit Americans' rights to only those listed within it? Explain.**
>
> _____
>
> _____

LIMITS ON CIVIL LIBERTIES AND RIGHTS

Although citizens are protected from many instances
of government interference by the Bill of Rights, an
individual's liberties can be limited when the person's
actions harm another person or conflict with civic
responsibilities. For example, smoking in a public
place or speaking about or printing confidential
information about the American military are instances
when an individual's actions can hurt the greater good
and therefore can be limited.

The courts, when presented with cases in which
individuals claim their rights are being violated, can
issue rulings that set a standard for how to balance

> **When can an American's civil liberties be limited?**
>
> _____
>
> _____

personal freedoms with the protection of all Americans. Most of these rulings have occurred since the early 1900s, and many are the result of cases brought to the courts' attention by interest groups, such as the National Association for the Advancement of Colored People (NAACP) and the American Civil Liberties Union (ACLU).

CIVIL LIBERTIES AND THE FOURTEENTH AMENDMENT

The Bill of Rights protects individuals from some actions by the federal government, not state and local governments. However, over the years, the Supreme Court has applied many of the protections within the Bill of Rights to state and local governments, based on the Fourteenth Amendment. This amendment, passed after the Civil War to protect the rights of formerly enslaved African Americans, forbids the states to deprive anyone of life, liberty, or property without **due process**—following established and complete legal procedures. The Court established the **incorporation doctrine** to justify merging much of the Bill of Rights with the Fourteenth Amendment, claiming that certain protections are essential to due process of the law.

> Why was the incorporation doctrine established?
> _____
> _____

This incorporation has taken place little by little. The first case to merge the Bill of Rights was *Chicago, Burlington & Quincy Railroad* v. *Chicago*. In this 1897 case, the Court ruled that the Fifth Amendment's "just compensation" clause also applied to the states. Later cases incorporated First Amendment freedoms, the Sixth Amendment, and parts of the Fourth, Fifth, and Eighth Amendments.

Civil Liberties

MAIN IDEA
The First Amendment protects five fundamental freedoms that are central to the American notion of liberty: the freedoms of religion, speech, the press, assembly, and petition.

Key Terms

establishment clause the part of the First Amendment that declares that government cannot take actions that create an official religion or support one religion over another

free exercise clause the part of the First Amendment that guarantees each person the right to hold any religious beliefs he or she chooses

slander a spoken defamatory statement

libel a printed defamatory statement

treason the crime of making war against the United States or giving "aid and comfort" to its enemies

sedition a legal term for speech or actions that inspire revolt against the government

prior restraint government action that seeks to prevent materials from being published

symbolic speech the communication of actions through symbols and actions

freedom of association the right to join with others, share ideas, and work toward a common purpose

Taking Notes

As you read, take notes on the five freedoms protected by the First Amendment. Record your notes in the graphic organizer below.

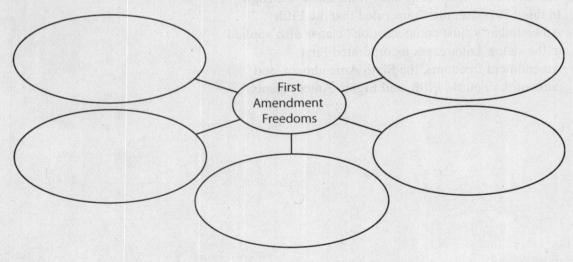

Section Summary

RELIGIOUS FREEDOM

The First Amendment freedom of religion guarantees two things. First, the government cannot establish an official religion or support one religion over another— this is the part of the First Amendment called the **establishment clause**. This clause created the separation of church and state, a thorny issue that the federal courts have dealt with a on a case-by-case basis. Many past cases have deal with government-sponsored religious displays. Several other important cases have involved how the establishment clause relates to education. For example, the Court has carefully examined how public funds should be used in relation to private schools, which can include religious schools. Justices have also struck down mandatory morning prayer and silent meditation in public schools, eventually developing the Lemon Test in 1971. Since then, the Court considers a law constitutional if it has a secular purpose, if its major effects neither advance nor inhibit religion, and if it does not encourage "excessive government entanglement with religion."

> **What does the establishment clause prevent?**
>
> _____
>
> _____

The second part of the First Amendment related to freedom of religion is the **free exercise clause**, which guarantees each person the right to hold any religious beliefs they choose—but does not allow them to practice these beliefs however that way. In recent decades, the Court has mainly ruled religious practices illegal only when the interest of enforcing a law is very strongly justified by the needs of society.

FREEDOM OF SPEECH AND OF THE PRESS

The First Amendment freedoms of speech and of the press allow Americans to participate in the democratic process with little fear of punishment by the government. These freedoms also make it possible for Americans to watch their government debate and act, as well as access most government documents.

> **How does freedom of speech give Americans access to politicians?**
>
> _____
>
> _____

While the freedom of speech protects most speech, including that which is racist or offensive, the government can limit obscene speech or printed materials, in addition to speech and printed materials that knowingly harm another person. These types of

speech and printed materials include instances of
slander—a spoken defamatory statement—and
libel—a printed defamatory statement. Also,
sedition—a legal term for speech or actions that
inspire revolt against the government—or speech or
writings that are considered examples of **treason**—the
crime of making war against the United States or
giving "aid and comfort" to its enemies—can be
prohibited. The Supreme Court and the country as a
whole have struggled with what constitutes seditious
speech and how to define "clear and present danger"
when evaluating the consequences of such speech

Freedom of the press helps the spread of
information in a democratic society. The government
regulates television and radio more closely than other
media forms. Historically, print media has mostly
been protected from **prior restraint**, or government
action that seeks to prevent materials from being
published. The Supreme Court has repeatedly ruled
that prior restraint can only be used when the
government can prove how the potentially printed
materials can cause immediate harm. Likewise, the
Court has ruled that **symbolic speech**, or the
communication of ideas through symbols and actions,
falls under the protection of the First Amendment
unless it threatens property or public order.

> **Explain prior restraint in your own words.**
> _____
> _____

FREEDOMS OF ASSEMBLY AND PETITION

The First Amendment freedoms of assembly and
petition allow Americans to meet and share ideas, as
well as create initiatives, or petitions designed to force
the government to consider an issue or allow a vote.
Various Supreme Court cases have confirmed these
two freedoms, even incorporating the right to
assembly into the Fourteenth Amendment. While the
government can almost never limit the content of an
assembly, it can restrict when, where, and how some
assemblies are held. The Supreme Court has also ruled
that while the **freedom of association**, or the right to
join with others, share ideas, and work toward a
common purpose, is not explicitly stated in the
Constitution, it is established simply by the presence
of the other First Amendment freedoms and the due
process clause.

> **What power does the government have over assemblies?**
> _____
> _____

Civil Liberties

MAIN IDEA
A key purpose of the Bill of Rights is to protect individuals from government abuses. Several amendments limit the government's power and protect individual rights against government actions.

Key Terms

probable cause the strong likelihood that a search would find evidence of a crime

search warrant a document that gives police legal authority to search private property

exclusionary rule the rule that evidence obtained illegally may not be used against a person in court

police power the government's ability to regulate behavior for the common good

procedural due process legal expectation that government follow certain procedures before punishing a person

substantive due process legal expectation that laws are fair and just

Taking Notes

As you read, take notes on the different amendments discussed in this section. Record your notes in the graphic organizer below.

Amendment	Protections
Second	
Third	
Fourth	
Fifth	

Section Summary

THE RIGHT TO KEEP AND BEAR ARMS

The Second Amendment was included in the Bill of Rights to allow states to form their own militias and to relieve Americans' fears of an overly powerful, federally-controlled standing army. Today, Americans continue to debate the true meaning of the amendment. Gun-rights advocates claim that it gives individuals the right to own whatever guns they choose. Gun-control advocates claim that nothing in the amendment prevents the government from limiting gun ownership. With the exception of one case in which it upheld a law restricting the possession of certain guns, the Supreme Court has left decisions about gun laws to the lower courts.

> **What was the original purpose of the Second Amendment?**
> _____
> _____

SECURITY OF HOME AND PERSON

The Third Amendment forbids the government from housing troops in private homes during peacetime without the owner's consent—the Constitution's response to earlier practices by the British army.

As with the Third Amendment, the Fourth Amendment, which forbids "unreasonable searches and seizures," was inspired by colonial British practices, such as conducting searches without **probable cause**, or reasonable grounds. The Fourth Amendment requires probable cause for **search warrants**, documents that give police legal authority to search public property. Fourth Amendment protections also limit police to searching only for evidence related to a crime they are investigating, allowing them to take other evidence only when it is in "plain view." In response to searches conducted illegally, the Supreme Court has established the **exclusionary rule**, which states that evidence obtained illegally may not be used against a person in court. However, this rule does not apply to police searches conducted outside or in a person's trash.

Stopping a person who is walking down the street or in a car in order to search them is legally considered a seizure, and is justifiable if police believe there is reasonable suspicion that the person may harm others. But under the protections of the Fourth Amendment, there must be probable cause to arrest

> **What does the exclusionary rule prevent?**
> _____
> _____

the person. Also, in order to search a car, police need to first stop the driver based on probable cause, such as a traffic violation. Any evidence then found during the search is allowable.

Other modern-day Fourth Amendment issues include how much freedom government agencies have to monitor electronic communications without warrants—especially since the passage of the USA PATRIOT Act—and which public and private employers can drug test their employees and when. The Supreme Court has ruled that schools may randomly drug test students, a segment of the American population that has fewer Fourth Amendment rights. For example, students and their belongings can be searched without probable cause.

THE RIGHT TO PRIVACY

While the right to privacy is not explicitly stated in the Constitution, many Americans and, at times, the Supreme Court feel that citizens are entitled to the right in certain situations. Some arguments point to the expectation of privacy built into the Fourth Amendment, as well as the guarantee of liberty in the due process clauses of the Fifth and Fourteenth Amendments. In the landmark cases *Griswold* v. *Connecticut* (1965) and *Roe* v. *Wade* (1973), the Supreme Court ruled that certain amendments indicate a "zone of privacy" and a right to privacy that can protect some decisions and behaviors.

What is one way the right to privacy has been established, even though it is not mentioned in the Constitution?
_____
_____

DUE PROCESS OF LAW

The concept of due process is inherent in both the Fifth Amendment, which applies due process to the federal government, and the Fourteenth Amendment, which applies it to state governments. Due process limits the government's **police power**, or ability to regulate behavior for the common good. **Procedural due process** requires that government follow certain procedures before punishing a person. **Substantive due process** requires that the laws potentially used to punish a person are fair and just. Either right can be limited in cases where the government's need to do something is strongly justified and is in the interest of the greater good.

What is the difference between procedural and substantive due process?
_____
_____

MAIN IDEA
The Constitution contains many features that help ensure that people accused of a crime receive fair and reasonable treatment—from arrest to trial to punishment.

Key Terms

civil law category of law that covers private disputes between people over property and relationships

criminal law category of law that deals with crimes and their punishments

indictment a formal complaint of criminal wrongdoing issued by a grand jury

bail money pledged by the accused as a guarantee that he or she will return to court for trial

capital punishment punishment by death

Miranda warnings a list of certain constitutional rights possessed by those accused of crimes

bench trial a trial in which the judge alone hears and decides a case

double jeopardy restriction on trying a person twice for the same offense

Taking Notes

As you read, take notes on the protected rights of people accused of crimes. Record your notes in the graphic organizer below.

```
┌─────────────────────────┐        ┌─────────────────────────┐
│                         │        │                         │
│   Rights of the Accused │ ─────> │                         │
│                         │        │                         │
└─────────────────────────┘        └─────────────────────────┘

┌─────────────────────────┐        ┌─────────────────────────┐
│                         │        │                         │
│                         │ ─────> │                         │
│                         │        │                         │
└─────────────────────────┘        └─────────────────────────┘

┌─────────────────────────┐        ┌─────────────────────────┐
│                         │        │                         │
│                         │ ─────> │                         │
│                         │        │                         │
└─────────────────────────┘        └─────────────────────────┘
```

Section Summary

THE U.S. JUSTICE SYSTEM

There are two categories of law: civil and criminal. **Civil law** involves private disputes between people over property or relationships. Subcategories of civil law include contract law, tort law, property law, and family law. Civil lawsuits can be settled by trial, mediation, arbitration, or negotiation. When civil lawsuits do go to trial, they typically follow five basic steps: the plaintiff hires a lawyer and files a complaint, the two sides try to settle the dispute before the trial begins, the two sides exchange information in discovery, a judge or jury hears the trial, and the judge or jury issues a ruling, which may be appealed later.

Criminal law is the system for dealing with crimes—both misdemeanors and felonies—and their punishments. In most federal criminal cases, per the Fifth Amendment, an accused person faces a grand jury. If it believes there is enough evidence of a crime, the grand jury issues an **indictment**, or formal complaint of criminal wrongdoing. Once an indictment is issued, the accused is arrested, goes through hearings, and may be allowed to temporarily go free by posting **bail**, or money pledged by the accused as a guarantee that he or she will return to court for trial. If the accused pleads guilty or accepts a plea bargain, he or she will be sentenced without a trial. If the accused pleads not guilty, a trial takes places, after which sentencing occurs if the person is found guilty. The harshest sentence is **capital punishment**, or punishment by death.

> **What are two different ways plaintiffs and defendants can settle civil lawsuits?**
>
> _____
>
> _____

> **What takes place first: sentencing or trial?**
>
> _____

RIGHTS OF THE ACCUSED

In the American justice system, a person accused of a crime is presumed innocent until proven guilty and afforded several protections under the Constitution. First, by almost never allowing the government to suspend the writ of habeas corpus, the Constitution ensures that the accused will have a chance to defend his or her actions in court. Second, under the Fifth Amendment, the accused needs to first be indicted by a grand jury before standing trial for most federal crimes. Third, the Fifth Amendment also prevents the accused from being forced to give spoken evidence of or testify about anything that suggests his or her own guilt. In response to violations of this third protection, police must now read the **Miranda warnings**, or list of constitutional rights possessed by the accused, to suspects before they are arrested.

The Constitution does not provide any protections for victims of crime. In recent years, several states have passed such laws, including some that give victims the right to be informed of related offenders' convictions, sentences, imprisonment, and release.

> **What do the Miranda warnings tell accused persons?**
> _____
> _____
> _____

GUARANTEES OF A FAIR TRIAL

The Sixth Amendment guarantees the right of Americans accused of a crime to a "speedy and public trial" and applies to both the federal government and the states. Delays that harm a defendant or give a prosecutor undue advantage can violate the Sixth Amendment. A "public" trial is considered one that is open to the public, although the court may limit press and public access in certain circumstances.

The Sixth Amendment also guarantees those accused of criminal charges the right to a trial by an impartial and local jury; a **bench trial**—one in which a judge alone hears and decides a case—may take place in specific situations. Additional Sixth Amendment—and Fourteenth Amendment—protections include the right to be informed of charges, the right to confront witnesses, and the right to an adequate, professional defense. Furthermore, the Fifth Amendment prohibits **double jeopardy**, or trying a person twice for the same offense.

> **Is a jury involved in a bench trial? Explain.**
> _____
> _____
> _____

PUNISHMENT

Americans convicted of crimes are also protected. The Eighth Amendment prohibits the government from imposing excessive fines; this protection does not apply to civil cases between private parties. The Eighth Amendment also bans "cruel and unusual punishment," the definition of which has mainly been left to the lower courts, particularly in cases involving capital punishment. Most states allow the death penalty, which the Supreme Court has declared constitutional, but only when applied to criminals fairly.

Civil Rights

Chapter Summary

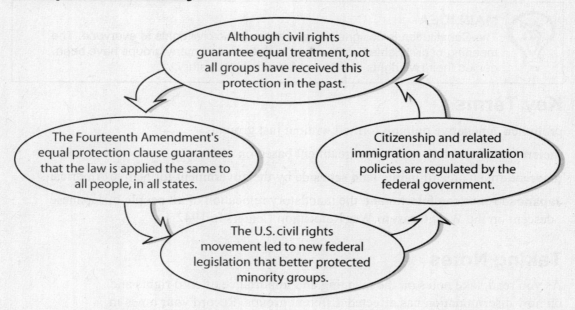

COMPREHENSION AND CRITICAL THINKING

Use information from the graphic organizer to answer the following questions.

1. **Describe** What was the result of the U.S. civil rights movement?

   _____

   _____

2. **Explain** Why is the idea behind the equal protection clause so important?

   _____

   _____

3. **Elaborate** American culture needed to change before all Americans were guaranteed the same civil rights. How do you think the civil rights movement helped these changes come about?

   _____

   _____

   _____

Civil Rights

MAIN IDEA
The Constitution is designed to guarantee basic civil rights to everyone. The meaning of civil rights has changed over time, and many groups have been denied their civil rights at different times in U.S. history.

Key Terms

prejudice a negative opinion formed without just grounds

racism discrimination and unfair treatment based on race

reservation an area of public land set aside by the government for Native Americans

Japanese American internment the mandatory relocation of all people of Japanese descent on the West Coast to War Relocation Centers in 1942

Taking Notes

As you read, take notes on the meaning and importance of civil rights and on how discrimination has affected different groups. Record your notes in the graphic organizer below.

Civil Rights	Discrimination

Section Summary

CIVIL RIGHTS IN THE UNITED STATES

Civil rights are rights that involve equal status and treatment. They protect people from discrimination, the act or practice of treating people unfairly based on their race, national origin, sex, religion, age, or other factors. Civil rights also give people the right to participate in government, such as voting and running for office.

In the United States, civil rights are protected by the law. Such laws are found in the Constitution and its amendments, federal and state laws, and Supreme Court decisions. However, for long periods of U.S. history, the government and much of American society did not consider certain groups entitled to guaranteed civil rights. Society's idea of fair and equal treatment has changed over the years, and women and ethnic and racial minorities have successfully fought for the rights to vote, participate in government, and be free from discrimination.

> **What American laws protect civil rights?**
> _____
> _____

A PATTERN OF DISCRIMINATION

In past centuries, the U.S. government operated with **prejudice**—a negative opinion formed without just grounds—toward certain groups. Such prejudice is primarily based on feelings of **racism**, or discrimination and unfair treatment based on race.

Enslaved for over 250 years, African Americans received horrible treatment for a good part of U.S. history. Until the 1860s, government and society considered them property and therefore unequal to white Americans. After the Civil War, the Thirteenth Amendment abolished slavery. This action was quickly followed by the passage of the Fourteenth and Fifteenth Amendments, which granted former slaves citizenship and the right to vote. Yet African Americans continued to suffer unfair treatment for decades, as attacks, new state laws, and court rulings produced new forms of discrimination.

Native Americans were long considered a group outside of American society and the protections of civil rights. Throughout the 1800s, the U.S. government consistently violated land treaties it made with Native Americans, eventually forcing them from

> **Why did the Thirteenth, Fourteenth, and Fifteenth Amendments fail to give adequate protection to African Americans?**
> _____
> _____
> _____

their traditional lands onto **reservations**, areas of public lands set aside by the government for Native Americans. Furthermore, Native Americans were often prevented from speaking their native languages, raising their own children, or following their traditional ways of life.

Asian Americans have also had to deal with discrimination, starting with the arrival of Chinese immigrants in the mid-1800s. As these immigrants took jobs in the mining and railroad industries, many Americans became angry about increased competition for jobs and discriminated against the Chinese in employment, housing, and access to public services. Chinese immigration was even temporarily banned in 1882. Similarly, Japanese immigration was halted in the early 1900s. Japanese Americans also experienced one of the worst violations of civil rights in U.S. history during an event known as **Japanese American internment**, when all people of Japanese descent on the West Coast were forced into War Relocation Centers from 1942 until the end of World War II.

Explain how Japanese American internment violated people's civil rights.
_____
_____
_____

Hispanics or Latinos—people with a Spanish-speaking background—are yet another group that has faced discrimination. As the United States took control of various lands where Hispanics lived, such as Texas and California, it treated the native people—now known as Mexican Americans—with disrespect, sometimes taking their land or segregating them. From the mid-1800s until modern times, several waves of Hispanic immigration have taken place, each of which has had to deal with the problem of discrimination.

Finally, women were denied equal treatment for years, as much of society—and the Supreme Court—considered them members of the "domestic sphere" only. Until 1920, when they won the right to vote, women could not actively participate in government, serve on juries, hold property or custody rights equal to men's, or pursue most educational and career opportunities.

Civil Rights

Section 2

MAIN IDEA
The Fourteenth Amendment was designed to bolster civil rights by requiring states to guarantee freed slaves "the equal protection of the laws." However, African Americans and women still struggled to win equal treatment in American society.

Key Terms

equal protection clause clause within the Fourteenth Amendment that requires states to apply the law the same way for one person that they would for another person in the same circumstances

suspect classification a classification based on race or national origin

segregation the separation of racial groups

Jim Crow laws segregation laws that reduced participation in government by African Americans

separate-but-equal doctrine the policy that laws requiring separate facilities for racial groups were legal so long as the facilities were "equal"

suffrage the right to vote

Seneca Falls Convention the first women's rights convention in the United States

de jure segregation segregation by law

desegregation ending the formal separation of groups based on race

de facto segregation segregation in fact, even without laws that require segregation

Taking Notes

As you read, take notes on the meaning of equal protection and its effects on the struggles of African Americans and women for equal rights. Record your notes in the graphic organizer below.

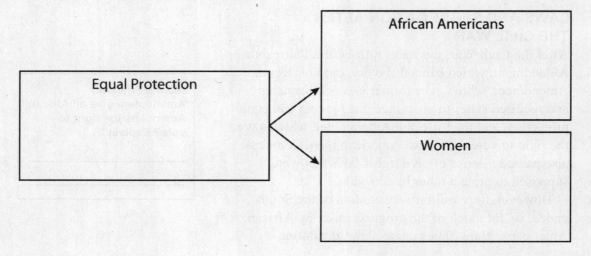

Section Summary

EQUAL PROTECTION OF THE LAW

The **equal protection clause** in the Fourteenth Amendment requires states to apply the law the same way for one person that they would for another person in the same circumstances. Passed after the Civil War to protect the rights of former slaves, the Fourteenth Amendment was the first addition to the Constitution specifically designed to protect people from abuses by state governments.

Yet the equal protection clause does not always require people to be considered equal. The government can sometimes make a reasonable distinction between groups. The courts consider three guidelines when evaluating reasonable distinction. First, they may use the rational basis test, which allows the government to treat groups differently if the law in question is proven to accomplish a legitimate goal, such as public safety. A higher standard to determine reasonable distinction—especially in cases involving gender—is the intermediate scrutiny test, which requires a compelling reason and "exceedingly persuasive justification." Finally, the strict scrutiny test is used when a fundamental right is restricted or when a classification is made based on race or national origin, known as a **suspect classification**. It is very difficult for a distinction to pass this test, which has been used in cases involving interracial marriages and Japanese American internment.

> **What does the equal protection clause prevent from happening?**
>
> _____
>
> _____

LAWS AND SEGREGATION AFTER THE CIVIL WAR

After the Civil War, the states ratified the Thirteenth Amendment, which banned slavery, the Fourteenth Amendment, which gave former slaves citizenship and required states to guarantee due process and equal protection, and the Fifteenth Amendment, which gave the right to vote to African American men. Congress also passed a series of civil rights laws that were supposed to protect other basic rights.

However, once military occupation of the South ended, so did much of the progress made by African Americans. Many states passed laws instituting

> **Did the Fifteenth Amendment give all African Americans the right to vote? Explain.**
>
> _____
>
> _____

segregation—the separation of racial groups—known as **Jim Crow laws** after a popular racist song. These laws targeted almost all areas of life, from participating in government to eating in restaurants. The Supreme Court upheld many Jim Crow laws, first ruling the Civil Rights Act of 1875 unconstitutional and then establishing—in *Plessy* v. *Ferguson* (1896)—the **separate-but-equal doctrine**, the policy that laws requiring separate facilities for racial groups were legal so long as the facilities were "equal."

VOTING RIGHTS FOR WOMEN

While fighting for equal rights for African Americans, many women in the North began to demand equal rights for themselves, especially **suffrage**, or the right to vote. The first U.S. women's rights convention was the **Seneca Falls Convention**, where delegates called for a number of rights and adopted the Declaration of Sentiments. Upset that the Fifteenth Amendment did not also give women the right to vote, women continued to fight for suffrage throughout the 1800s. Although many western states and territories gave women suffrage by the late 1800s, the women's rights movement experienced little progress at the federal level. Finally, in 1920, the Nineteenth Amendment was ratified, which granted women the right to vote.

> Was the fight for women's suffrage more successful at the state or federal level in the 1800s?
> _____
> _____

ROLLING BACK SEGREGATION

De jure segregation, or segregation by law, continued well into the 1900s. African American activist groups began challenging segregation in court, first insisting that the "equal" in "separate but equal" be a reality. The courts soon found segregated facilities consistently unequal. In the 1954 landmark case *Brown* v. *Board of Education of Topeka, Kansas*, the Supreme Court overturned *Plessy* and declared segregation in public schools unconstitutional. Schools slowly began the process of **desegregation**, or ending the formal separation of groups based on race, although in many places whites resisted this change. Today, all segregation is illegal but **de facto segregation**, or segregation in fact if not law, still exists. Americans continue to work to overcome this challenge.

> What is the difference between de jure segregation and de facto segregation?
> _____
> _____
> _____

Civil Rights

MAIN IDEA
In the 1950s and 1960s, an organized movement demanding civil rights changed American society and led to a series of new federal laws that protected the civil rights of African Americans and other groups.

Key Terms

civil rights movement a mass movement in the 1950s and 1960s to guarantee the civil rights of African Americans

civil disobedience nonviolent refusals to obey the law as a way to advocate change

poll tax a tax levied on someone who wants to vote

affirmative action a policy that requires employers and institutions to provide opportunities for members of certain historically underrepresented groups

reverse discrimination discrimination against the majority group

quota a fixed number or percentage

Taking Notes

As you read, take notes on the civil rights movement and how it led to new civil rights laws. Record your notes in the graphic organizer below.

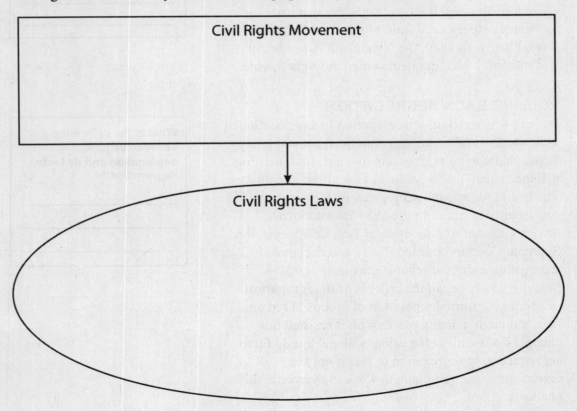

Section Summary

THE CIVIL RIGHTS MOVEMENT

The **civil rights movement** was a mass movement in the 1950s and 1960s to guarantee the civil rights of African Americans. To communicate their message, members used acts of **civil disobedience**—nonviolent refusals to obey the law as a way to advocate change—such as sit-ins and boycotts. One of the most important boycotts of the movement involved civil rights leader Martin Luther King, Jr., and the Montgomery, Alabama, public buses, on one of which African American Rosa Parks refused to give up her seat to a white person. Parks' refusal and subsequent arrest led to the boycott and a Supreme Court ruling against the city that became the first major success of the civil rights movement. A 1963 March on Washington and the Selma to Montgomery marches also helped lead to the passage of laws that better protected the civil rights of minorities.

> **What is an example of an act of civil disobedience?**
> _____
> _____

NEW FEDERAL LAWS

The strength of the civil rights movement inspired a series of new laws. The Civil Rights Act of 1957 included several federal anti-discrimination measures and created the Civil Rights Commission. The Civil Rights Act of 1960 let the federal government monitor places known for voter discrimination and made it illegal for anyone to restrict the right to vote. Both laws lacked enforcement strength, however, mainly due to the opposition of southerners in Congress.

The landmark Civil Rights Act of 1964 was much more powerful, passed under the authority of Congress's commerce clause. This legislation banned discrimination based on race, color, religion, sex, national origin—and, by 1967, age—in voting, employment, public accommodations, and government programs—and applied to individuals and businesses, not just actions by the states.

Eventually the courts began to strike down unfair southern voting laws. Additionally, the Twenty-fourth Amendment banned **poll taxes**, taxes levied on someone who wants to vote. One year later, in 1965, the Voting Rights Act banned literacy tests and gave the federal government oversight power to change

> **What kinds of discrimination did the Civil Rights Act of 1964 ban?**
> _____
> _____

voting laws, voter registration, and elections anywhere Congress believed discrimination was widespread.

EXTENDING CIVIL RIGHTS

The civil rights era also resulted in extended civil rights for other minority groups. Various legislation and court rulings banned discrimination against women in many areas, including education and personal finance; required equal pay for men and women in the same jobs; and confirmed that women have a constitutional right to an abortion and that sexual harassment is illegal. Hispanics also saw improvements in treatment, especially in better application of the equal protection clause. The Voting Rights Act of 1975 made ballots available in Spanish, and migrant farm workers, many of whom were Hispanic, also gained new rights.

In the interest of Native Americans, Congress passed several laws, including some that allowed Native American groups more control over programs in their communities and confirmed their religious freedom. Finally, the Americans with Disabilities Act of 1990 required public buildings and transportation to be fully accessible and prohibited discrimination against people with disabilities.

> **What civil rights were extended to women as a result of the civil rights era?**
>
> _____
>
> _____

AFFIRMATIVE ACTION

Affirmative action is a policy that requires employers and institutions to provide opportunities for members of certain historically underrepresented groups, first used in the 1960s to improve diversity in private and public workplaces. But by the late 1970s, some people claimed affirmative action policies were a form of **reverse discrimination**, or discrimination against the majority group. In 1978—in a case involving a **quota**, or fixed number or percentage, of minority students— and then again in 2003, the Supreme Court considered the role of affirmative action in higher education, ruling against the use of strict quota systems but declaring the use of race and diversity as factors in the admissions process constitutional. In some states, voters have passed ballot measures to restrict the use of affirmative action policies.

> **Explain in your own words why some people thought affirmative action was a form of reverse discrimination.**
>
> _____
>
> _____
>
> _____
>
> _____

Section 4

 MAIN IDEA
Being a U.S. citizen includes certain rights and responsibilities. The federal government regulates citizenship through its immigration and naturalization policies.

Key Terms

jus soli a principle of citizenship by birthplace

jus sanguinis a principle of citizenship by parentage

naturalization the legal process by which an immigrant becomes a citizen

denaturalization the process through which a naturalized person loses citizenship

expatriation the legal process of giving up one's citizenship

undocumented alien someone living in a country without authorization from the government

deportation the legal process of forcing a noncitizen to leave a country

Taking Notes

As you read, take notes on American citizenship and immigration issues. Record your notes in the graphic organizer below.

Citizenship	Immigration

Section Summary

U.S. CITIZENSHIP

Both citizens and noncitizens—also known as aliens—are guaranteed civil rights in the United States, although aliens cannot vote. Most people become citizens by being born in the United States or a U.S. territory—a principle of citizenship by birth, called **jus soli**—or by being born on foreign soil to U.S. citizens—a principle of citizenship by parentage, called **jus sanguinis**.

Naturalization is the legal process by which an immigrant becomes a citizen. Naturalized citizens have all of the same rights as native-born citizens, although the Constitution does not allow them to become president or vice president. The naturalization process involves legal entry into the country; a period of residence in the country; the ability to read, write, and speak English; good moral character; belief in the Constitution; and positive feelings toward the country. Additionally, an exam and an oath are required. Also, there are some instances in which the government can grant collective naturalization to an entire group of people, such as when the United States gained new territories.

> **What is the difference between a naturalized citizen and a person who received citizenship through jus soli?**
>
> _____
>
> _____
>
> _____

Although it is uncommon, a citizen can also lose his or her citizenship through a process called **denaturalization**. This is typically the result of becoming a citizen by fraud, by committing serious crimes against the U.S. government, or by working for or swearing allegiance to another country's government or military. In cases where a citizen willingly gives up citizenship, the legal process is called **expatriation**.

Americans share a civic identity in their devotion to American ideals, such as democracy, and to civic responsibilities, such as voting, respecting laws and others' rights, and paying taxes. Meeting civic responsibilities helps preserve and protect U.S. society.

> **What are two examples of civic responsibilities?**
>
> _____
>
> _____

IMMIGRATION POLICIES

Until the late 1800s, the U.S. government barely regulated immigration, often encouraging it instead. Once the U.S. population reached new heights and immigrants from outside of northern and western Europe began arriving in waves, American society and government became stricter about immigration. In 1875 Congress passed a law that barred entry to criminals, then a law that ended immigration from China—for 10 years—in 1882.

In the 1920s, new quota laws set the total number of legal immigrants at 165,000 a year, with quotas for specific European countries based on the national origin of the U.S. population in 1890. Immigration dropped as Asian, African, and Latin American immigrants were restricted. In 1965 the Immigration and Nationality Act Amendments—updated in 1990—abolished the quota system, set a new annual total, and gave preference to immigrants with certain skills or relatives in the United States. Today 675,000 immigrants are allowed per year, with many arriving from Asia and Latin America. Refugees and people seeking political asylum are subject to different immigration policies.

> **How did U.S. immigration policy change during the 1800s?**
>
> _____
>
> _____
>
> _____

ILLEGAL IMMIGRATION

Illegal immigration is a major problem facing the United States. Most **undocumented aliens**, or unauthorized immigrants, have entered the country by crossing the U.S.-Mexico border or by overstaying legally issued visas. The government is unable to keep track of these approximately 12 million people, who are subject to **deportation**, or the legal process of forcing a noncitizen to leave the country, if caught. Some Americans feel that illegally entering the United States is wrong, and that illegal immigrants take away jobs from American citizens and strain government services. Others argue that illegal immigrants are just trying to build better lives for themselves and take otherwise undesirable jobs. The government has tried various tactics to stem illegal immigration, from creating and increasing the Border Patrol to granting one-time amnesty to undocumented aliens to making deportation easier. Yet officials still struggle over the problem and the best way to solve it.

> **What is one argument against illegal immigration? What is one argument in defense of illegal immigrants?**
>
> _____
>
> _____
>
> _____
>
> _____

Understanding Elections

Chapter Summary

Candidates	Voters
• Work with staff to create message • Deliver message via various media • Raise funds from variety of sources • Appeal to voters for support	• Educate selves about candidates and issues • Register to vote and cast ballots • Work on campaigns or at polls • Run for office

COMPREHENSION AND CRITICAL THINKING

Use information from the graphic organizer to answer the following questions.

1. **Identify** Which duties do voters undertake in the election process?

   _____

   _____

2. **Draw Conclusions** How do you think different types of media outlets help candidates in different ways?

   _____

   _____

3. **Elaborate** Voting is considered the most basic form of political participation. Why do you think this is?

   _____

   _____

Understanding Elections

READING FOCUS
The purpose of election campaigns is to help the public learn about the candidates, so that voters can make an informed decision on election day. Candidates today take advantage of media exposure and polling in order to influence the voters and get elected to public office.

Key Terms

platform a party's stand on important issues and the party's general principles

focus group a small gathering of people whose response to something is studied and used to predict the response of a larger population

swing states states where support for each candidate is about equal

stump speech a standard speech that candidates give during a campaign

negative campaigning attacking the opponent during a campaign

sound bite a very brief segment of a speech or statement

demographic a population group defined by a specific characteristic or set of characteristics

Taking Notes

As you read the summaries, use your Student Casebook to take notes on the section.

Case Study Summary

TELEVISION AND THE 1960 ELECTION

The first televised presidential debates were held in 1960. Candidates Senator John F. Kennedy and Vice President Richard Nixon, whom voters already considered very different from one another, appeared in stark contrast during the debate. Kennedy looked tan and healthy, but Nixon looked tired and pale. While polls showed that people who had only listened to the debate on the radio thought had Nixon performed better, those who watched the debate claimed that Kennedy had won. The debate and its possible effect on the outcome of the election— Kennedy won by a slight margin—is still used today as an example of how powerful a role television plays in revealing a candidate's personality and overall public appeal.

What You Need to Know Summary

CAMPAIGN PLANNING

Candidates run campaigns to help the public get to know them and their **platform**, their party's stand on important issues and general principles. Running a campaign requires a dedicated, hard-working staff, the size of which can vary from campaign to campaign.

There are several key figures who work on campaigns. The campaign manager coordinates the entire campaign. He or she develops and executes the campaign plan and supervises other key staffers. The finance chair is charged with the responsibility of raising money to fund the campaign. The pollster creates scientific polls whose results then guide the direction of the campaign. The media coordinator arranges free and paid advertising to get the candidate's message to the public in as many ways possible. The scheduler manages the candidate's time to ensure that he or she attends the events necessary for a successful campaign. Issue advisers educate the candidate and write campaign position papers on major issues important to the voting public. The treasurer manages the money a campaign raises and spends. The volunteer coordinator recruits and manages volunteer staff. The press secretary creates press releases about the campaign and tracks media coverage. The speechwriter reviews and writes some of the candidate's speeches.

No matter what their role, staff members need to identify *how* and *where* they can make sure their candidate wins. Knowing this ahead of time helps a campaign develop and deliver their candidate's message. A large part of creating a winning message is knowing who will want to hear it, mainly by conducting polls and determining who is likely to vote for the candidate. Likewise, targeting the message to this select group of people is essential. Campaigns often use **focus groups**, small gatherings of people whose response to something is studied and used to predict the response of a larger population. Once a campaign staff knows how people feel about the candidate and the platform, they can "package" the candidate's image and create advertisements geared toward these feelings.

Why is it important that a candidate has a platform?
_____
_____
_____

What do focus groups tell campaign staff?
_____
_____
_____

CONDUCTING A CAMPAIGN

Geography can help determine the direction a campaign takes. Presidential candidates will often spend more time in states with several electoral votes, in states where support for opponents is weak, or in **swing states**, those states where support for each candidate is about equal. Similarly, when visiting a state, a candidate is more likely to speak about those issues most important to the population. In addition to issue speeches, candidate regularly give **stump speeches**, or standard speeches delivered throughout the campaign.

Some of these speeches, as well as much of a candidate's advertising, may involve **negative campaigning**. When employing this strategy, a candidate attacks an opponent in hopes of decreasing his or her support and forcing the opponent to spend time and energy responding to the attack.

Whether negative or positive, advertising and other media coverage are among a campaign's key features. Television ads, interviews, and even simple photo opportunities are integral to a campaign's publicity. Radio spots and interviews can also be good publicity within a certain demographic. Campaign staff use newspapers to target older voters and the Internet to target younger voters, using both mediums to explain their candidate's message in greater depth.

One disadvantage of widespread media coverage, however, is the inability to control the **sound bites**, or brief segments of speeches or statements, that media might use. When used in a certain way, these sound bites can have a devastating or uplifting effect on a campaign.

Polls influence the direction of a campaign from start to finish. Early polls can identify **demographics**, or population groups defined by a specific characteristic or set of characteristics, that will or will not support a candidate. Polls also monitor public opinion and can potentially influence voter behavior.

> **What are two places candidates might speak in hopes of persuading voters?**
> _____
> _____

> **How can sound bites be dangerous to a campaign?**
> _____
> _____
> _____

Simulation

Use your Student Casebook to help you complete the simulation.

Undestanding Elections

READING FOCUS
Money plays a major role in election campaigns. Candidates and their staff must carefully decide where the campaign will get money and how they will use this money.

Key Terms

Federal Election Commission government agency created to enforce the Federal Election Campaign Act and administer the related public-funding program

party-building activities political party activities that do not support specific candidates

issue ads advertisements that support or oppose candidates' views without specifically calling for their election or defeat

leadership PACs groups formed by officeholders that are separate from the officeholders' campaign organizations

527 group a tax-exempt organization created to influence an election

Taking Notes

As you read the summaries, use your Student Casebook to take notes on the section.

Case Study Summary

CONTROVERIES OVER CAMPAIGN FUNDING

In the early twenty-first century, two scandals involving members of Congress emphasized the need for campaign reform. In 2002 Ohio Representative James Traficant was found guilty of and convicted on 10 felony counts, some of which involved taking money donated to his campaign for personal use. Traficant was then expelled from the Senate by a vote of 420 to 1.

In 2005 Texas Representative Tom DeLay and one of his political action committees, TRMPAC, were indicted for making illegal campaign contributions. Delay had helped move corporate donations made to the National Republican Party to Republican candidates in Texas, where corporate contributions to state campaigns are illegal. After his indictment, Tom DeLay resigned from the House of Representatives.

> **How did Traficant and DeLay use campaign donations improperly?**
>
> _____
>
> _____
>
> _____

What You Need to Know Summary

FUNDING ELECTION CAMPAIGNS

Running an election campaign can be very expensive; currently, there is no limit in the United States on how much a candidate can spend. To raise money, candidates turn to four sources. First, candidates can accept individual donations. These donations are the largest funding source and only need to be reported if in excess of $200. Second, candidates can receive contributions from political action committees, or PACs. Third, the political party that a candidate represents can donate a limited amount of money. Finally, a presidential candidate can receive public funding, if he or she agrees to certain limits on any other money raised or spent.

In order to reduce the dependence of candidates on big donors, the government has initiated various campaign finance reforms. In the first half of the twentieth century, Congress banned corporations and labor unions from making campaign contributions. Then, in 1971, Congress passed the landmark Federal Election Campaign Act (FECA). This legislation established strict contribution limits and reporting responsibilities, created the current system of public funding for presidential campaigns, and instituted the **Federal Election Commission** (FEC) to enforce the FECA and administer the public funding program.

Congress amended the FECA multiple times during the 1970s, including a change in 1979 that allows parties to spend unlimited money on **party-building activities**—those that do not directly support candidates. This change in election law created a new kind of donation—soft money, or money not given directly to candidates. Unregulated by the FEC, soft-money donations are unlimited, can come from corporations, and often end up funding **issue ads**, which support or oppose candidates' views without specifically calling for their election or defeat.

Soft-money donations skyrocketed between 1996 and 2002, so much so that Congress passed legislation to curb it. The 2002 Bipartisan Campaign Reform Act (BCRA) banned soft-money contributions to political parties for advertising.

What is a campaign's largest funding source?

_____

_____

What is the difference between an individual donation to a campaign and soft money?

_____

_____

_____

INTEREST GROUPS AND ELECTION CAMPAIGNS

Since the role of interest groups in the campaign fundraising process is limited, it is up to the groups' PACs to collect money from members and donate it to specific campaigns. Donations to a national PAC are limited to $5,000 per year per donor, but many state PACs have no such limits. Similarly, **leadership PACs**, groups that officeholders can form to raise soft money, are also not subject to limits.

Critics of PACs question whether PAC donations give interest groups undue influence over candidates. But supporters point to the fact that interest-group members have more of a voice in the political process thanks to PACs.

527 groups are another source of campaign contributions. These groups are named for a section of the U.S. tax code that allows certain kinds of groups to pay no taxes. 527 groups, through a loophole in the 2002 BCRA, work to influence voters' opinions about candidates or issues without calling for a candidate's election or defeat outright. As long as a 527 is not directly connected to a candidate or party, it is allowed to raise and spend unlimited amounts of money without reporting its activities to the FEC. In the 2004 presidential campaigns, 527 groups mostly created ads that attacked a specific candidate, prompting a debate over the regulation of donations versus donors' freedom of speech.

Unlike 527s, campaign advertising is limited. The BCRA requires that all campaign media advertisements include a visual or oral message that identifies who is paying for the ad. If an ad comes directly from a campaign, the candidate must appear in the ad, along with audio of the candidate saying that he or she approves of the message.

> **What worries critics of PACs?**
> _____
> _____
> _____

> **How can you tell if a television advertisement comes directly from a campaign?**
> _____
> _____
> _____

Simulation

Use your Student Casebook to help you complete the simulation.

Understanding Elections

Section 3

READING FOCUS
Voting is one of the main responsibilities of U.S. citizenship. Being a part of the voting process and taking an active role in electing public officials helps give all Americans a voice in their government.

Key Terms

poll workers people hired by local election officials to manage voting on election day

poll watchers volunteers whom a party or candidate sends to polling places to ensure that elections are being run fairly

redistricting the process of drawing new boundaries for legislative districts

Taking Notes

As you read the summaries, use your Student Casebook to take notes on the section.

Case Study Summary

ELECTION 2000

In the 2000 presidential election, the race between Republican George W. Bush and Democrat Al Gore was so close that the result would depend upon who won Florida's 25 electoral votes. Yet the Florida race itself was so close that a recount was called in order to count every ballot once again.

When the recount was complete, results showed that Bush had won by about 1,500 votes. Democrats objected, claiming that the recount machines could not always accurately read the ballots, which Florida voters cast by punching a hole in them. Democrats then demanded a recount by hand, which Republicans opposed.

Both sides took their case to the Florida Supreme Court, which ordered the hand recount on December 8. The Bush campaign appealed the ruling to the U.S. Supreme Court, which ruled 5—4 on December 12 that the Florida court's ruling was unconstitutional. In the majority opinion, justices explained that the Florida court did not include standards for how votes should be recounted. The Court also declared that there was not enough time to resolve the controversy according to a deadline set by Florida law. Al Gore publicly accepted defeat on December 9.

> **Why did Democrats demand a hand recount in Florida during the 2000 presidential election?**
>
> _____
> _____
> _____

What You Need to Know Summary

POLITICAL PARTICIPATION

In a democratic republic, where political power belongs to the people, citizen participation is essential. Voting is a basic, extremely important form of participation. However, millions of eligible Americans choose not to vote, despite the fact that segments of the U.S. population struggled for years to win the right to vote.

Several factors might explain low voter turnout. First, the type of election affects voting. Presidential elections traditionally attract more voters than state elections and local elections. Age is another factor— older Americans are much more likely to go to the polls than those under the age of 25. Third, not all voters are aware of the impact of their individual vote. As the 2000 presidential election proved, there are times when every vote does count, particularly in local elections, where the outcome of often very close races has an impact on everyday life.

Besides voting, citizens can participate in the political process by volunteering to support campaigns, or to support or oppose specific issues. Citizens can also work at the polls on election day as **poll workers**—people hired by local election officials to manage the voting—or **poll watchers**—mostly volunteers whom a party or candidate sends to polling places to ensure that the election is running fairly.

Running for office is yet another way citizens can become involved in politics. At the local, state, or national level, many Americans become political candidates in hopes of helping to affect change in their government.

How does age affect voter turnout?
_____
_____

THE VOTING PROCESS

There are three steps to the voting process. First, voters should educate themselves about the candidates, from their experience and background to their stance on major issues.

Second, voters need to register to vote, the process for which can vary from state to state. Some states now allow on-site, election-day registration; others give people the opportunity to register while applying for a driver's license. People are often asked to

What should a person know about the candidates before voting?
_____
_____

declare a political party when registering. This is not required information. A person who does not declare a party is simply listed as an independent.

Third, voters need to cast a ballot. The balloting method may involve marking a paper ballot or using a mechanical voting machine.

To ensure that every vote has equal weight, the law requires that every district in a legislative body, federal or state, contains about the same amount of people. Since the population of areas change, the government, by order of the Constitution, conducts a census every 10 years to keep track of these changes. If necessary, seats in the House of Representatives and the state legislatures are reassigned based on census results. This process of drawing new boundaries for legislative districts is called **redistricting**. In instances where state legislatures draw boundaries so that the majority of voters in a district favor one political party over another, the process is called gerrymandering.

Election day is typically one of the busiest days in a campaign. Staff focus their activities around three pieces of information: the places where their candidate has strong support, the places where support for their candidate's opponent is strong, and the places where the voting could go either way. Often avoiding areas where support for an opponent is strong, the candidate and campaign volunteers usually gather near polling places to summon last-minute support. Campaign staff also spends much time and energy on get out the vote, or GOTV, activities. These efforts may consist of phoning voters to ask for their support or offering them a ride to the polls. If poll watchers are allowed at the polls, they alert other staff as to who has not voted yet. Additional GOTV efforts might then be directed at this group of people.

Why is redistricting necessary?
_____
_____
_____

What are two ways campaign members try to "get out the vote"?
_____
_____
_____

Simulation

Use your Student Casebook to help you complete the simulation.

Supreme Court Cases

Chapter Summary

First Amendment
• Freedom of expression and assembly
• Student speech and school prayer

Fourth Amendment
• Unreasonable search and seizure
• Expectations of privacy

Important Supreme Court Decisions

Fourteenth Amendment
• Equal protection under the law
• Substantive and procedural due process

Commerce Clause
• Doctrine of selective exclusiveness
• Questions of regulation

COMPREHENSION AND CRITICAL THINKING

Use information from the graphic organizer to answer the following questions.

1. **Describe** What First and Fourth Amendment issues have been influenced by Supreme Court decisions?

_____

_____

2. **Make Inferences** The doctrine of selective exclusiveness identifies when Congress has the power to regulate commerce. Explain why you think this issue would need to be decided by the Supreme Court.

_____

_____

_____

3. **Rate** What is your opinion about the importance of the Fourteenth Amendment? Why do you think "due process" and "equal protection" are essential to Americans?

_____

_____

_____

Supreme Court Cases

READING FOCUS
Your freedom of expression—the right to practice your religious beliefs; to hold, express, and publish ideas and opinions; to gather with others; and to ask the government to correct its mistakes—is the cornerstone of our democracy. Through its power to interpret the Constitution, the Supreme Court can expand or limit your rights.

Key Terms

freedom of expression the right of citizens to hold, explore, exchange, express, and debate ideas

redress of grievances to remove the cause of a complaint and make things right

right of assembly the right to form and join groups to gather for any peaceful and lawful purpose

Taking Notes

As you read the summaries, use your Student Casebook to take notes on the section.

Case Study Summary

STUDENTS' RIGHT OF EXPRESSION

In 1965 despite their school's ban on armbands, John and Mary Beth Tinker and other students wore black armbands to school to protest the Vietnam War. When the students were suspended, their families sued the school district, claiming that the teenagers' First Amendment right to free expression had been violated. The district countered that the school had reasonably used its power to preserve order.

The case, *Tinker* v. *Des Moines School District*, was eventually appealed to the Supreme Court. In 1969 the Court reversed the lower courts' rulings, deciding in favor of the students. In the 7–2 majority opinion, justices explained that although schools had the right to maintain order, the expression in question did not substantially interfere with school operation—a standard that has become known as the Tinker test and is still used in free-expression cases involving public-school students. In the decades since the *Tinker* case, though, the Court has ruled against students in cases involving vulgar speech, school-newspaper censorship, and off-campus expression.

> **Explain the Tinker test in your own words.**
>
> _____
>
> _____

What You Need to Know Summary

FREEDOM OF RELIGION

Freedom of expression is the right of American citizens to hold, explore, exchange, express, and debate ideas. This freedom is guaranteed within the First Amendment. The First Amendment also contains the establishment clause and the free exercise clause when it states that "Congress shall make no law respecting an establishment of religion or the free exercise thereof."

These two clauses have been at the center of many controversial Supreme Court decisions. The establishment clause is most often cited in cases involving the separation of church and state. In 1962 the Court banned a prayer required in public schools, soon following that decision with others that declared certain required prayers and periods of silent meditation illegal—including prayer before school athletic events. The Court has not banned private, voluntary school prayer, however, requiring public schools to allow students to form private religious groups with the stipulation that school employees may not take part. The Court has also ruled that teaching about the religion or the Bible is constitutional, as long as the instruction itself is nonreligious in nature.

While the free exercise clause allows people to believe whatever they want, it does not allow them to *express* their beliefs however they want. The Supreme Court has developed and employs the "compelling interest test," which requires the government to have a compelling reason for banning a religious practice to protect society. This test has been used to decide cases involving polygamy—ruled illegal—and the right to wear religious headwear in the military while on duty—also ruled illegal—as well as many other cases in which the Court declared that what society gained from making a person follow a law was less important that that person's religious freedom.

Which part of the Constitution protects freedom of expression?
_____

What does the free-exercise clause *not* allow people to do?
_____

FREEDOM OF SPEECH

Although the First Amendment states that "Congress shall make no law . . . abridging freedom of speech," the Supreme Court has deemed some speech unprotected over the years, including speech with

Section 1 *continued*

little or no social value, speech that may inspire violence, speech that defames a person orally (slander) or in print (libel), and speech that is lewd.

Furthermore, the Court has ruled that schools can control the time, place, and content of student expression. The Court and American schools continue to carefully use the Tinker test when considering whether to ban student political speech. The Court has been less open-minded when it comes to vulgar and obscene speech, ruling that it is contrary to a school's mission of teaching socially acceptable behavior. While the Court has not yet ruled on speech codes, it has declared that cyberspeech—speech on the Internet—has the same protections as printed materials. The lower courts have heard several cases involving cyberspeech and have ruled both for and against a school's right to suspend a student for criticizing school officials online.

FREEDOM OF PETITION AND ASSEMBLY

The freedom of petition—the right to ask the government for a **redress of grievances**, or to remove the cause of a complaint and make things right—and the **right of assembly**, or the right to gather for any peaceful and lawful purpose, are additional guarantees included in the First Amendment. However, the Supreme Court has ruled that the government may sometimes regulate the time, place, and behavior of assemblies on public property, as well as the kinds of groups to which a person may belong.

> **When can the government regulate assemblies?**
> _____

STUDENT ASSEMBLY

Freedom of assembly is also sometimes limited in schools. The Supreme Court has ruled that schools have the right to regulate the time, place, and manner of student gatherings; set restrictions on student clubs; and, in some instances, deny students permission to form a new club. Furthermore, the Court holds that schools cannot discriminate against clubs because of their religious or philosophical viewpoints.

Simulation

Use your Student Casebook to help you complete the simulation.

Supreme Court Cases

Section 2

READING FOCUS
The Fourth Amendment guarantees your right to be secure against unreasonable searches and seizures—in other words, it guarantees that you have rights to some forms of privacy. As with First Amendment rights, Fourth Amendment rights are not absolute and are subject to judicial interpretation. In this cyber age, protection of these rights is perhaps more important than ever.

Key Terms

search any action by government to find evidence of criminal activity

seizure when authorities keep something found during a search

plain view doctrine an assumption under the law that if an object is in plain view, the owner does not consider it private

Terry stop when the police stop a person and pat down him or her down for weapons due to the fact that he or she is acting suspiciously and may be a threat to the public interest

special needs test standard to determine whether a search serves some safety or security need for society

cyber-surveillance searches of wireless communications

National Security Letter a document signed, issued and used by the Federal Bureau of Investigation and other agencies to search for information about a person

Taking Notes

As you read the summaries, use your Student Casebook to take notes on the section.

Case Study Summary

THE RIGHT TO PRIVACY

In 1998 Roy Caballes was pulled over by an Illinois state trooper for speeding. While performing a routine check for outstanding warrants, the officer discovered that Caballes had been arrested twice for selling drugs. A nearby officer with a drug-sniffing dog joined the first trooper, and when the dog barked near Caballes's trunk, the officers searched the car, found drugs, and arrested Caballes.

Caballes was convicted and sentenced, but in 2003, the Illinois Supreme Court reversed the conviction, claiming that using the dog at a routine stop was a violation of Caballes's Fourth Amendment rights. The state appealed the ruling to the Supreme Court in *Illinois* v. *Caballes*.

> **Why did the Illinois Supreme Court reverse Caballes's conviction?**
>
> _____
> _____

In a 6–2 decision issued in 2005, the Court reversed the Illinois Supreme Court's decision and upheld Caballes's conviction, stating that a dog sniff did not constitute a search and that a person has no privacy when in possession of drugs or other contraband. The justices in the majority ruled that because the traffic stop was legal and because the dog had barked as trained to, the state police had enough reasonable suspicion to search Caballes's car.

What You Need to Know Summary

UNDERSTANDING SEARCH AND SEIZURE

The Fourth Amendment protects a citizen's rights against unreasonable **searches**—any actions by the government to find evidence of criminal activity—and **seizures**—when authorities keep something. This protection extends only to searches and seizures made by the government, which can include everything from listening in on phone conversations to seizing drugs. A person is seized when his or her movement is restrained by physical force or someone's authority.

The Fourth Amendment also guarantees that warrants—or court orders to search for something or seize someone—can only be obtained if there is probable cause, or good reason, that a search or seizure will produce evidence of a crime or a criminal. In order to prevent what the Constitution calls "unreasonable search and seizure," a warrant must state what authorities are looking for and where. Warrants are not required—although probable cause is—for all searches, seizures, or arrests. For example, the law assumes that if an object is in plain view, its owner does not consider it private and the police therefore do not need a warrant—an assumption called the **plain view doctrine**.

THE FOURTH AMENDMENT AND PRIVACY

A person's right to privacy has limits. The Supreme Court has ruled that a person has an expectation of privacy in certain places, like his or her home and yard, but not in others, such as public places, anywhere when in possession of illegal drugs, or someone else's home.

> **What is the difference between a search and a seizure?**
> _____
> _____

> **Imagine that the police find drugs in a bathroom drawer. Is this an example of the plain-view doctrine? Explain.**
> _____
> _____

The privacy a person has over his or her body has also been interpreted in different ways by the Supreme Court. Since the ruling in the 1968 case *Terry* v. *Ohio*, in which the Court decided that police could stop a person who was acting suspiciously and pat them down for weapons, police only need reasonable suspicion for a so-called **Terry stop**. Subsequent rulings have varied as to what authorities can remove from a person's body—and how. In such Fourth Amendment cases, the Court seems to consider a person's legal status, the invasiveness of the search, and whether the search served some safety or security need for society—a standard called the **special needs test**. DNA, blood, and urine tests are typically considered intrusive, although the Court has ruled that it is legal to conduct random drugs tests on some public-safety workers and student athletes. Public-school students—and sometimes their lockers—can also be searched by school officials if the circumstances behind the search are reasonable.

> **What issues does the Supreme Court consider when deciding if a search of a person's body was legal?**
>
> _____
>
> _____

Recent technology has made it necessary to apply the Fourth Amendment in new ways. The Supreme Court has yet to hear a case involving **cyber-surveillance**, or searches of wireless communications. Currently, authorities must obtain a warrant to intercept wireless communications, although the 2001 USA PATRIOT Act relaxed the process for getting warrants, as well as searches and seizures. The PATRIOT Act makes it possible for the Federal Bureau of Investigation and other government agencies to issue and use a document called a **National Security Letter** (NSL), instead of a warrant granted by a judge, to require almost anyone to turn over consumer records and other information. Authorities do not need probable cause to get a NSL. Given these new developments, the Supreme Court is likely to hear several cases challenging government surveillance programs currently in the federal courts, a task that will involve balancing citizens' Fourth Amendment rights with the government's responsibility for national security.

> **Who issues a National Security Letter?**
>
> _____

Simulation

Use your Student Casebook to help you complete the simulation.

Section 3

READING FOCUS
The Fourteenth Amendment requires that states provide due process and equal protection under the law. These requirements have made this amendment one of the most important parts of the Constitution.

Key Terms

unenumerated rights those rights that are not explicitly stated in the Constitution

Taking Notes

As you read the summaries, use your Student Casebook to take notes on the section.

Case Study Summary

DUE PROCESS AND PUBLIC SCHOOLS

In 1971 a Columbus, Ohio, high school suspended several students for misconduct. One of the students, Dwight Lopez, claimed he had been an innocent bystander and filed a lawsuit—with several other students as additional plaintiffs—that claimed he should have been entitled to a hearing. When a district court ruled that due process had been denied, the school system appealed to the Supreme Court.

In *Goss* v. *Lopez*, school official Norval Goss argued that Ohio students did not have a constitutional right to public education and therefore no expectation of due process. The students' lawyers countered that Ohio law requires the state to provide free education and that a lack of due process potentially deprived students of this education. The Supreme Court sided with the students, ruling that before or shortly after a suspension, students must be allowed a hearing—although they are not allowed to call or cross-examine witnesses.

> **Why did Lopez claim his right to due process was violated?**
> _____
> _____
> _____

What You Need to Know Summary

DUE PROCESS AND EQUAL PROTECTION

The Fourteenth Amendment declares that no state will deprive a person of "life, liberty, or property, without due process of law," nor deny a person "equal protection of laws"—including against actions of the

federal government. The due-process clause means
that laws and the processes and procedures for
applying and enforcing laws must be fair—known as
substantive due process and procedural due process,
respectively. The equal opportunity clause means that
the law must be applied the same way to every person.

> **How does the equal-opportunity clause protect Americans?**
> _____
> _____

SUBSTANTIVE DUE PROCESS

The Ninth Amendment has been interpreted to protect
rights that are not explicitly stated, known as
unenumerated rights. Through the doctrine of
substantive due process, the Supreme Court has
recognized some of these rights.

In the landmark 1896 case *Lochner* v. *New York*,
the Supreme Court addressed property rights. Bakery
owner Joseph Lochner was arrested for requiring an
employee to work more than 60 hours a week—a
situation illegal in bakeries under New York law.
Lochner appealed his conviction to the Supreme
Court, arguing that since the New York law applied
only to bakery workers, it violated the equal-
protection clause. He also argued that the law violated
the due-process clause, since it deprived him of his
property rights—here, the right to negotiate an
employment contract—without due process. The
Supreme Court agreed with Lochner, ruling 5–4 that
New York's public-health regulation was not truly
reasonable or necessary and interfered with the rights
of employers and employees to make contracts.

> **According to the Supreme Court's ruling in *Lochner*, how did the New York law violate residents' property rights?**
> _____
> _____

Backlash over *Lochner* and later Supreme Court
property-rights cases prompted the Court to announce
in 1938 that it would apply only a rational basis test
for economic regulations going forward. For the Court
to uphold a law, the government would only have to
show that the law had a rational basis.

After 1938 the Court used substantive due process
to define personal unenumerated rights, including the
privacy right to die in the 1990 case *Cruzan* v.
Director, Missouri State Department of Health.
Missouri resident Nancy Beth Cruzan was seriously
injured in a car accident in 1983. After Cruzan spent
years unconscious, her parents asked the hospital to
remove her feeding tube and allow her to die. When
the hospital refused, Cruzan's parents successfully

sued, but the Missouri Supreme Court overturned the ruling. The U.S. Supreme Court upheld the lower court of appeals ruling, noting that although the privacy right to refuse medical treatment was protected under the Fourteenth Amendment, the lack of evidence that ending life support was what Cruzan wanted violated her right to due process.

PROCEDURAL DUE PROCESS

Two landmark cases established minimum standards for procedural due process in cases involving property rights. In the 1970 case *Goldberg* v. *Kelly*, the Supreme Court declared government payments a kind of property, of which a person cannot be denied or have terminated without due process of law, such as a hearing. In the 1972 case *Stanley* v. *Illinois*, the court ruled that unwed fathers are entitled to due process hearings to determine their fitness as a parent before their children can be taken away, a decision that established that every American is entitled to at least a formal notice and hearing before the government can deprive him or her of rights or property.

> **Why was the Court's decision in *Stanley* v. *Illinois* important to all Americans?**
>
> _____
>
> _____

The Supreme Court has also clearly defined procedural due process in cases involving juveniles, particularly in the case *In re Gault*. This case involved Arizona teenager Gerald Gault, who, after being accused of making an obscene phone call, was found guilty and sentenced to six years in a state industrial school. Gault was not advised he could have an attorney, his family did not testify, no one testified under oath, no record was made of the hearing, and Gault was not given his Sixth Amendment right to confront his accuser.

Since Gault did not have the right to appeal under Arizona law, his parents petitioned the Supreme Court for his release. In a 8–1 decision in favor of the petitioners, the Court declared that the Fourteenth Amendment applied to minors and adults alike. This ruling gave juveniles almost all of the same due process rights as adult defendants.

> **Name two ways Gault's Fourteenth Amendment rights were violated.**
>
> _____
>
> _____

Simulation

Use your Student Casebook to help you complete the simulation.

Supreme Court Cases

Section 4

READING FOCUS

In Chapter 4 you read that federalism is a system of government in which power is divided between a central government and regional governments. The Constitution gives the national government power over some issues and reserves to the state governments power over other issues. The balance of power between the national government and states shifts from time to time as a result of legislation and Supreme Court decisions.

Key Terms

selective exclusiveness a doctrine that states that only Congress may regulate commerce that requires national, uniform regulation

Taking Notes

As you read the summaries, use your Student Casebook to take notes on the section.

Case Study Summary

TREATIES AND STATES' RIGHTS

In 1916 the United States and Great Britain signed a treaty to protect birds that migrated between the United States and Canada. Two years later Congress passed the Migratory Bird Treaty Act to implement the treaty and make it illegal to kill or capture any bird mentioned in the treaty. Missouri state officials tried to prevent federal game warden Ray Holland from enforcing the act, claiming that it was an unconstitutional use of federal power. A federal district court disagreed. Missouri then appealed the decision to the Supreme Court.

In *Missouri* v. *Holland* federal attorneys argued that the Constitution gives the president the power to make treaties and also, through the supremacy clause, makes the Constitution, treaties, and federal laws the supreme law of the land. Missouri's attorneys argued that Congress had passed legislation that violated the Tenth Amendment and intruded upon Missouri's sovereign powers. They also argued that Congress should not be able to use the president's treaty power to pass a law that would otherwise be unconstitutional.

In 1920 the Supreme Court upheld the lower court's decision, stating that the supremacy clause

What made it possible for Congress to pass the Migratory Bird Treaty Act?

_____

_____

gives Congress the right to implement treaties, including regulating activities within states.

What You Need to Know Summary

EXPANDING FEDERAL AUTHORITY

Article I, Section 8, Clause 3 of the Constitution, known as the commerce clause, states that Congress has the right "to regulate commerce with foreign nations, and among the several states, and with the Indian tribes." Over the years, the way Congress has used and the Supreme Court has interpreted this clause has defined the U.S. system of federalism. For example, Congress used its right to control commerce between states—known as interstate commerce—to help end racial discrimination—with the help of the Supreme Court. In 1964 the Court ruled that part of the recently passed Civil Rights Act of 1964 could be applied to private businesses—such as motels with guests from several states—to force them from discriminating against African Americans.

> **How does the commerce clause help define federalism?**
>
> _____
>
> _____

THE COMMERCE CLAUSE AND THE COURT

Until the mid-1800s, Congress hardly ever employed the commerce clause to expand federal power. But in 1852, in *Cooley* v. *Board Warden*, the Supreme Court established the doctrine of **selective exclusiveness**, which states that when commerce requires national, uniform regulation, only Congress may regulate it. Otherwise states may regulate it.

After *Cooley*, Congress became more secure in regulating commerce that fell under its jurisdiction. However, as *United States* v. *Lopez* and *Gonzales* v. *Raich* show, selective exclusiveness is not always applied exactly the same way by the Supreme Court.

In 1992 San Antonio, Texas teenager Alfonso Lopez brought a gun to school. Once questioned by school officials, Lopez admitted he had a gun and was arrested under Texas law with firearm possession on school property. The next day all state charges were dropped so that federal officials could charge Lopez with violating Section 922(q) of the federal Gun-Free School Zones Act of 1990. Lopez was convicted and sentenced in federal court, but the conviction was reversed upon appeal. Federal officials appealed this

> **According to the doctrine of selective exclusiveness, when can states regulate commerce?**
>
> _____
>
> _____

reversal to the Supreme Court in *United States* v. *Lopez*, arguing that guns in school zones could lead to violent crime and interrupt students' learning, both outcomes that could affect the economy and therefore were Congress's responsibility to regulate under the commerce clause. Lopez's lawyers argued that having a gun in school was a criminal offense but had nothing to do with interstate commerce. In a 5–4 decision, the Supreme Court agreed with Lopez and declared the Gun-Free School Zones Act unconstitutional. This was the first time Congress's use of the commerce clause had been limited since the 1930s.

The Supreme Court again debated Congress's use of the commerce clause in the 2005 case *Gonzales* v. *Reich*. In 1996 California voters approved the use of marijuana, illegal under federal law, for medical purposes. Two California residents, Diane Monson and Angel Raich, began growing marijuana at home to relieve chronic pain. In 2002, federal authorities seized their plants, prompting Monson and Raich to successfully sue the federal government.

After the court of appeals also ruled in the plaintiffs' favor, the government appealed to the Supreme Court. Monson and Raich's lawyers argued that the federal law allowing the seizure overstepped Congress's power to regulate interstate commerce, since everything used to grow the plants was from California. Federal lawyers countered that, through the supremacy clause, federal law took precedence over state law. They also argued that homegrown marijuana could affect the illegal trade in marijuana coming into California from other states and countries, therefore giving the federal government the right to regulate it.

In a 6–3 decision—and in spite of a strong dissent saying that the principles of federalism should protect California's actions—the Supreme Court agreed with the federal government that marijuana, although illegal, is a part of commerce and that the commerce clause therefore applied to the situation.

> **Why did the federal government believe that guns in school zones should be regulated by Congress?**
>
> _____
>
> _____

> **How was the Court's decision in *Gonzales* v. *Raich* different than in *United States* v. *Lopez*?**
>
> _____
>
> _____

Simulation

Use your Student Casebook to help you complete the simulation.

Making Foreign Policy

Chapter Summary

U.S. Foreign Policy	
Goals	Protect national security, establish free and open trade, promote world peace, support democracy, and provide aid to people in need
Influences	President, Congress, Departments of State and Defense, CIA, interest groups, public opinion, media
Past and Present	Transition from isolationism to important role in international politics, supporting developing democracies and global foreign-aid efforts
Role in United Nations	Help to maintain international peace and security, develop friendly relations among nations, and achieve international cooperation

COMPREHENSION AND CRITICAL THINKING

Use information from the graphic organizer to answer the following questions.

1. **Recall** What are the primary goals of U.S. foreign policy?

_____

_____

2. **Analyze** Why do you think international cooperation is a key UN goal?

_____

_____

3. **Predict** How might public opinion contribute to foreign policy decisions?

_____

_____

Making Foreign Policy

READING FOCUS
Foreign policy is a nation's plans and procedures for dealing with other countries. Although U.S. foreign policy has changed over time, it has been guided by five basic goals and formulated through a set of theories, tools, and strategies.

Key Terms

foreign policy a nation's set of plans and procedures for dealing with foreign countries

isolationism an approach to foreign policy in which a government's leaders look after domestic issues and stay out of world affairs in order to avoid war

internationalist an approach to foreign policy in which a country takes an active role in international politics as the best way to pursue national security

embassies diplomatic centers

defense alliance an agreement between nations to come to each other's aid in the event of an attack

collective security attempts at keeping international peace and order

economic sanctions acts of withholding money

just war theory a theory of warfare in which a state may justly got o war under certain specific circumstances and must limit its conduct according to certain standards

Taking Notes

As you read the summaries, use your Student Casebook to take notes on the section.

Case Study Summary

GENOCIDE IN RWANDA

Once Rwanda gained its independence from Belgium in 1962, the Hutus, the largest ethnic group, took control of the government, killing or exiling thousands of Tutsis, the chief minority. By 1990 a Tutsi rebel group had formed, and after an unsuccessful attempt to overthrow the Hutus, began talks with Hutu leader Juvénal Habyarimana. After Habyarimana died in a plane crash in 1994, however, the country slipped into chaos. Hutu extremists killed both moderate members of their own group and 800,000 Tutsi people and sympathizers.

Despite the fact that it had signed a United Nations convention to prevent genocide, the United States and President Bill Clinton decided only to issue a

> **Who controlled the Rwandan government once the country gained independence?**
>
> _____
>
> _____

Section 1 *continued*

statement of shock and sadness about the Rwanda killings, instead of intervening. The United States had recently lost U.S. forces during a peacekeeping mission in Somalia and was reluctant to repeat that tragedy. In July 1994, President Clinton sent 200 troops to Rwanda for humanitarian relief, but the genocide was already over.

What You Need to Know Summary

THE BASICS OF FOREIGN POLICY

The **foreign policy** of the United States is its plans and procedures for dealing with foreign countries. Although it varies from president to president, foreign policy ultimately has five goals: protect national security, establish free and open trade, promote world peace, support democracy in the interest of stability and open markets, and provide aid to people in need.

There are many theories as to how the United States should approach foreign policy. Up until World War I, the U.S. government followed a policy of **isolationism**, mostly staying out of world affairs in order to avoid war. Since then, however, the country has been heavily involved in international politics. Americans who consider themselves realists prefer the **internationalist** approach, which promotes international cooperation, such as alliances, to protect national security. Others believe neoisolationism is the best course of action, by which the United States refrains from most involvement in foreign affairs in the interest of itself and other countries. Finally, idealists are split on the idea of military action but firmly believe in foreign policy as a method for promoting democracy and supporting human rights.

> How is the internationalist approach to foreign policy different than the isolationist approach?
>
> _____
> _____
> _____
> _____

THE TOOLS OF FOREIGN POLICY

Besides persuasion and power, the United States relies on diplomatic, economic, and military tools to accomplish its foreign policy.

Diplomacy helps the country protect itself by maintaining healthy relationships with other nations. The United States has more than 160 **embassies**, or diplomatic centers, around the world. American presidents have also signed treaties with leaders all over the globe. Additionally, the country belongs to

> Why is diplomacy so important?
>
> _____
> _____
> _____

defensive alliances. All nations within an alliance agree to come to each other's aid in the event of an attack. This is an example of **collective security**, or attempts at keeping international peace and order.

Economic foreign-policy tools include foreign aid and sanctions. By offering nonmilitary aid to countries in need through the United States Agency for International Development (USAID), the United States helps spread democracy and expands free markets. Military aid is also sometimes provided to other nations' armed forces. **Economic sanctions** occur when a country or countries withhold money—by restricting imports, exports, trade, or financial transactions—to pressure another nation to make social or political changes.

Using military force within another nation is an extremely important decision. Although Congress is the governmental body with the power to declare war, it has primarily been the president who has initiated most American military action. When considering such action, the president may listen to several advisers, including the secretary of state, the secretary of defense, the Joint Chiefs of Staff, and members of the Central Intelligence Agency and the National Security Council.

What is the purpose of economic sanctions?
_____
_____
_____

JUST WAR THEORY

According to the **just war theory**, a state may justly—or fairly—go to war under certain specific circumstances and must limit its conduct according to certain standards. War theorists call the justification of a war *jus ad bellum* and how to conduct it *jus in bello*. *Jud as bellum* is defined by four principles: a state must openly declare war and have a just cause for doing so; justice must be the purpose of the war; the state must have considered all costs and benefits of warfare and any other possible resolutions before declaring war; and the war's only goal must be an outcome of just peace. *Jus in bello* limits the conduct of war to military targets only and forbids any action beyond what is necessary to achieve the war's goal.

According to the just war theory, what should the only goal of war be?
_____

Simulation

Use your Student Casebook to help you complete the simulation.

Making Foreign Policy

READING FOCUS

U.S. foreign policy is directed and shaped by the executive branch and Congress and is carried out by a large bureaucracy. Domestic influences such as interest groups also play a role in foreign policy.

Key Terms

foreign service the approximately 20,000 State Department employees who work overseas

presidential doctrines foreign policy statements that guide the direction of U.S. foreign policy

diplomatic recognition the act of acknowledging a government as the proper representative of its country's people

Taking Notes

As you read the summaries, use your Student Casebook to take notes on the section.

Case Study Summary

ELIÁN GONZÁLEZ

In November 1999, two American fishermen discovered a six-year-old Cuban boy named Elián González floating off the coast of Florida. The refugee boat he had been on with his mother and stepfather had capsized and he was one of only three survivors. Elián was placed with Cuban-American relatives in Miami, who wished for him to remain in the United States. However, back in Cuba, Elián's father and Cuban president Fidel Castro demanded that he be returned.

For many Cuban Americans, Elián became a symbol in their struggle with Fidel Castro, against whose communist government they wished to place an embargo. Elián's Miami family made several attempts to keep him in the United States, yet the fact remained that he had entered the country illegally. In early 2000, the U.S. Immigration and Naturalization Service (ISN) announced that Elián's father was responsible for his custody. The Department of State then allowed Elián's father to come to the United States, where the U.S. Attorney General met with him. Yet the Miami relatives did not agree to release Elián to his father.

> **What did Elián González come to symbolize for some Cuban Americans?**
>
> _____
>
> _____
>
> _____

INS agents finally stormed the home where Elián was being held, removed him, and returned him to his father. Protests broke out in Miami, and Elián's American relatives appealed to the Supreme Court. The Court rejected the case only hours before Elián and his father returned to Cuba.

What You Need to Know Summary

THE FOREIGN POLICY BUREAUCRACY

There are many players involved in the U.S. foreign-policy bureaucracy, the administrative structure that carries out U.S. foreign policy on a day-to-day basis.

The most important foreign-policy agency is the Department of State, which manages all international relations and diplomatic efforts within the executive departments. Many of the department's bureaus and agencies are outside the United States. In fact, about 20,000 employees from the Department of State work overseas in what is known as the **foreign service**. These employees carry out foreign policy abroad and relay information about other countries to U.S. policymakers.

The Department of Defense supervises U.S. military actions and advises the president on related issues. Included within the department are its head, the secretary of defense, and the Joint Chiefs of Staff—the leaders of every branch of the military.

The Central Intelligence Agency (CIA) is the third major player in U.S. foreign policy. Through both transparent and covert activities, the CIA collects and analyzes information about other nations.

At times, foreign policy can also be affected by domestic influences. While creating legislation concerning foreign policy, policymakers may feel pressured by constituents and by their own political party. Lobbyists can also influence policymakers.

THE PRESIDENT, CONGRESS, AND FOREIGN POLICY

As the country's ambassador to the world, the president regularly spends time building international relationships that benefit American security and the economy. The Constitution grants the president the power to negotiate treaties, which are later ratified by

> **Who makes up the foreign service?**
> _____
> _____

> **Explain the purpose of the Central Intelligence Agency.**
> _____
> _____
> _____

Congress; issue **presidential doctrines**, or foreign policy statements that guide foreign policy; make executive, or informal, agreements with the heads of other nations; and decide whether to grant a nation **diplomatic recognition**, or an official acknowledgement by the United States that a government is the proper representative of its people.

As commander in chief, the president also has the power to initiate military action against and within foreign nations—such as short-term military strikes— even without a declaration of war issued by Congress. Since the passage of the War Powers Act in 1973, however, presidents have been limited in how they can take independent action. If a president commits troops, he or she now must work closely with Congress to determine further action.

In terms of foreign policy, the Constitution grants Congress the power to declare war, appropriate or deny funds, ratify treaties, and confirm presidential appointments. Congress can also initiate foreign policy by introducing resolutions, establishing programs, setting guidelines, directing the executive branch, and making funding requests. Policymakers can also give advice and use legislation and funding restrictions to support or change the president's foreign-policy actions. Additionally, Congress holds oversight hearings and investigations on how well executive agencies are carrying out foreign policy.

> **Why are more limits placed on how presidents authorize military activity today than there were 50 years ago?**
>
> _____
> _____
> _____
> _____

INTEREST GROUPS AND FOREIGN POLICY

Interest groups are another force that can affect the way policymakers approach foreign policy. These groups provide specialized information to both policymakers and the public in hopes of influencing relevant legislation. Similarly, public opinion and the ways in which public opinion is shaped by various media outlets can have an impact on foreign-policy decisions-making.

> **Why do interest groups attempt to educate policymakers?**
>
> _____
> _____

Simulation

Use your Student Casebook to help you complete the simulation.

Making Foreign Policy

READING FOCUS
The United States is a member of international organizations that work to maintain peace and political stability around the world.

Key Terms

UN Security Council a 15-member division of the United Nations that is charged with maintaining international peace and security

trust territory a colony or territory placed under administration by another country or countries

Taking Notes

As you read the summaries, use your Student Casebook to take notes on the section.

Case Study Summary

MAKING THE CASE FOR WAR

In 1990 a U.S.-led coalition attacked Iraq in response to the country's invasion of Kuwait. The United Nations (UN) authorized the attacks, and at the cease-fire, required Iraq to stop developing nuclear weapons.

In October 2002, Congress voted to authorize President George W. Bush to use force in Iraq if it was proven that Iraq had violated the UN requirement. Although the UN warned Iraq to fully disarm and continued its weapons inspections, the international organization did not agree to pass a resolution to attack Iraq.

President Bush decided to attack without formally asking the UN Security Council to issue a resolution authorizing military action, and without asking for the help of other member nations. Some international critics claimed this decision should not have been made by the United States alone and that it marginalized the value and efforts of international organizations like the United Nations.

> **Why did some critics believe President Bush's actions marginalized the United Nations?**
>
> _____
> _____
> _____
> _____

What You Need to Know Summary

THE UNITED NATIONS

The United Nations (UN) was established in 1945, at the end of World War II, as a replacement for the

League of Nations. It includes 192 member nations. The UN's charter breaks the organization's purpose into four goals: maintain international peace and security; develop friendly relations among nations based on respect for equal rights and the self-determination of peoples; achieve international cooperation in solving economic, social, cultural, and humanitarian problems; and be a center for harmonizing how members' actions attain these common goals.

There are six major divisions in the UN, within which are dozens of smaller agencies. First, all states meet as the General Assembly to discuss and vote on what to do about important international matters. Critical matters require a two-thirds majority, but less critical votes need only a simple majority. All votes and their consequences are advisory, not binding.

Second, 15 member nations form the **UN Security Council**. These members are responsible for maintaining international peace and security, and the decisions they make—a supermajority, or nine votes, is required—do hold authority. Such decisions may include economic sanctions or collective military action. There are 10 elected member nations and five permanent member nations: China, France, the Russian Federation, the United Kingdom, and the United States.

The third division of the UN is the Economic and Social Council (ECOSOC), which coordinates dozens of UN organizations and thousands of nongovernmental organizations (NGOs) that work to increase living standards in developing countries and universal respect for human rights.

The International Court of Justice (ICJ), or World Court, is the fourth UN division. Fifteen judges elected by the General Assembly and Security Council hear cases voluntarily presented by both member and nonmember states, then issue final, binding verdicts based on international law.

The fifth division is the Trusteeship Council. Tasked with administering the UN **trust territories**—colonies or territories placed under administration by another country or countries—the Council now only

---

Summarize the purpose of the United Nations in your own words.

_____

_____

_____

_____

How are votes by the Security Council different than those by the General Assembly?

_____

_____

_____

_____

meets on an as-needed basis, since all former trust territories are now independent.

Finally, the Secretariat is the sixth UN division. This group is responsible for the administration and coordination of UN efforts. Staff members are considered part of an international civil service and only take orders from the UN. The Secretariat is headed by the Secretary General, who is elected every five years—with the chance of reelection—by the General Assembly, on the recommendation of the Security Council. The Secretary-General is a very public figure and acts as the chief administrative officer at meetings held by all other UN divisions except the ICJ.

> **Name the six main divisions of the United Nations.**
> _____
> _____
> _____
> _____
> _____

OTHER INTERNATIONAL INSTITUTIONS

Large organizations affiliated with the United Nations govern the world's economic and judicial systems. The World Trade Organization's (WTO) 151 members make up about 97 percent of world trade. The WTO works to ensure equal-access trade among countries. The International Monetary Fund (IMF) includes almost all world nations and mainly loans money to less-developed countries whose economies are stuck in debt. Similarly, the World Bank works to assist developing nations meet specific goals, such as road construction or additional funding for agriculture.

> **Who do the International Monetary Fund and the World Bank try to help?**
> _____
> _____

In addition to the UN's World Court, the International Criminal Court (ICC) and international tribunals act as world judicial organizations. The ICC, established in 2002, is considered "a court of last resort" and hears cases that UN member nations cannot or will not prosecute, as well as cases referred by the UN Security Council. The ICC is treaty-based and prosecutes individuals accused of genocide, war crimes, and crimes against humanity. International tribunals were formed before the existence of the ICC to prosecute specific atrocities in Yugoslavia and Rwanda and will expire when their work is complete.

Simulation

Use your Student Casebook to help you complete the simulation.

Making Foreign Policy

READING FOCUS
Helping countries make the transition to democracy and overcome poverty are some foreign policy challenges facing the United States.

Key Terms

Monroe Doctrine a foreign-policy statement issued in 1823 in which the United States proclaimed its intention to remain neutral during European conflicts

deterrence a policy of building up the U.S. armed forces in order to discourage acts of military aggression by other nations

containment a policy based on the view that communism threatened democratic values and that Soviet expansion must be stopped

détente a relaxing of tensions

preemptive strike the potential use of force before an attack occurs

democratization the establishment of democratic governments

food security an adequate food supply at the national, household, and individual level

Taking Notes

As you read the summaries, use your Student Casebook to take notes on the section.

Case Study Summary

THE CZECH REPUBLIC

Still a young nation at the end of World War II, Czechoslovakia fell under Communist control by 1948, ending its history as the only democracy in Eastern Europe. By the 1960s, the Soviet-style Czech economy was in crisis. Attempts by a reform movement within the country's Communist party to initiate economic and democratic reforms were quickly squelched by Soviet troops.

One of the loudest voices to speak out against Czechoslovakia's communist government belonged to Václav Havel. Havel became a leader in the 1970s and 1980s human-rights movement, demanding with other dissidents that citizens be granted the civil and political rights to which they were entitled. He also started the hugely popular Civic Reform, an antigovernment coalition of reform groups.

What did Václav Havel wish for his people?
_____
_____
_____

By 1989 huge demonstrations led to the collapse of the country's communist government, a mostly nonviolent event now called the Velvet Revolution. Havel was elected interim president. In 1993 the Czech and Slovak republics peacefully separated and became independent states.

What You Need to Know Summary

PAST FOREIGN POLICY CHANGES

For several decades after the United States won its independence, the country mostly maintained a policy of isolationism and neutrality. In 1823 the government issued the **Monroe Doctrine** to proclaim America's intentions to remain neutral during European conflicts. U.S. foreign policy followed this doctrine until the late 1800s, when the country began to shift to more of an internationalist policy, best seen by its role in the Spanish-American War of 1898, from which the United States emerged a world power. After German attacks on U.S. ships, the country also entered World War I in 1917. Resentment over the brutality of World War I kept the country from participating in World War II until Japanese planes attacked Hawaii in 1941, at which point Congress declared war.

After World War II, U.S. foreign policy began to center around collective security—working with other nations to keep international peace and order—and **deterrence**, the policy of building up the U.S. armed forces to discourage acts of military aggression by other nations. Deterrence was in large part directed at the Soviet Union, which began taking control of Eastern Europe after World War II. Determined to stop the spread of communism, which reached Asia by 1949, the United States also began following a policy of **containment**, which was based on the view that communism threatened democratic values and that Soviet expansion must be stopped.

As part of this policy, the United States became involved in two undeclared wars, the Korean War and the Vietnam War, during the 1950s, 1960s, and 1970s. The country was also briefly involved with Communist Cuba in 1962, eventually persuading the Soviet Union to remove nuclear missiles it had been planning to place there.

> Describe U.S. foreign policy up until the late 1800s.
>
> _____
>
> _____
>
> _____

> What did the United States hope to achieve by following a policy of containment?
>
> _____
>
> _____
>
> _____
>
> _____

The Soviet Union began to collapse from within by the late 1980s. This followed a period of U.S.-Soviet **détente**, or a relaxing of tensions. By the early 1990s, the tension between the two countries, long known as the Cold War, had largely disappeared.

CONTEMPORARY FOREIGN POLICY CHANGES

Although the Cold War is over, the United States still faces many foreign-policy challenges, including how to stop the spread of nuclear weapons. U.S. leaders also struggle to maintain relationships with oil-rich but typically non-democratic countries in the Middle East. The U.S.-Israel alliance bothers many Muslims in the region. The U.S. invasions of Afghanistan and Iraq following the September 11, 2001, terrorist attacks are another point of contention, although the United States considers both actions part of a **preemptive strike** doctrine, or the potential use of force before an attack occurs.

What factors currently strain the relationship between the United Sates and some Middle Eastern nations?
_____
_____
_____
_____

Current U.S. foreign policy also includes support of **democratization**, or the establishment of democratic governments. The United States works on supporting the economies of the former Soviet republics; the struggling democracies that replaced dictatorships in some Latin America countries; the shaky democratic governments of Afghanistan and Iraq, both affected by political and religious sects; and transitional African democracies, many of which still need to firmly establish the idea of the rule of law.

Giving foreign aid to overcome poverty remains a huge part of U.S. foreign policy. Current efforts include working with other nations to promote **food security**, or an adequate food supply at the national, household, and individual level, in poor regions of the globe. The United States also runs literacy programs around the world, including some that specifically promote gender equality in education. Additionally, the United States is part of several international organizations intent on eradicating the three deadly diseases of malaria, tuberculosis, and HIV/AIDS.

Name two goals of U.S. foreign aid.
_____
_____
_____
_____

Simulation

Use your Student Casebook to help you complete the simulation.

Comparative Political and Economic Systems

Chapter Summary

System	Characteristics
Democratic government	social welfare policies, protection of human rights, stable structure
Authoritarian government	disregard for civil and human rights, unequal power concentration
Traditional economy	economic choices made according to custom
Market economy	economic choices made by individuals and businesses
Command economy	economic choices made by the government
Mixed economy	elements of traditional, market, and command economies

COMPREHENSION AND CRITICAL THINKING

Use information from the graphic organizer to answer the following questions.

1. **Define** What is a mixed economy?

_____

_____

2. **Make Generalizations** What adjectives could you use to describe democratic governments?

_____

_____

3. **Predict** Why does it make sense that civil and human rights are considered unimportant in a government where power is unevenly distributed?

_____

_____

_____

Comparative Political and Economic Systems

READING FOCUS
Today many of the world's countries are democracies. Democracies consist of two basic forms of government: presidential and parliamentary. All democratic governments share certain characteristics, but no two governments are exactly alike.

Key Terms

authoritarian a type of government in which power is concentrated in the hands of a single leader or small group

coalition a temporary alliance for political purposes

apartheid a system of racial segregation and oppression in place in South African before the 1990s

Taking Notes

As you read the summaries, use your Student Casebook to take notes on the section.

Case Study Summary

EMERGING DEMOCRACY IN NIGERIA

After years as a British colony, Nigeria gained independence in 1960. Its first government, a parliamentary system, suffered many setbacks, ranging from a bloody civil war between different regional, ethnic, and religious groups to dictatorships and assassinations. In the 1970s, Nigeria switched its government to a form more closely resembling that of the United States, establishing three independent branches of government and allowing for the popular election of the president.

Yet for years the country continued to lack a stable government, and a series of takeovers and fraudulent elections ensued. However, the election of General Olusegan Obasanjo—a former military ruler who became a reform and human rights leader—in the late 1990s and the first peaceful presidential election in 2007 have both been signs of Nigeria's gradual political stability. After years of dishonest government, the country's leaders will now need to work diligently to earn the people's trust and ensure free, open, and fair elections.

What challenges do Nigeria's leaders face today?

_____

_____

_____

What You Need to Know Summary

DEMOCRATIC SYSTEMS

Governments are categorized by who holds power and how it is distributed. In a democracy, much power rests with the voters and the leaders they elect, whereas in an **authoritarian** government, power is concentrated in the hands of one ruler or small group. Today nearly half of the countries in the world are democracies. While the power of the head of state can vary, all democracies include social welfare policies, protection of basic human rights, and the ability to withstand national crises without changing structure.

MEXICO AND BRAZIL

Like the United States, both Mexico and Brazil are democracies with a presidential form of government, three branches, and a federal system. In Mexico, three-fifths of the seats in the bicameral legislature are elected, with the rest distributed in proportion to parties' share of the popular vote. The president is directly elected and the judicial branch is independent. For many years, the Institutional Revolutionary Party (PRI) held power, but recently the National Action Party (PAN) has taken control of the presidency. Although the country has a fairly stable economy, Mexico's government faces many challenges, including modernization and job growth.

> How are members of Mexico's legislature chosen?
>
> _____
>
> _____

After years of political upheaval, Brazil enacted a revised constitution in 1985. The elected legislature is made up of a senate and a chamber of deputies, and the president and vice president are also directly elected. The judicial branch consists of three levels. Voting is mandatory for people between 18 and 70. Brazil's four major parties make it necessary for politicians to work together to achieve goals.

THE UNITED KINGDOM AND JAPAN

The United Kingdom and Japan are both examples of the world's most common form of democracy, the parliamentary system. In this system, the legislature is the most powerful branch and is responsible for choosing—and possibly removing—the chief executive, known as the prime minister or premier.

> What control does the legislature have over the executive branch in a parliamentary system?
>
> _____
>
> _____

Over the centuries, the United Kingdom has developed into a constitutional monarchy—the hereditary monarch is largely ceremonial—with a unitary government; local governments have only as much power as the central government gives them. The legislature, Parliament, is made up of the elected House of Commons and the limited House of Lords, where members are chosen by political parties or inheritance. Given the number of parties in Parliament, politicians often must set aside their differences and form **coalitions**, or temporary alliances made for political purposes. The prime minister is the leader of the majority party in Parliament and the nation's head of state.

After World War II and with the help of the United States, Japan enacted a democratic constitution in 1947. Japan's unitary system of government is similar to that of the United Kingdom. A bicameral legislature called the Diet is mostly elected, although some seats are distributed based on a party's share of the popular vote. The prime minister is the head of government and the emperor is the head of state.

> **Why do politicians in Parliament need to form coalitions?**
>
> _____
>
> _____

EMERGING DEMOCRACIES

Young democracies face many challenges as they develop. In Latin America, several nations are struggling to establish constitutional democracies while overcoming a long history of authoritarian leadership. Similarly, in Africa, where authoritarian governments were common after countries achieved independence in the years following World War II, democracies are still developing. The country of South Africa, after years of **apartheid**—a system of racial segregation and oppression—successfully established a democracy in 1994 with the election of Nelson Mandela, the country's first black president. In Asia, the change from colony to democracy has also been gradual and sometimes bloody, as countries such as Cambodia have endured civil war and other serious roadblocks on the path to democracy.

> **Why do you think South Africa might be a symbol of hope for other African nations?**
>
> _____
>
> _____

Simulation

Use your Student Casebook to help you complete the simulation.

Comparative Political and Economic Systems

READING FOCUS
Democracy has spread throughout the world in recent decades, but some countries are still under the rule of authoritarian governments. Citizens in these countries have little control over their own government and, in some cases, over their own lives.

Key Terms

theocracy a government that is ruled by religious leaders

totalitarianism authoritarian rule that controls nearly every aspect of public and private life in a country

communism an economic and political system in which government owns all property and controls economic planning

Taking Notes

As you read the summaries, use your Student Casebook to take notes on the section.

Case Study Summary

TOTALITARIAN RULE IN NORTH KOREA

After World War II, the United States and the Soviet Union divided the country of Korea into two parts. Occupied by the Soviet Union, North Korea established a government partially based on Soviet communism. Kim Il Sung became the country's leader, a totalitarian dictator who worked to control all aspects of life.

Today, Kim Il Jung's son, Kim Jong Il, rules North Korea much as his father did. The country is isolated from the rest of the world but is known for its widespread civil and human rights abuses. Citizens' "right to vote" is limited to voting for the one candidate the country's ruling political party, the Korean Workers' Party, chooses for the ballot. Many North Koreans live in extreme poverty, and failed government programs, natural disasters, and the collapse of the Soviet Union have led to millions of deaths from starvation. The country rarely receives foreign aid, and up until recently, its work on nuclear weapons has further harmed its relations with other countries.

> **What is North Korea's relationship with other countries?**
> _____
> _____

What You Need to Know Summary

AUTHORITARIAN SYSTEMS

In an authoritarian system, all power rests with a single leader or small group—citizens have no way to influence or change government, even if there is the appearance of democratic rule. There are many forms of authoritarianism. In a **theocracy**, a government is ruled by religious leaders, who believe that government authority rests with God or some divine power, not the people. In a dictatorship, the most common form of authoritarian rule, dictators may take power by overthrowing the previous government or even by first being elected. **Totalitarianism** occurs when authoritarian rule controls nearly every aspect of public and private life in a country. The government controls everything, and citizens have no freedom of choice.

Authoritarian systems, though they can vary, share some common features. Citizens' civil and human rights are rarely or never protected and rulers may use force to squelch opposition. Also, authoritarian governments are not limited by existing law—rulers can change or ignore any restrictions on their power.

> **What do authoritarian systems have in common?**
> _____
> _____
> _____

THE SOVIET UNION AND CHINA

In 1922 revolutionaries led by Vladimir Lenin formed the Soviet Union around the theory of **communism**, an economic and political system in which government owns all property and controls economic planning. The Soviet government severely limited citizens' rights and allowed only one political party, the Communist Party of the Soviet Union (CPSU), which was controlled by the Central Committee. This committee elected the Politburo, the chief decision-making body. The Politburo was headed by a general secretary who was also the Soviet leader. In 1928 Joseph Stalin took control of the country, instituting a totalitarian regime under which millions of citizens were killed and imprisoned. After Stalin's death in 1953, restrictions on Soviet citizens were eased a bit, but it was not until reforms took place in the 1980s that Soviet power truly began to weaken.

The People's Republic of China was established in 1949, led by Mao Zedong, who imprisoned or killed

> **Describe the structure of the Soviet Union's government.**
> _____
> _____
> _____

those who spoke out against his policies—including a failed five-year Soviet-style plan for economic development that led to deadly food shortages. After Zedong's death in 1976, some economic and political reforms were put into place by leader Deng Xiaoping. Today while some changes have been made, the communist government still limits citizens' basic rights and freedoms. The Chinese Communist Party (CCP) rules the country, electing a Central Committee, which elects the Politburo—a small decision-making body led by a general secretary who is often also China's president. The State Council is the country's chief executive body, led by a premier chosen by the president. The National People's Congress consists of elected representatives, who mainly carry out State Council and CCP decisions.

> **Does the National People's Congress carry out its constituents' wishes? Explain.**
>
> _____
> _____

OTHER AUTHORITARIAN NATIONS

Although it is now a democracy, Chile was under authoritarian rule for years, most recently under General Augusto Pinochet, a military leader who overthrew the socialist government in 1973. For years, Pinochet's government committed human rights abuses, and thousands were tortured and killed. In 1988 Pinochet allowed Chileans to vote as to whether he should stay in power. He was quickly voted out in favor of open elections.

Italy and Germany, also both modern democracies, first underwent periods of fascism—the glorification of the state above all else, including individual needs—in the years between World Wars I and II. Italian dictator Benito Mussolini and German fascist leader Adolf Hitler—under whom millions of Jews were killed—were both defeated during World War II.

Saudi Arabia, an oil-rich U.S. ally, remains an authoritarian nation. Its monarch has near-absolute power but must also follow the Qur'an, the sacred text of Islam, and the laws of Islam. The government tightly controls its people and spends much of its money on social programs and the military. Regular elections and political parties do not exist.

> **Who led the fascist governments of Italy and Germany?**
>
> _____
> _____
> _____

Simulation

Use your Student Casebook to help you complete the simulation.

Comparative Political and Economic Systems

READING FOCUS

Economic systems can be characterized as three basic types: traditional, market, and command. Nearly all nations today have mixed economies, meaning they have some combination of traditional, market, and command features.

Key Terms

factors of production the basic resources that make up an economy—land and natural resources, labor, and capital

traditional economy an economy in which people answer the basic economic questions by custom

market economy an economy in which individuals and businesses make most economic decisions

command economy an economy in which the government makes most economic decisions

mixed economy an economy that combines elements of traditional, market, and command economies

capitalism a type of mixed economy in which individuals and businesses make most economic decisions

laissez-faire a concept popularized by Adam Smith that calls for minimal government involvement in economic affairs

socialism an economic and political system in which the state controls most productive resources

proletariat working class

bourgeoisie the people who own the means of production in a capitalist system

Taking Notes

As you read the summaries, use your Student Casebook to take notes on the section.

Case Study Summary

A CHANGING INDIA

Once India won its independence from Great Britain in 1947, leaders established socialist policies in hopes of encouraging economic growth and spreading wealth equally among the population. The government took control of and regulated all key industries, a move that resulted in economic slowdown starting in the 1960s.

By the 1970s, India began making the transition to an economy based on free markets, leaving more economic decisions to individuals and businesses. The Indian economy accelerated in the 1990s. As the government lowered barriers to foreign trade, there was a dramatic increase in competition, efficiency, and foreign investment. Today India's economy is booming, and a widespread middle class has developed. However, the country still faces many challenges, including how to help the 30 percent of the population living in poverty and how to adequately expand the national infrastructure.

> **What change did India's government make to turn around its economy?**
> _____
> _____

What you Need to Know Summary

MAKING ECONOMIC DECISIONS

Economics is the study of how people produce, distribute, and consume goods and services. The basic resources that make up an economy—land and natural resources, labor, and capital—are known as the **factors of production**. All societies consider the questions of what should be produced, how, and for whom when deciding how to use resources to provide goods and services. In a **traditional economy**, people answer these questions by custom, or what has always been done. In a **market economy**, individuals and businesses make most economic decisions based on the needs and wants of others. Finally, in a **command economy**, the government makes most economic decisions. Today most countries have a **mixed economy**, which combines elements of traditional, market, and command economies.

MIXED ECONOMIES

There are three main types of mixed economies: capitalism, socialism, and communism. The U.S. economy is largely based on **capitalism**, in which individuals and businesses make most economic decisions and competition is encouraged. Philosopher Adam Smith founded capitalism, encouraging **laissez-faire** practices, or minimal government involvement in economic affairs. While government still plays an important role in all capitalist economies—such as by encouraging job creation—the United States and many other governments are working toward reduced government involvement in international trade and encouraging global competition.

> **What role do individuals play in a capitalist economy?**
> _____
> _____

The second type of mixed economy is **socialism**, an economic and political system in which the state controls most productive resources, mainly in order to distribute wealth throughout society for the benefit of the majority of its citizens. German theorist Karl Marx founded modern socialism, arguing that in a capitalist society, the **proletariat**, or working class, receives unfair treatment from the **bourgeoisie**, or the people who own the means of production. Today most socialist countries are democratic, resolving any injustices of capitalism with regulation and plentiful social services, such as retirement benefits and child care. Opponents of socialism argue that all of these social programs lead to high taxes, and that since everyone has to pay these taxes, there is little incentive to work harder or more creatively. Supporters counter that capitalism produces inequalities, an ill fixed by the economic democracy of socialism.

Karl Marx believed that the proletariat would overthrow capitalism, resulting in a classless society he called *Communist*. Today communism is the third type of mixed economy, first adopted by the leaders of the Soviet Union. There the government owned most businesses and resources and controlled all economic planning. This system resulted in increased industrialization and a powerful military, but also created inefficiencies and high costs. The Soviet empire collapsed in 1991.

However, Communist China, established in 1949, still exists, having gradually moved away from central planning and communism toward increased economic freedoms for businesses and foreign investment. China is now projected to be the second largest economy in the world.

While communism is basically an extreme authoritarian form of socialism, it can allow countries to develop their economies quickly. Yet in an economy that does not allow competition, poor product quality and shortages of consumer goods can become worrisome problems.

> **What are the arguments for and against socialism?**
> _____
> _____
> _____

> **How might a lack of competition hurt an economy?**
> _____
> _____
> _____

Simulation

Use your Student Casebook to help you complete the simulation.

State and Local Government

Chapter Summary

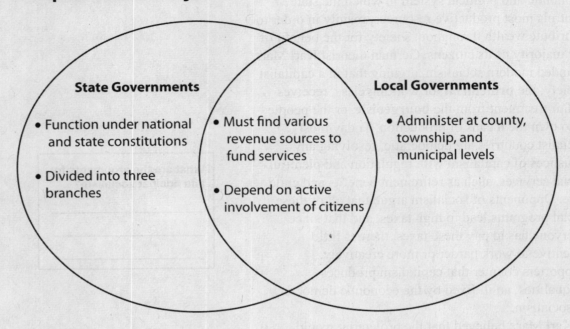

State Governments

- Function under national and state constitutions

- Divided into three branches

Must find various revenue sources to fund services

Depend on active involvement of citizens

Local Governments

- Administer at county, township, and municipal levels

COMPREHENSION AND CRITICAL THINKING
Use information from the graphic organizer to answer the following questions.

1. **Recall** How is power divided in state governments?

   _____

   _____

2. **Analyze** Local governments must provide many services. How do you think active citizen participation affects the delivery of these services?

   _____

   _____

3. **Evaluate** Why do you think the structure of state government is so similar to that of the federal government?

   _____

   _____

   _____

State and Local Government

READING FOCUS
As you have learned, the word *federalism* is used to describe the relationship between the national and state governments. State governments function under the national constitution and a state constitution. State constitutions share important similarities as well as strengths and weaknesses.

Key Terms

guarantee clause another name for Article IV, Section 4, of the Constitution, which "guarantee[s] to every state in [the] Union a Republic Form of Government"

fundamental law law that determines the basic political principles of a government

statutory law law found in state constitutions that is very detailed and specific

Taking Notes

As you read the summaries, use your Student Casebook to take notes on the section.

Case Study Summary

THE NULLIFICATION CRISIS

In 1828 Congress raised a tariff on British imports to help goods produced in the northern states seem less expensive. The southern states quickly protested what they called the Tariff of Abominations, claiming that the tariff hurt them in favor of the northern states. Even after a new, lower tariff was passed, the South Carolina legislature remained furious and voted to test the doctrine of nullification, only a theory up until that point. By passing the Ordinance of Nullification in November 1832, the state nullified, or disregarded, the federal tariff, judging them to be against the state's best interests.

President Andrew Jackson issued the Nullification Proclamation the next month, declaring South Carolina's ordinance illegal. Tensions between South Carolina and the federal government remained strained until the Compromise Tariff of 1833, which gradually reduced tariff rates, went into effect. Yet states' rights remained a national issue, eventually becoming one of the causes of the Civil War. While the Supreme Court ruled in *Texas* v. *White* (1869) that the United States was "an indestructible Union, composed of indestructible states," states' rights are

> **Why did South Carolina's legislature nullify the 1828 tariff?**
> _____
> _____
> _____

still the focus of many political debates today,
including those surrounding civil rights and gun laws.

What You Need to Know Summary

STATES IN THE FEDERAL SYSTEM

Although the Constitution grants delegated powers to
the national government and reserves all other powers
to the states—besides those powers held concurrently
by both levels of government—it was inevitable that
conflicts would arise between the national and state
governments. The Framers anticipated this and
included the supremacy clause in Article 6, Section 2,
of the Constitution, which declares the laws of the
national government the "supreme law of the land."
The Framers also anticipated the need for guidelines
for relationships between states, exemplified by their
inclusion of the full faith and credit clause. This
clause requires that each state recognize the civil laws
and acts, as well as the decisions of the courts, of the
other states. The full faith and credit clause was
intended to promote and ease cooperation between the
states.

> **What does the inclusion of the supremacy clause in the Constitution show about the Framers?**
> _____
> _____

STATE CONSTITUTIONS

Article IV, Section 4, of the Constitution, also known
as the **guarantee clause**, "guarantees to every state in
[the] Union a Republican Form of Government."
Through this clause, the Constitution ensures that state
governments will be limited and representative like
the national government, but leaves all other decisions
about the framework of state and local governments to
each state's constitution.

State constitutions vary in length and how many
times they have been rewritten, but all express basic
civic principles and practices and include a bill of
rights. While the government outlined by each state
constitution is different from those of other states,
every state government is limited, with power shared
between its legislative, executive, and judicial
branches.

> **What do state constitutions have in common?**
> _____
> _____

The state constitutions have been amended many
more times than the U.S. Constitution, primarily
because the process for making changes is easier.
Most state constitutions have also been rewritten more

than once, although some states still have original constitutions, including Massachusetts, which has the world's oldest constitution still in effect.

The number of rewrites most state constitutions have undergone over the centuries has resulted in some problems. Many constitutions are extremely long, due to the fact that they contain both **fundamental law**—law determining the fundamental political principles of a government, as in the U.S. Constitution—and **statutory law**—detailed, specific, and often obsolete law. To address the problem of excessive statutory law, several states have revised or completely rewritten their constitutions, sometimes through the amendment process.

> **Why is statutory law sometimes a problem in state constitutions?**
> _____
> _____

Simulation

Use your Student Casebook to help you complete the simulation.

State and Local Government

Section 2

READING FOCUS

State governments, like the federal government, divide power among legislative, executive, and judicial branches. In terms of their structure and functions, these state branches mirror the branches of the federal government. Also like the federal government, state governments must find funding for expensive yet essential programs and services.

Key Terms

governor the chief executive in a state government

citizen legislatures part-time legislatures, in which legislators meet only once every other year and for a period of about two months

professional legislatures legislature in which sessions may be held annually and may last for much of the year

line-item veto a type of veto by which a governor can reject specific parts of legislation while signing the rest of a bill into law

executive clemency powers granted to a governor, including the power to grant pardons and commutations

Missouri Plan a system for selecting judges involving both election and appointment

Taking Notes

As you read the summaries, use your Student Casebook to take notes on the section.

Case Study Summary

TEEN DRIVING LAWS

In July 2003, 17-year-old Joshua Brown from Georgia lost control of his car on a wet road and died upon colliding with a tree. In response to this tragedy, the state legislature passed Joshua's Law, legislation that expanded Georgia's already strict licensing system for teen drivers. Sixteen-year-olds now have to take driver education classes to apply for unrestricted licenses and all teen drivers must undergo hours of supervised driving.

As the history of Joshua's Law shows, driving laws are the responsibility of the state—and these laws vary widely. In some states, teens can drive without supervision at 14 and a half, while the beginner's age is 16 and a half in other states. Most states have

> How did Joshua's Law change Georgia's licensing system for teen drivers?
>
> _____
>
> _____

---

graduated licensing systems, which usually involve a
learner's permit and periods of restricted driving.

What You Need to Know Summary

ORGANIZATION OF STATE GOVERNMENTS

As in the federal government, power is divided
between three branches in state government. State
legislatures are bicameral, except in Nebraska, where
the legislature is unicameral. The lower house is
usually called the House of Representatives and the
upper house the Senate. Total number of legislators,
terms of office, and session lengths vary, but state
legislatures share some common features. State
executive branches are also similar. All 50 states have
an elected **governor**, who serves as chief executive of
state. The state judicial branch is the third arm of state
government and includes both trial and appellate
courts. State courts hear cases involving state law,
which make up 99 percent of all U.S. court cases.

> Name three ways in which
> the structure of state
> governments is similar to
> that of the federal
> government.
>
> _____
>
> _____
>
> _____
>
> _____

STATE LEGISLATIVE BRANCHES

State legislatures can be citizen legislatures,
professional legislatures, or a combination of both.
There are 17 **citizen legislatures,** in which legislators
meet only once every other year and for a period of
about two months. There are 11 **professional
legislatures**, in which sessions may be held annually
and last for much of the year. Legislators in this type
of legislature do not usually hold other jobs, as do
those in citizen legislatures.

A state legislature is granted all of the reserved
powers not granted to another branch by the state
constitution and not denied it by the state constitution
or the U.S. Constitution. The power to make laws is
key to state legislatures, whose actions often influence
the U.S. Congress. Also, the legislatures' approval and
impeachment powers allow them to check the other
state branches. The organization and law-making
processes of state legislatures resemble those of the
U.S. Congress, including the roles of presiding
officers and committees and how a bill becomes law.

> What is the difference
> between citizen and
> professional legislatures?
>
> _____
>
> _____
>
> _____

STATE EXECUTIVE BRANCHES

Governors have many powers, including the power to enforce state law and mobilize the state's units of the National Guard. The governor can check the other branches by vetoing legislation—in most states, a **line-item veto** allows the governor to reject only specific parts of legislation—and using the powers of **executive clemency**. Most governors serve four-year terms. Governors work closely with other key executive officers, which can include the lieutenant governor, secretary of state, state treasurers, and attorney general.

> **What is the purpose of a line-item veto?**
> _____
> _____
> _____

STATE JUDICIAL BRANCHES

State courts hear both civil and criminal cases. In criminal cases, a grand jury decides if there is enough evidence to indict a person. A petit jury then hears the case. If a person is found guilty, he or she may appeal the decision to the state's intermediate appellate court and sometimes then to the state supreme court. From there, a very few cases involving federal law or the Constitution can move to the federal court system.

State judges are either appointed by the governor or legislature, elected, or both appointed and elected under a form of the **Missouri Plan**. Under this plan, the governor appoints a judge based on a list compiled by a nonpartisan commission. At the next election, voters can then choose to keep or replace the judge.

> **Explain the Missouri Plan in your own words.**
> _____
> _____
> _____
> _____

STATE SERVICES AND FINANCES

States must provide many essential government services, ranging from funding and shaping education to maintaining roads. To fund services, most states collect income and sales taxes, as well as charge user fees, receive federal grants, sell bonds, and run a lottery. The state budget—which must be balanced in many states—is developed by the governor, revised by the legislature, and approved by the governor.

Simulation

Use your Student Casebook to help you complete the simulation.

State and Local Government

Section 3

READING FOCUS
A variety of local governments provide many of the services you rely on every day. These services are paid for by local, state, and federal revenue. Direct citizen participation in government is often easiest at the local level.

Key Terms

counties the most basic units of government, except for in parts of New England

parishes counties in Louisiana

boroughs counties in Alaska

townships divisions of counties

municipalities the nation's cities, towns, and villages

incorporation process by which municipalities are given their legal authority by the state

mayor-council system a form of municipal government in which citizens elect a mayor to serve as the chief executive and a city council to serve as the local legislature

council-manager system a form of municipal government in which the city council appoints a city manager to be the chief executive and the mayor leads the city council

commission system a form of municipal government in which a group of elected commissioners lead city departments and set local policies

special districts local governments that provide a single service to defined area

zoning laws laws passed by cities and towns to regulate land use

initiative a process through which citizens propose and enact state and local laws directly

referendum a popular vote on a proposal that has already been considered by the legislature

recall a process through which citizens remove government officials from office before the end of a term

Taking Notes

As you read the summaries, use your Student Casebook to take notes on the section.

Case Study Summary

LAND USE IN EASTON, MARYLAND

In the United States, local governments regularly make decisions about how land should be used and how to balance economic growth with potential community concerns. In 1999 the town of Easton, Maryland, was faced with the dilemma of whether it should allow three "big-box" retail stores to locate to their 14,000-person town. Residents raised many concerns, such as whether local roads could handle the increased traffic the stores would attract and how the large stores would affect the town's smaller retailers and overall charm.

In order to address these concerns, the town government issued a moratorium on the construction of big-box stores, then held hearings and commissioned a study on the effects of large-scale development on Easton. When the local government determined that stores larger than 65,000 feet would indeed harm the town, the Easton Planning and Zoning Commissions recommended prohibiting the building of stores that size. In response, the Easton Town Council issued an ordinance that made this recommendation into law.

> **What steps did the Easton town government take to address residents' concerns?**
>
> _____
> _____
> _____

What You Need to Know Summary

LOCAL GOVERNMENT

There are approximately 88,000 local governments in the United States, each created by its home state. There are various levels of local government. All states are divided into **counties**, which are the most basic units of government except in parts of New England; counties are called **parishes** in Louisiana and **boroughs** in Alaska. Most counties are governed by county boards. In certain parts of the country where counties are divided into **townships**, township governments help the county government deliver services, especially to rural areas.

In addition to counties and townships, Americans also live in **municipalities**—the nation's nearly 20,000 cities, towns, and villages, each given legal authority by the state through a process called **incorporation**. There are three forms of municipal government. First, in the **mayor-council system**, citizens elect a mayor to serve as the chief executive and a city council to serve as the local legislature. Second, in the **council-manager system**, the city council appoints a city manager to be the chief executive and the mayor leads the city council. Finally, in a **commission system**, a group of elected commissioners lead city departments and set local

> **Which level of government do you think would best be able to meet citizens' specific needs: county or municipal government? Explain.**
>
> _____
> _____
> _____
> _____

policies. In certain parts of New England where towns, not counties, are the most basic units of government, a board of three to five selectmen presides over town meetings and manages the town's affairs. The greatest number of local governments are **special districts**, which provide a single service to a defined area, such as school districts.

County governments provide many essential services, such as public safety, record keeping, and election supervision. Municipal governments provide additional services, including libraries and garbage collection. Municipal governments also regulate land use in the area through **zoning laws**.

Local governments need to raise money to cover the costs of these services. They do this mainly by collecting property taxes on much of the land, homes, cars, and business property within their boundaries. A local government may also levy additional sales and income taxes, tax corporations, charge certain user fees, or sell municipal bonds. Intergovernmental revenue, such as federal and state grants, can also help local governments fund services.

> **What is the purpose of zoning laws?**
>
> _____
>
> _____

PARTICIPATING IN STATE AND LOCAL GOVERNMENT

When citizens monitor public policy and make their interests known to government officials, they are taking part in a process called participatory citizenship. Voting, running for office, volunteering, and testifying before state or local boards are all ways to be an active citizen. Some citizen actions actually have the force of law, such as an **initiative**, a process through which citizens propose and enact state and local laws directly. In an initiative, citizens collect signatures on a petition supporting a bill, then either pass it to the state legislature or the state's voters for approval. Citizens can also make laws through a **referendum**, a popular vote on a proposal that has already been considered by the legislature, and remove government officials from office before the end of a term through a **recall**.

> **What can citizens accomplish through an initiative?**
>
> _____
>
> _____

Simulation

Use your Student Casebook to help you complete the simulation.

SCORE!

Mountain Challenge

MATH WORKBOOK

KAPLAN

PUBLISHING

New York

Contributing Editor: Justin Serrano
Editorial Director: Jennifer Farthing
Editorial Development Manager: Tonya Lobato
Assistant Editor: Eric Titner
Production Editor: Dominique Polfliet
Production Artist: Creative Pages, Inc.
Cover Designer: Carly Schnur

© 2007 by Kaplan, Inc.

Published by Kaplan Publishing, a division of Kaplan, Inc.
888 Seventh Ave.
New York, NY 10106

Printed in the United States of America

May 2007
10 9 8 7 6 5 4 3 2 1

ISBN-978-1-4195-9458-8
ISBN-10: 1-4195-9458-3

Kaplan Publishing books are available at special quantity discounts to use for sales promotions, employee premiums, or educational purposes. Please email our Special Sales Department to order or for more information at kaplanpublishing@kaplan.com, or write to Kaplan Publishing, 888 Seventh Avenue, 22nd Floor, New York, NY 10106.

Table of Contents

Are you ready for a fun and challenging trip up *SCORE!* Mountain?

Getting Started

This exciting, interactive workbook will guide you through 6 unique base camps as you make your way up *SCORE!* Mountain. Along the way to the top you will have the opportunity to challenge yourself with over 150 math questions, activities, and brain busters as you work toward conquering *SCORE!* Mountain.

To help you figure out the answer to each question, use the blank space on the page or the extra pages at the back of your workbook. If you need extra space, use a piece of scrap paper.

Base Camp

SCORE! Mountain is divided into 6 base camps—each covering an essential math topic—and is aligned to the educational standards set forth by the National Council of Teachers of Mathematics. The final base camp in this book, Everyday Math, has a special focus on the many ways we might use math each day.

Your trip through base camp will take you through 19 questions related to the base camp topic, a Challenge Activity designed to give your brain an extra workout, and a 5-question test to see how much you've learned during your climb.

Each question comes with helpful hints to guide you to the right answer. Use these hints to make your climb up *SCORE!* Mountain a successful learning experience!

The Answer Hider

We encourage you to give each question your best effort before looking at the answer; that's why your *SCORE! Mountain Challenge Workbook* comes equipped with a handy answer hider.

Tear out the answer hider and, while you work on each question, use your answer hider to cover up the solution until you're finished. Then, uncover the answer and see how well you did!

Celebrate!

At the end of each base camp, there's a fun celebration as a reward for successfully making it through. It's the perfect opportunity to take a break and refresh yourself before tackling the next base camp!

SCORE! Mountain Challenge Online Companion

Don't forget—more fun awaits you online! Each base camp comes with a set of 10 online questions and interactive activities, plus a mountain-climbing study partner who will encourage you and help you track your progress as you get closer to the top of *SCORE!* Mountain!

SCORE! online base camps are designed to supplement the educational themes of each base camp from the book. As you reach the end of each base camp in the book, we encourage you to go to your computer to round out your *SCORE!* Mountain Challenge experience. Plus, after you successfully complete the last online session you are awarded a Certificate of Achievement.

Certificate of Achievement

Upon completion of the entire book and online program, you will receive your very own Certificate of Achievement that can be shared with family and friends!

Time Management

In addition to all of the great math practice that your *SCORE! Mountain Challenge Workbook* has to offer, you'll find an array of helpful tips and strategies at the front of the book on how you can best organize and manage your time to stay on top of your busy schedule, do well at school, get all of your homework and chores done, and still have time for fun, family, and friends! It's a great way to help you perform at your best every day!

Tools

Every mountain climber needs a set of tools to help him or her reach the mountaintop! Your *SCORE! Mountain Challenge Workbook* has a special set of tools for you. In the back of your book you'll find a handy guide to help you get through each base camp. Turn to the back of the book and use these tools whenever you need a helping hand during your climb up *SCORE!* Mountain.

Enjoy your trip up *SCORE!* Mountain. We hope that it's a fun and educational learning experience!

GOOD LUCK!

Being organized and managing your time well are very important skills to learn. They are a valuable key to success!

Here are some tips to help.

Getting Started

- *Be realistic.* We all wish that we had an endless number of hours in the day to take care of all of our responsibilities and still have time for all of the fun things we want to do. The truth is that every person in the world has the same amount of time to work with. Each of us gets 24 hours a day, 7 days a week, so how you budget your time is important!

- *Keep a schedule.* To help keep track of your time, try creating a weekly schedule. You can use a calendar or organizer, or you can make your own schedule on a blank piece of paper. Your weekly schedule might look like this:

My Weekly Schedule

	MON.	TUES.	WED.	THURS.	FRI.	SAT.	SUN.
6:00 A.M.							
7:00 A.M.							
8:00 A.M.							
9:00 A.M.							
10:00 A.M.							
11:00 A.M.							
12:00 P.M.							
1:00 P.M.							
2:00 P.M.							
3:00 P.M.							
4:00 P.M.							
5:00 P.M.							
6:00 P.M.							
7:00 P.M.							
8:00 P.M.							
9:00 P.M.							
10:00 P.M.							

- *Budget time.* Set aside time on your schedule for all of your regular daily activities. For instance, if you go to school between 7:00 A.M. and 2:30 P.M. each weekday, write that on your schedule. Be sure to include any important chores, responsibilities, after-school clubs, and special events. Budget time for homework and school assignments as well, but also make time for fun with your friends and family!

Staying Organized:

- *Write it down.* The best way to keep track of new activities or assignments is to write them down. Whenever something new comes up, add it to your schedule!

  You can also try keeping a "To Do" list to make sure you remember everything. Try to estimate the amount of time it will take to complete your assignments. It's a good way to budget your time!

- *Have a daily plan.* Each day, plan out what chores, assignments, and activities you have to do that day. Use your "To Do" list to help. Some activities may take up more time, so make sure you have enough time that day to complete everything. Your daily plan might look something like this:

Sample Daily Plan

MONDAY	
6:00 A.M.	Get up, get dressed
7:00 A.M.	Eat breakfast Go to school
7:40 A.M.	School starts
2:30 P.M.	School ends Karate Club meeting – gym
3:30 P.M.	Get home from school
4:00 P.M.	Homework, and chores (see "To Do" list)
6:30 P.M.	Dinner
7:30 P.M.	Call friends and watch TV
8:45 P.M.	Get ready for bed
9:00 P.M.	Bed

Doing Homework

- *Set homework time.* Your schedule should include a block of time for doing homework. If possible, make this block of time for right after you get home from school, so you're sure to have enough time to complete your assignments. How much time do you usually need for homework? Write that on your weekly schedule.

- *Get right to it!* When it's time to do your homework, stay focused. Try to work straight through until you get it done. You'll be happy to finish, so you can move on to other fun things! Sometimes a small, healthful snack can help keep you going and energized!

- *Stay organized.* Set up your homework space in a well-lit area with all the things you'll need to do a great job. This includes your schoolbooks, a dictionary, a calculator, pens, and extra paper. If you keep these items handy, it makes learning a lot more organized and fun!

- *Improve your skills.* Good students develop their skills both inside and outside the classroom. Your *SCORE! Mountain Challenge Workbook* can help. Set aside part of your homework time each day for completing sections from the workbook. Check your progress with the online quizzes as well.

Chores and Activities

- *Keep your commitments.* Remember to include your chores in your daily schedule. You might even set aside a "chore time." Be sure to include chores on your daily "To Do" list as well.

- *Know your limits.* How many school activities can you manage? Be realistic when you join clubs or sign up for activities. Activities are fun, but you must make time for all of the other things going on in your life.

- *Set priorities.* If you don't have many commitments, you can get everything done in your free time. But what if you're committed to more things than you have time for? Then you must set priorities.

  A **priority** is something that's important to you. When you set priorities, you choose the items from your list that are most important to complete.

Use the worksheet below to help you determine your priorities.

Priorities Worksheet

Review the list of activities below. Write your own activities in the blank spaces next to Clubs, Sports, and Classes. Add any other activities on the lines next to Other.

In the column marked Priority, give each activity a letter: **A**, **B**, or **C**:

- **Priority A** = very important to me
- **Priority B** = important to me
- **Priority C** = less important to me

Priority	Activity	Priority	Activity
_____	Homework _____	_____	Sports _____
	_____	_____	_____
_____	Chores _____		
_____	_____	_____	Other _____
	_____	_____	_____
_____	Clubs _____	_____	_____
	_____	_____	_____
_____	Classes _____	_____	_____
_____	_____	_____	_____

List your top 5 priorities below. These items are the most important to you. You should always focus on getting these done.

Priority	Activity
1	
2	
3	
4	
5	

Once you know what's important to you, make sure the things that are top priority get done first!

Setting Goals

- Even though you're busy, it's also great to try new things Setting goals will help you with this!

- Maybe you want to try a new sport, join a new club at school, or read a new book. Fill in the spaces below to help you get started reaching your goals. Every time you reach a goal, make a new goal for yourself. You'll be amazed at how much you can do!

What is your #1 goal?

_____

_____

How are you going to reach your #1 goal?

_____

_____

Leaving Time for Fun!

- Everyone needs time to relax and recharge. Include some time in your schedule for relaxing and just having fun with your family and friends. You'll be glad you did!

Your *SCORE! Mountain Challenge Workbook* comes with a fun, interactive online companion. Parents, go online to register your child at **kaptest.com/scorebooksonline**. Here your child can access 60 exciting math activities and a cool mountain-climbing study partner.

Children, when you log on, you'll be brought to a page where you will find your *SCORE! Mountain Challenge Workbook* cover. You'll also be asked for a **password**, which you will get from a passage in this workbook. So have your workbook handy when you're ready to continue your *SCORE!* Mountain Challenge online, and follow the directions.

Good luck and have fun climbing!

Base Camp

Number Sense

Are you ready to begin climbing *SCORE!* Mountain? Let's get started! Good luck!

SCORE! MOUNTAIN TOP

BASE CAMP 5

BASE CAMP 4

BASE CAMP 3

BASE CAMP 2

BASE CAMP 1

1. Amanda is taking a **20-mile hike**. She hikes for **12 miles** and then she stops for lunch. What **percent** of the hike has she done so far?

_____

Hint #1:

A **percentage** is a ratio that compares a **part** to a **whole**, where the whole is **100**.

Hint #2:

Set up a **proportion** to show that $\frac{part}{whole} = \frac{percent}{100}$, plug in the information given in the problem, and solve.

Answer: Amanda has traveled **60 percent** of the hike.

By the time she stops for lunch, Amanda has traveled 12 of the 20 miles. Set up the **proportion** $\frac{part}{whole} = \frac{percent}{100}$, with the information given. Use the variable **n** to represent the missing percent: $\frac{12}{20} = \frac{n}{100}$. You can use equivalent fractions in this problem. $20 \times 5 = 100$: $\frac{12 \times 5}{20 \times 5} = \frac{60}{100}$. Therefore, percent **n** is **60**.

The proportion can also be solved by **cross multiplication**: $12 \times 100 = 20n$, which becomes $1200 = 20n$. Divide both sides of this equation by 20, and you have $1200 \div 20 = n$, or **60 = n**.

2. Max spent $\frac{2}{3}$ of an hour on homework **Monday**. He spent $1\frac{1}{6}$ hours on **Tuesday**, and $2\frac{1}{3}$ hours on **Wednesday**. On **Thursday**, Max spent $\frac{7}{12}$ of an hour on homework, and on **Friday** he spent $\frac{1}{2}$ of an hour.

Order these amounts of time from **shortest** to **longest**.

_____

Hint #1:

Two of the time values can be easily ordered—the times that are **mixed numbers**. By looking at the whole number part, they are easily ordered as the two longest times.

Hint #2:

Find a **common denominator** for the proper fractional times. This is the **least common multiple** of **2**, **3**, and **12**. Once the fractions are converted to the same denominator, they are easily ordered.

Answer: $\frac{1}{2}$, $\frac{7}{12}$, $\frac{2}{3}$, $1\frac{1}{6}$, $2\frac{1}{3}$

As described in the hints, the **mixed numbers** of $1\frac{1}{6}$ and $2\frac{1}{3}$ are easily seen to be the **longest times**, because the three proper fractions are all less than 1. Because $2 > 1$, the mixed number $2\frac{1}{3}$ hours is the **longest time**, and $1\frac{1}{6}$ hours is the **second longest time**.

To order the other three fractions, find the **common denominator**. The least common multiple of 2, 3, and 12 is **12**. So convert each fraction so it has a denominator of 12: $\frac{1 \times 6}{2 \times 6} = \frac{6}{12}$, and $\frac{2 \times 4}{3 \times 4} = \frac{8}{12}$. Now that they all have the same denominator, look at the **numerators** of each fraction. Because $6 < 7 < 8$, the order of the fractions, from **least** to **greatest** is: $\frac{6}{12}$, $\frac{7}{12}$, $\frac{8}{12}$, $1\frac{1}{6}$, $2\frac{1}{3}$, which is $\frac{1}{2}$, $\frac{7}{12}$, $\frac{2}{3}$, $1\frac{1}{6}$, $2\frac{1}{3}$.

3. Use the **commutative property of addition** to find the sum of the following numbers:

$$16 + 23 + 84$$

_____

Hint #1:

The **commutative property of addition** states that you can change the order of **addends** in an addition problem to find a sum.

Hint #2:

Look for addends that are easy to add. One method is to look for digits in the ones place that add to ten.

Answer: The correct answer is **123**.

To find the sum, you could use the order of operations and add from left to right. The problem, however, asks you to use the **commutative property of addition**. The commutative property of addition states that you can change the order of the addends. This can make addition easier.

Look at the addends. The first, **16**, and the third, **84**, can be added first to make the problem easier, because adding the **6** and the **4** produces a **10**. So order the numbers as follows: **16 + 84 + 23**.

16 plus 84 is 100, plus 23 is **123**.

4. Write the number **four trillion, 50 billion, two thousand thirty**.

_____

Hint #1:

When writing numbers, consider the **place values**, which are **powers of ten**. The numbers are grouped in **sets of three**, separated by commas.

XXX,   XXX,   XXX,   XXX,   XXX

Trillions   Billions   Millions   Thousands   Units

Hint #2:

Each set of three has a **hundreds**, **tens**, and **units** place. One trillion is the **13th place** to the left of the decimal point. Ten billion is the **11th place** to the left of the decimal point. One thousand is the **4th place** to the left of the decimal point, and ten is **2 places** to the left of the decimal point.

Answer: 4,050,000,002,030

5. A car travels at a constant rate of **50 miles per hour**. How far will the car travel in **4 hours**?

_____

Hint #1:

A **rate** is a special ratio that compares two unlike quantities. In this example, it is **miles** and **hours**.

Hint #2:

You are given a **unit rate** that states that every hour the car travels 50 miles. Use **multiplication** to find how far the car travels in 4 hours.

Answer: In 4 hours, the car will travel **200 miles**.

A rate is a **ratio**. Using this ratio, you can set up a **proportion** to find how far the car travels in 4 hours: $\frac{miles}{hours} = \frac{miles}{hours}$; $\frac{50}{1} = \frac{n}{4}$.

Cross multiply to get $50 \times 4 = n$, or $n = 200$.

6. Barbara ate $\frac{3}{4}$ of a bag of candy. What **percent** of the candy did she eat?

_____

Hint #1:

Imagine that the candy is separated into **4 equal sections**. Barbara ate **3** of the **4** sections. A **percent** is a part of a whole, where the whole is **100**.

Hint #2:

Set up a **proportion** where $\frac{3}{4} = \frac{n}{100}$, and solve for **n**.

Answer: Barbara ate **75%** of the bag of candy.

A percent is a **ratio**, so set up the **proportion**: $\frac{3}{4} = \frac{n}{100}$. You can use **equivalent fractions** to solve this percent question. Multiply $\frac{3}{4}$ by $\frac{25}{25}$ to get the denominator to be 100, which gives you $\frac{75}{100}$.

Your numerator, **n**, is therefore **3 × 25 = 75**. $\frac{75}{100}$ is **75%**.

7. Simplify:

$$| \, 90 - 42 \, |$$

_____

Hint #1:

The symbol $| \, n \, |$ stands for the **absolute value** of some quantity, n.

Hint #2:

The **absolute value** of any quantity is **always** positive. Simplify any expression within the absolute value symbols and make the quantity positive.

Answer: The value of $| \, 90 - 42 \, |$ is **48**.

Simplify by first performing the subtraction, **90 − 42 = 48**. This is also the **absolute value**, since it is already positive.

8. What is the value of $|-18|$?

_____

Hint #1:

Remember, the symbol $|n|$ stands for the absolute value of some quantity, n.

Hint #2:

Remember that absolute value is **always** positive. Simplify any expression within the absolute value symbols and make the quantity positive.

Answer: The value of $|-18|$ is **18**.

The **absolute value** of a quantity is that number, **not** counting the sign, or its "distance" from 0. Any negative value is changed to a positive value, and a positive value remains positive.

9. Where is $-1\frac{1}{4}$ on the following number line?

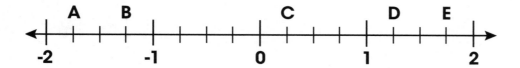

Hint #1:

Negative numbers are to the **left** of zero on a number line.

Hint #2:

$-1\frac{1}{4}$ is $\frac{1}{4}$ smaller than -1; therefore, it is to the **left** of -1.

Answer: $-1\frac{1}{4}$ is at point **B** on the number line.

There are 4 spaces between each integer, so each mark is $\frac{1}{4}$. Because $-1\frac{1}{4}$ is less than -1, it is one mark to the left of -1 on the number line.

10. What is the **multiplicative inverse** of 8?

_____

Hint #1:

The **multiplicative inverse** of a number is the number you multiply by to get a **product of 1**. The multiplicative inverse is also called the **reciprocal**.

Hint #2:

To find the multiplicative inverse for any number, write the number as a **fraction** and then find the reciprocal by switching the numerator and the denominator.

Answer: The multiplicative inverse of 8 is $\frac{1}{8}$.

The **multiplicative inverse** of a number is the number you multiply by to get a product of 1. To find the multiplicative inverse for any number, write the number as a **fraction** and then find the reciprocal by switching the numerator and the denominator.

The number 8 written as a fraction is $\frac{8}{1}$, and its reciprocal is $\frac{1}{8}$.

11. Express $\frac{5}{8}$ as a **decimal**.

_____

Hint #1:

The fraction $\frac{5}{8}$ can be read as **"five divided by eight."**

Hint #2:

Use **division** to find the decimal equivalent. Your answer should be less than 1, because $\frac{5}{8} < \frac{8}{8}$.

Answer: $\frac{5}{8}$ expressed as a decimal is **0.625**.

Because $\frac{5}{8}$ means 5 ÷ 8, perform division to get **0.625**.

12. **Eighty percent** of the baseball team is right-handed. If there are **thirty members** on the baseball team, how many members are **left-handed**?

_____

Hint #1:

Eighty percent means $\frac{80}{100}$, so **80** out of every **100** players are right-handed. How many are left-handed then?

Hint #2:

To find the number of left-handed players, set up a **proportion** using ratios comparing left-handed players to the total number of players. You can use the variable **n** to represent the number of left-handed players. Cross multiply to find the number of left-handed players out of a total of 30.

Answer: **6 members of the baseball team are left-handed.**

If 80 out of every 100 players are right-handed, then $100 - 80 = 20$ out of every 100 players are left-handed.

Set up a **proportion** comparing left-handed players to the total number of players: $\frac{20}{100} = \frac{n}{30}$. Cross multiply to get $600 = 100n$.

Divide both sides by 100 and **n = 6**.

13. What is the **decimal equivalent** of **7%**?

_____

Hint #1:

Seven percent means **7 out of 100**, or $\frac{7}{100}$.

$\frac{7}{100}$ = seven hundredths

Hint #2:

To change a fraction to a decimal equivalent, **divide** the numerator by the denominator.

Answer: 7% = 0.07

Seven percent means $\frac{7}{100}$, or **7 divided by 100**. When you divide a number by 100, you can simply move the decimal point two places to the left. The decimal equivalent of 7% is **0.07**.

14. Use the **distributive property** to multiply $12(10 + 5)$.

_____

© Kaplan Publishing, Inc.

Hint #1:

Multiplication distributes over addition.

Hint #2:

Distribute the 12 to both addends in the parentheses.

Answer: 180

The problem asks you to use the **distributive property** to multiply. **Distribute** the 12 to both addends in parentheses. The problem is now $12 \times 10 + 12 \times 5$. Use the order of operations to get $120 + 60 = 180$.

15. What number is the **additive identity**?

_____

What is
additive identity?

Hint #1:

The **additive identity** is the value that can be added to any number without changing its value.

Hint #2:

The **additive identity is** ☐ , where $5 + ☐ = 5$, and $22 + ☐ = 22$.

Answer: The additive identity is **0**.

The **additive identity** is the number that can be added to any other number without changing its value. That number is **0**.

16. Which of the following is an example of the **associative property of multiplication**?

(A) $(5 \times 3) \times 2 = 5 \times (3 \times 2)$

(B) $5 \times 3 \times 2 = 5 \times 2 \times 3$

(C) $5(3 + 2) = 5 \times 3 + 5 \times 2$

(D) $5 \times 1 = 5$

Hint #1:

The **associative property** always uses **grouping symbols**, such as **parentheses**.

Hint #2:

The **associative property** states that you can change the grouping of factors in a multiplication problem without changing the product.

Answer: Choice **A** is correct.

The **associative property** states that you can change the grouping (parentheses) in a multiplication problem without changing the product. This is shown in choice **A**.

17. The **length** and **width** of a television screen are **15 inches** and **20 inches**. The **length** and **width** of a projection screen are **75 inches** and **100 inches**.

True or False:
The television and projection screens are **proportional** to each other. Circle your answer.

True   False

Hint #1:

A **proportion** states that two ratios are equal. If the screens are proportional, their ratios of length to width will be equal.

Hint #2:

Set up the proportion $\frac{length}{width} = \frac{length}{width}$ and cross multiply to verify that it is a proportion.

Answer: The statement is **True**. The television and projection screens are **proportional** to each other.

Set up the proportion $\frac{length}{width} = \frac{length}{width}$ with the given dimensions: $\frac{15}{20} = \frac{75}{100}$.

Now, cross multiply to see if the products are equal.
15 × 100 = 20 × 75

The two screens are proportional because the products are equal: **1500 = 1500**.

18. What is the **identity element of multiplication**?

_____

Hint #1:

When you perform an operation on a number (in this case multiplication) and the result is the **same** as the original number, the other number you used in the operation is called the **identity element**.

Hint #2:

Let ☐ represent the identity element for multiplication. What value would fit into the ☐ for these problems: $3 \times \square = 3$ and $14 \times \square = 14$?

Answer: The identity element of multiplication is **1**.

The **multiplicative identity** is the special number that can be multiplied by any number to get that number.

That special number is **1**.

19. Give the **word equivalent** of the number 104,000,200,603.

_____

Hint #1:

Starting from the **left**, determine the value of each non-zero digit according to its placement. Each subgroup of three digits, separated by commas, has a word value.

Hint #2:

The subgroups of three read "**trillions, billions, millions, thousands**, and **hundreds, tens, units**." Within each subgroup, the three digits represent, from left to right: **hundreds, tens**, and **units**. The place value words are shown in the figure below:

XXX,	XXX,	XXX,	XXX,	XXX
Trillions	Billions	Millions	Thousands	Units

Answer: One hundred four billion, two hundred thousand, six hundred three.

Within each group of three digits that are separated by commas, the word values are, reading from left to right, hundreds, tens, and ones. Since the subgroup **104** is the fourth group to the left, it is the **billions group**, and 104 represents "**one hundred four billion.**"

The subgroup of **200** is the second group to the left, so it is the **thousands group**, and 200 represents "**two hundred thousand.**" The subgroup **603** is the first grouping from the left, so it represents simply "**six hundred three.**"

You're doing a great job so far!
Are you ready for a Challenge Activity?
Good luck!

a) Place the following numbers on the number line below.

$$\frac{4}{5}, \ -1\frac{3}{5}, \ 40\%, \ 150\%, \ \frac{11}{5}$$

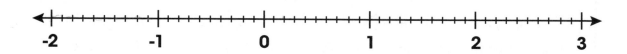

| -2 | -1 | 0 | 1 | 2 | 3 |

b) Which number belongs farthest to the **right** on the number line?

c) Which number belongs farthest to the **left** on the number line?

Hint #1:

The number line is divided into **tenths** between each integer. Remember that negative numbers are always to the **left** of zero.

Hint #2:

You can turn each number into an **equivalent decimal**. Convert **percentages** into **decimals** by dividing the percentage by 100. To divide by 100, you can move the decimal point two places to the left. To convert a **fraction** to a **decimal**, divide the numerator by the denominator. To convert a **mixed number**, keep the whole number portion, and change the proper fractional part as described above.

See answers on following page.

Answers to Challenge Activity:

a)

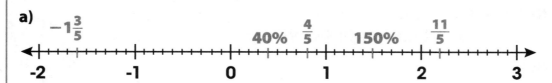

This question is best handled by breaking it down into steps.

The **first step** is to recognize that the number line is divided into **tenths** between each integer. Thus, it would be helpful to turn each number into an **equivalent decimal** in order to determine its place on the number line.

The **next step** is to convert the **fractions** to decimals and then to find their locations on the line. To convert a fraction to a decimal, divide the numerator by the denominator. The value $\frac{4}{5}$ is $4 \div 5 = $ **0.8**. This value is at the eight-tenths mark (the eighth mark right of zero). The value $\frac{11}{5}$ is $11 \div 5 = $ **2.2**. This value is between the integers 2 and 3, at the two-tenths mark to the right of 2.

To convert a **mixed number**, keep the whole number portion and change the proper fractional part as described above. Take the fractional part of the mixed number $-1\frac{3}{5}$ and divide -3 by 5 to get -0.6 (The number is negative, so both the integer and fractional parts are negative). Add this to -1 to get **-1.6.** This number is between -1 and -2, at the six-tenths mark to the left of -1.

Then, convert the **percentages** into decimals by dividing each percentage by 100. To divide by 100, you can move the decimal point two places to the left. Forty percent, 40%, has the decimal equivalent **0.4**; 150% has the decimal equivalent **1.5**. The number 0.4 is four-tenths past zero, and 1.5 is halfway between 1 and 2.

By converting the numbers to equivalent decimals, they become much easier to place on the number line. After doing so, you can clearly see that **b)** $\frac{11}{5}$, or **2.2**, belongs farthest to the **right** on the number line and **c)** $-1\frac{3}{5}$, or $-$**1.6**, belongs farthest to the left on the number line.

Let's take a quick test and see how much you've learned during this climb up *SCORE!* Mountain.

Good luck!

1. Order these numbers from least to greatest:

$$\frac{5}{7} \text{ , } 2.52, 2.09, \pi, 2\frac{1}{3}$$

2. It will take Manuel 6 hours to travel 330 miles. At this rate, how long will it take him to travel 247.5 miles?

3. Use the commutative property of multiplication to find the product of $8 \times 25 \times 7 \times 4$.

4. An 8×10 picture frame has a width of 8 inches and a length of 10 inches. A 5×7 picture frame has a width of 5 inches and a length of 7 inches.

True or **False**: These two frames are proportional to each other.

Circle your answer.　　　　True　　　　False

5. A hockey stick is on sale for 30% off the original price of $76.00. What is the discount, or the amount of money saved on this sale?

See answers on following page.

Answers to test questions:

1. The order of the numbers from least to greatest is:

$$\frac{5}{7}, 2.09, 2\frac{1}{3}, 2.52, \pi$$

Let's look at $\frac{5}{7}$ first. This is the only number less than 2, so it is the least.

An easy way to order the remaining numbers is to convert each number to a **decimal equivalent**.

The next number, **2.52**, is already a decimal and it represents "**2 and 52 hundredths**."

2.09 represents "**2 and 9 hundredths**," which is **less** than 2 and 52 hundredths, but **greater** than $\frac{5}{7}$, or 71 hundredths.

So far the order is $\frac{5}{7}$, 2.09, 2.52.

The next number, **π**, is **3.14** when rounded to the nearest hundredth, or "**3 and 14 hundredths**," the **largest value** so far.

The final number is **$2\frac{1}{3}$**, which is "**2 and one-third**." Convert the fractional part to a decimal: 1 ÷ 3, which, rounded to the nearest hundredth, is 0.33. Thus, this number is "**2 and 33 hundredths**," so it lies between 2 and 9 hundredths and 2 and 52 hundredths.

The correct order is $\frac{5}{7}$, 2.09, $2\frac{1}{3}$, 2.52, π.

2. It will take Manuel **4.5 hours** to travel **247.5 miles**.

This is a **rate** question. A rate is a special ratio that compares two unlike quantities. In this problem, it is miles and hours.

Set up a proportion: $\frac{miles}{hours} = \frac{miles}{hours}$. Let **n** represent the number of hours it will take to travel 247.5 miles. The proportion is $\frac{330}{6} = \frac{247.5}{n}$.

Cross multiply to get **330n = 6 × 247.5**. Multiply on the right to get **330n = 1485**.

Divide both sides of the equation by 330 to get **n = 4.5 hours**.

Answers to test questions *continued*:

3. 5,600

The **commutative property** states that you can change the order of factors in a multiplication problem without changing the value of the expression. Therefore, you can change the order to make the multiplication easier.

Look for a pair of factors that have a convenient product. In this problem, the factors **25** and **4** will create a product of **100**, and 100 is easy to multiply by other numbers.

Use the commutative property to have the expression read **25 × 4 × 8 × 7**. Multiply left to right: 100 × 8 × 7. Next, multiply 100 × 8 to get 800. Finally, multiply **800 × 7 = 5,600**.

4. False

The frames are **not** proportional to each other.

If two objects are proportional, the ratios of their dimensions will be **equal**. To solve this problem, set up a proportion such as $\frac{width}{length} = \frac{width}{length}$. When you set up this proportion, there will be no variable term.

To determine if the frames are proportional, **cross multiply** to see if the resulting equation is true. The proportion is $\frac{8}{10} = \frac{5}{7}$. Cross multiply to get $8 \times 7 = 10 \times 5$. Multiply to get **56 = 50**. This is a **false statement** since **56 ≠ 50**. Thus, the frames are **not proportional**.

5. The discount is $22.80.

The discount, or the money saved on this sale, is **30%** of the original price. A percent is a special ratio of $\frac{part}{whole}$, where the whole is 100. Let **n** represent the discount and set up a proportion: $\frac{30}{100} = \frac{n}{76}$.

Cross multiply to get **30 × 76 = 100n**.

Multiply the left side of the equation to get **2,280 = 100n**.

Divide both sides by 100, and **n = $22.80**, the money off the original price.

Celebrate!

Let's take a fun break before we go to the next base camp. You've earned it!

Now that you have exercised your brain in this session, how about some exercise for your body?

Congratulations!
You're on your way up *SCORE!* Mountain.

Write down your favorite exercise or activity. Maybe you like baseball, running, soccer, or even dancing. It can be anything, as long as it gets you moving!

My favorite activity is: _____

Now, grab some fresh air and have fun doing your favorite activity for a while!

Ask a friend or family member to join you in the fun!

Also, think about some ways you can improve your skills in your favorite activity. Maybe you can join a team or club, take a class, or read a book about it!

Good luck and have fun!
You deserve it for working so hard!

Base Camp

2

Number Operations

Let's continue the climb up *SCORE!* Mountain. Are you ready? Let's get started! Good luck!

1. Find the **value** of the expression $10 + 20 \div 5 \times 2$.

_____

Hint #1:

Remember to use the order of operations, which is:

Parentheses, **E**xponents, **M**ultiplication and **D**ivision (in order from left to right), **A**ddition and **S**ubtraction (in order from left to right). A good way to remember this order is to remember the "word" **PEMDAS**. There are no parentheses or exponents in this expression, so what should the first operation be?

Hint #2:

The second operation here should be **multiplication**.

Answer: The correct answer is **18**.

To evaluate the expression, use the order of operations. **Division** comes before multiplication in this expression because the division symbol is to the **left** of the multiplication symbol. 20 divided by 5 is **4**. The expression is now simplified to $10 + 4 \times 2$.

Next multiply 4 by 2 to get 8.

Finally, add: $10 + 8 = 18$.

2. Lara ate $\frac{5}{8}$ of the pizza.

Katy ate $\frac{1}{4}$ of the pizza.

What **fraction** of the pizza was left over?

_____

Hint #1:

Add the amounts that were eaten. First, find a **common denominator** for the given fractions. Convert them both to this denominator and then add only the numerators. The denominator of the sum will be the same as the common denominator you find.

Hint #2:

Subtract the amount eaten from one whole pizza to find what is left over.

Answer: $\frac{1}{8}$ of the pizza is left over.

The **least common multiple** of 4 and 8 is **8**. Convert $\frac{1}{4}$ to eighths: $\frac{1 \times 2}{4 \times 2} = \frac{2}{8}$.

Add the two fractions by adding the numerators and keeping the common denominator: $\frac{5}{8} + \frac{2}{8} = \frac{7}{8}$.

Finally, to find the amount of pizza left over, subtract the amount eaten from one whole: $\frac{8}{8} - \frac{7}{8} = \mathbf{\frac{1}{8}}$.

3. Solve:

$$\frac{3}{8} = \frac{n}{56}$$

_____

Hint #1:

Notice that the problem states that the fractions are **equivalent**.

Hint #2:

Think $8 \times \square = 56$, so $\square = 56 \div 8$. Multiply the numerator and the denominator of $\frac{3}{8}$ by this number to find **n**.

Answer: $n = 21$

You can use **equivalent fractions** to solve for **n**. Recognizing that $8 \times 7 = 56$, you can multiply the numerator and the denominator of $\frac{3}{8}$ by **7**: $\frac{3 \times 7}{8 \times 7} = \frac{21}{56}$. So **n = 21**.

© Kaplan Publishing, Inc.

4. The hostess at a popular restaurant receives **10%** of each of the waitresses' total tips for the night. How much will the hostess receive if the total tips for the night from all waitresses were **$450.00**?

_____

Hint #1:

The word "*of*" means to **multiply**.

Hint #2:

Ten percent is $\frac{1}{10}$, or 0.10. What math operation should be done next?

Answer: The hostess receives **$45.00**.

The phrase "**10% of each of the waitresses' total tips**" tells you to multiply the total tips by **10%**. 10% can be written as the decimal **0.10**, because you move the decimal point two places to the left when you change a percent into a decimal.

$450.00 × 0.10 = $45.00

5. Simplify:

$$|28| - |-14|$$

_____

Hint #1:

Remember, the symbol $|n|$ means "**the absolute value**" of n, the enclosed simplified number. Absolute value is the number **without** regard to the sign. It is **always** positive.

Hint #2:

First, find the absolute values of 28 and −14, then subtract.

Answer: 14

As described in hint #1, the symbol $|n|$ means "**the absolute value**" of n, the enclosed simplified number. Absolute value is the number without regard to the sign and it is **always** positive. The absolute value symbol is also considered to be a **grouping symbol**. Therefore, it is done first in the order of operations.

So, find the absolute values of **28** and **−14**, which are 28 and 14, then subtract. **28 − 14 = 14**.

6. To make a party mix, $5\frac{2}{3}$ **cups** of cereal are mixed with $2\frac{3}{4}$ **cups** of nuts and $1\frac{5}{12}$ **cups** of pretzels. How many **total** cups of mix does this make?

_____

Hint #1:

To combine these mixed numbers, find a **common denominator** that is the least common multiple of **3**, **4**, and **12**.

Hint #2:

After finding a common denominator, **add** the fractions. Convert to a mixed number if needed. Add this to the whole number parts.

Answer: There are a total of $9\frac{5}{6}$ **cups** of mix.

To find the total number of cups of mix, add the mixed numbers. One way to do this is to first add the fractional parts. Find a common denominator that is the **least common multiple (LCM)** of **3**, **4**, and **12**, the denominators of the fractions. The LCM is **12**.

Convert each fraction to an equivalent fraction with the common denominator: $\frac{2}{3} = \frac{8}{12}$, $\frac{3}{4} = \frac{9}{12}$, and $\frac{5}{12}$ remains the same.

Add the fractional parts: $\frac{8}{12} + \frac{9}{12} + \frac{5}{12} = \frac{22}{12}$.

Convert to the mixed number $1\frac{10}{12}$, which is $1\frac{5}{6}$ in lowest terms.

Finally, add this to the whole number parts: $1\frac{5}{6} + 5 + 2 + 1 = 9\frac{5}{6}$.

© Kaplan Publishing, Inc.

7. What is $\frac{1}{4}$ of $\frac{5}{8}$?

_____

Hint #1:

In this problem, the key word "**of**" means **to multiply**.

Hint #2:

To multiply fractions, multiply the numerators, multiply the denominators, then simplify to lowest terms.

Answer: $\frac{5}{32}$

To multiply fractions, multiply the numerators, multiply the denominators, then simplify to lowest terms: $\frac{1}{4} \times \frac{5}{8} = \frac{1 \times 5}{4 \times 8} = \frac{5}{32}$, which can't be simplified.

8. Divide the following fractions:

$$3\frac{1}{2} \div 1\frac{3}{5}$$

_____

Hint #1:

First, convert each mixed number to an **improper fraction**.

Hint #2:

To **divide** fractions, multiply the first fraction by the **reciprocal**, or **multiplicative inverse**, of the second fraction. Then simplify to lowest terms.

Answer: $2\frac{3}{16}$

First, convert each mixed number to an **improper fraction**:
$3\frac{1}{2} = \frac{(3 \times 2) + 1}{2} = \frac{7}{2}$, and $1\frac{5}{3} = \frac{(1 \times 5) + 3}{5} = \frac{8}{5}$.

To divide fractions, multiply the first fraction by the reciprocal, or multiplicative inverse, of the second fraction: $\frac{7}{2} \times \frac{5}{8}$.

To multiply these fractions, multiply the numerators and multiply the denominators to get $\frac{35}{16} = \mathbf{2\frac{3}{16}}$. The fractional part, $\frac{3}{16}$, can't be simplified.

9. Liz has $7\frac{1}{2}$ **yards** of fabric. She wants to cut it into $\frac{3}{4}$ **yard** pieces. How many $\frac{3}{4}$ yard pieces will she have after cutting?

Hint #1:

First, divide the amount of fabric by $\frac{3}{4}$.

Hint #2:

To divide, first change the mixed number to an **improper fraction**. Then, multiply the first fraction by the reciprocal of the second fraction.

Answer: Liz will have **10 pieces** after cutting.

She wants to divide up the large piece of fabric, so divide $7\frac{1}{2}$ by $\frac{3}{4}$. Change the mixed number to an **improper fraction**:

To divide, multiply the first fraction by the reciprocal of the divisor:
$\frac{15}{2} \times \frac{4}{3} = \frac{60}{6}$.
Simplify this fraction: **60 ÷ 6 = 10**.

10. Simplify:

$$100 - 24 \div 2^3 + 3$$

_____

Hint #1:

Remember to use the order of operations, which is:
Parentheses, **E**xponents, **M**ultiplication and **D**ivision (in order from left to right), **A**ddition and **S**ubtraction (in order from left to right). The exponent is the operation that will be done **first** in this problem.

Hint #2:

The second operation to do here is **division**. Then subtract and add from left to right.

Answer: 100

To evaluate the expression, use the order of operations (**PEMDAS**). There are no parentheses, so evaluate the **exponent** first:

$2^3 = 2 \times 2 \times 2 = 8$.

Next, perform the division operation: $24 \div 8 = 3$.

The problem is now $100 - 3 + 3$.

Finally, do addition and subtraction: $(100 - 3) + 3 = 97 + 3 = 100$.

11. Write $4 \times 7 \times 7 \times 7 \times 7 \times 7 \times 4 \times 4 \times 7$ in **exponential notation**.

_____

Hint #1:

First, use the **commutative property** to change the order so that all the **4's** are together, and all the **7's** are together.

Hint #2:

Exponential form is **base^{exponent}**. The **base** is the number being multiplied, and the **exponent** is how many factors there are of that base. For example, **5^4** means **5 × 5 × 5 × 5**.

Answer: $4^3 \times 7^6$

Use the **commutative property** to change the order so that all of the 4's are together and all of the 7's are together: **4 × 4 × 4 × 7 × 7 × 7 × 7 × 7 × 7**. Count the number of 4's, and the number of 7's.

There are **three 4's** and **six 7's**. Exponential form is **base^{exponent}**. The base is the number being multiplied and the exponent is how many factors there are of that base. The exponential form is **$4^3 \times 7^6$**.

12. Find the **prime factorization of 360**. Then write your results in **exponential form**.

_____

Hint #1:

Make a **factor tree**, breaking each sub-product into two factors. Continue this until all factors are **prime**.

Hint #2:

If there are duplicate prime factors, write them in exponential form, For example, **2 × 2 × 2 × 2 × 5 × 5 = 2⁴ × 5²**. Remember that if the exponent is one, you do **not** have to show it.

Answer: 2³ × 3² × 5

Make a **factor tree**, breaking each sub-product into two factors. Continue this until all factors are **prime**.

The result shown on the factor tree is that **360 = 2 × 2 × 2 × 3 × 3 × 5**. Write this in exponential form. There are three factors of 2, two factors of 3, and one factor of 5: **2³ × 3² × 5**.

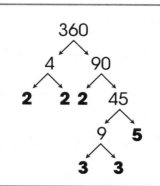

13. What is the value of 2^6?

_____

Hint #1:

This expression is in **exponential form**: **base^{exponent}**. The **base** is the number that is repeatedly multiplied, and the **exponent** is the number of factors of that base.

Hint #2:

Expand the exponential form and then multiply to get a simplified answer.

Answer: $2^6 = 64$

$2^6 = 2 \times 2 \times 2 \times 2 \times 2 \times 2$. Perform the multiplication and you get $2^6 = 64$.

14. Evaluate y^3 where $y = 5$.

_____

© Kaplan Publishing, Inc.

Hint #1:

Substitute **5** for **y** in the expression.

Hint #2:

Expand the exponential form **y³**.

Answer: 125

y³ means **y × y × y**.

Substitute **5** for **y** in the expression to get **5 × 5 × 5 = 25 × 5 = 125**.

15. Miguel has an English assignment to read a **250-page novel**.

On **Monday**, he reads **10%** of the total pages.
On **Tuesday**, he reads **20%** of the total pages.

How many pages of the book does Miguel still need to read?

_____

Hint #1:

Add the percentages read so far to find the percentage of the book Miguel has read.

Hint #2:

Convert the percentage of pages read to a **decimal equivalent**. Use multiplication to find the number of pages that Miguel has read so far. Use subtraction to determine how many more pages Miguel still has to read.

Answer: Miguel still has **175 pages** to read.

By the end of **Tuesday**, Miguel has read **10% + 20% = 30%** of the total pages in the book. 30% written as a decimal is **0.30**. Multiply this by the total number of pages in the book to find out how many pages Miguel has already read: **250 × 0.30 = 75 pages**. Because there are a total of 250 pages in the book, Miguel still has **250 − 75 = 175 pages to read**.

16. **Seventy-six percent** of the student body voted in the election for student council president. If there are **1,200 students** in the school, how many voted?

_____

Hint #1:

Seventy six percent, or 76%, can be written as a **decimal equivalent** by moving the decimal point two places to the **left**.

Hint #2:

Look at the phrase "**76% of the student body**" from the problem. The key word "**of**" tells you to **multiply**.

Answer: 912 students voted.

First, change the percent into a **decimal**. 76% can be written as a decimal by moving the decimal point two places to the left: **0.76**.

76% of the student body means **0.76 × 1,200 = 912 students**.

© Kaplan Publishing, Inc.

17. Jason can do **6 sit-ups** in **3 seconds**. At this rate, how many sit-ups can he do in **8 seconds**?

_____

Hint #1:

Express the relationship as a **rate** of $\frac{sit\text{-}ups}{seconds}$.

Hint #2:

Write a proportion $(\frac{sit\text{-}ups}{seconds} = \frac{sit\text{-}ups}{seconds})$ and substitute the given information.

Answer: Jason can do **16 sit-ups** in 8 seconds.

Write and solve the proportion: $\frac{sit\text{-}ups}{seconds} = \frac{sit\text{-}ups}{seconds}$. Substitute in the given information. Use a variable, such as **n**, to represent the number of sit-ups in 8 seconds: $\frac{6}{3} = \frac{n}{8}$.

Cross-multiply to get **$6 \times 8 = 3n$**, or **$48 = 3n$**.

Divide both sides by 3 to get **$n = 16$**.

Another way to arrive at the answer is to realize that if he does 6 sit-ups in 3 seconds, he can do **2 sit-ups** every second.

Multiply **$2 \times 8 = 16$ sit-ups**.

18. Clarence, Brittany, and Althea were asked to evaluate $5n^2$, where $n = 3$.

Clarence arrived at an answer of **30**.
Brittany got an answer of **45**.
Althea got at an answer of **225**.

Who is correct?

Hint #1:

You have to use the order of operations to simplify the expression.

Hint #2:

An exponent of 2 means to multiply the base number times itself. For example, $2^2 = 2 \times 2 = 4$. According to the order of operations (**PEMDAS**), should the exponentiation be done first?

Answer: Brittany is correct.

To evaluate the expression, substitute in the value of **3** for **n** to get

5×3^2. To simplify the expression, use the correct order of operations, which is:

Parentheses

Exponents

Multiplication and **D**ivision, left to right

Addition and **S**ubtraction, left to right

There are no parentheses, so find the value of 3^2 first to get

$5 \times 9 = 45$, so **Brittany** is correct.

Clarence arrived at the wrong answer of 30 by handling the exponent incorrectly. He multiplied 3×2 instead of 3×3.

Althea was incorrect because she didn't use the order of operations. She multiplied first and then performed the exponentiation.

19. Simplify:

$$\frac{2}{3} + \frac{7}{15} - \left(\frac{4}{5} + \frac{1}{10}\right)$$

_____

Hint #1:

Remember, to add and subtract fractions, find a **common denominator**. This is the least common multiple of **3**, **5**, **10**, and **15**.

Hint #2:

Follow the order of operations. First, do the operation in parentheses. Then, add and subtract from left to right.

Answer: $\frac{7}{30}$

The first step in adding or subtracting fractions is to convert each fraction to an equivalent fraction with a common denominator.

The least common multiple of **3**, **5**, **10**, and **15** is **30**.

Convert each fraction to have the denominator of 30:

$\frac{2}{3} = \frac{20}{30}$, $\frac{7}{15} = \frac{14}{30}$, $\frac{4}{5} = \frac{24}{30}$, and $\frac{1}{10} = \frac{3}{30}$.

The problem now reads $\frac{20}{30} + \frac{14}{30} - \left(\frac{24}{30} + \frac{3}{30}\right)$.

Follow order of operations. First, do the operation in parentheses: $\frac{24}{30} + \frac{3}{30} = \frac{27}{30}$. The expression becomes $\frac{20}{30} + \frac{14}{30} - \frac{27}{30}$.

Then, adding and subtracting from left to right gives $\frac{34}{30} - \frac{27}{30} = \frac{7}{30}$.

Challenge Activity

You're doing a great job so far!
Are you ready for a Challenge Activity?

Good luck!

Dustin has a model train that is **proportional** to a real train.
The **scale ratio** on the model train is **1:48**. This means that the
real train is precisely **48 times bigger** than the model in every
dimension.

a) Using the scale, what is the **ratio** of the model train to the
real train, **written as a fraction**?

b) The model train is **18 inches** in length. Using your answer to
part **a**, use a **proportion** to find the **length** of the real train in
inches.

c) If the **height** of the real train is **180 inches**, what is the **height**
of the model train?

Hint #1:

You are given the **scale ratio**, which you can write as a fraction in the form $\frac{toy}{real}$.

Hint #2:

To find the length of the real train, set up the proportion $\frac{toy}{real} = \frac{1}{48}$, and solve for the real length after substituting in the length of the model train.

See answers on following page.

Answers to Challenge Activity:

a) Written as a fraction, the ratio of the model train to the real train is $\frac{1}{48}$.

The ratio **1:48** can be changed to a fraction in the form $\frac{toy}{real}$ by making the number before the colon the numerator and the number after the colon the denominator.

b) The length of the real train is **864 inches**.

Set up the proportion $\frac{toy}{real} = \frac{1}{48}$, substituting **18 inches** for the model (toy) length, and using the variable *n* to represent the real train's length. Now, solve the proportion $\frac{18}{n} = \frac{1}{48}$.

Cross-multiply to get *n* = **864 inches**.

c) The height of the model train is **3.75 inches**.

Set up another proportion, this time substituting **180 inches** for the real train height, and use the variable *n* to represent the height of the model (toy) train, $\frac{n}{180} = \frac{1}{48}$. Cross multiply to get 48*n* = 180.

Solve this equation by dividing both sides by 48, and *n* = 180 ÷ **48**, or *n* = **3.75 inches**.

© Kaplan Publishing, Inc.

Let's take a quick test and see how much you've learned during this climb up *SCORE!* Mountain.

Good luck!

1. Simplify: $4\frac{1}{3} - 2\frac{1}{2}$

2. Evaluate $6n^3$, where $n = 4$.

3. Jess is teaching her friends how to tie various kinds of knots. Each person needs $1\frac{2}{3}$ feet of rope. What total length of rope is needed for Jess and her 8 friends?

4. Tom can mow a lawn in 80 minutes. How many lawns can he mow in an 8-hour work shift?

5. Five percent of all popcorn kernels do not pop. If there are 9 unpopped kernels in the bowl, how many total kernels are there?

See answers on following page.

Answers to test questions:

1. $1\frac{5}{6}$

One way to **subtract mixed numbers** is to first subtract the fractional parts and then subtract the whole number parts. However, because $\frac{1}{3} < \frac{1}{2}$, you would have to borrow from the whole number part, so this is **not** a good approach for this problem.

Instead, convert the mixed numbers to improper fractions: $4\frac{1}{3} = \frac{(4 \times 3) + 1}{3} = \frac{13}{3}$, and $2\frac{1}{2} = \frac{(2 \times 2) + 1}{2} = \frac{5}{2}$. The problem is now $\frac{13}{3} - \frac{5}{2}$.

Convert each of these fractions to have a common denominator of 6: $\frac{26}{6} - \frac{15}{6}$

Subtract the numerators and keep the denominator, to get $\frac{26 - 15}{6} = \frac{11}{6} = \mathbf{1\frac{5}{6}}$.

2. **384**

To evaluate the expression, substitute the given value, **4**, for the variable **n**. The expression is now **6 × 4³**. Follow the order of operations, which is:

Parentheses

Exponents

Multiplication and Division, left to right

Addition and Subtraction, left to right

There are no parentheses, so first do the exponentiation, and then multiply by **6**. The term **4³** is simplified as **4 × 4 × 4 = 64**. Finish evaluating the expression to get **6 × 64 = 384**.

3. **15 feet** of rope is needed.

Each person needs $1\frac{2}{3}$ feet of rope, and there are 8 + 1, or **9 people**. The total amount of rope needed is therefore $9 \times 1\frac{2}{3}$. To multiply fractions, first convert each whole or mixed number into an improper fraction: $9 = \frac{9}{1}$, and $1\frac{2}{3} = \frac{(1 \times 3) + 2}{3} = \frac{5}{3}$. Multiply the numerators, multiply the denominators, and then simplify if needed. $\frac{9}{1} \times \frac{5}{3} = \frac{45}{3}$.

$45 \div 3 = \mathbf{15}$.

Answers to test questions *continued*:

4. Tom can mow **6 lawns** in an 8-hour work shift.

The problem states that Tom can mow **one lawn in 80 minutes**, and you are to find how many lawns he can mow in **8 hours**. There are 60 minutes in an hour, so express the number of minutes as a fraction to determine that it takes Tom: $\frac{80}{60} = \frac{4}{3}$ hour to mow one lawn. If Tom has 8 hours available, and each lawn requires $\frac{4}{3}$ of an hour to mow, divide 8 by $\frac{4}{3}$. Remember, to divide fractions, multiply the first fraction by the **reciprocal** of the second fraction: $\frac{8}{1} \times \frac{3}{4} = \frac{24}{4}$.

This can be simplified to **6 lawns** in an 8-hour work shift.

5. 180 kernels

A **percent** is a ratio of $\frac{part}{whole}$, where the whole is 100.

Set up the **proportion** $\frac{part}{whole} = \frac{part}{whole}$ where the *part* is the **unpopped kernels**, and the *whole* is the **total number of kernels**. The whole is the value that is unknown, so assign it a variable, like n. The proportion is $\frac{9}{n} = \frac{5}{100}$. Cross-multiply to get **5n = 9 × 100**, or **5n = 900**.

Divide both sides by 5, and get $n = 180$.

Celebrate!

Let's take a fun break before we go to the next base camp. You've earned it!

Let's plan a **Game Night** with friends and family!

Make a list of your favorite games and activities below and gather them up for a night of fun!

Or you can ask people to bring their favorite games!

Make a list of the snacks you want to have for your **Game Night**. Or you can ask people to bring their favorite snacks and share!

Congratulations!
You're getting closer to the top of *SCORE!* Mountain.

© Kaplan Publishing, Inc.

Game Night Activities

_____
_____
_____
_____
_____
_____
_____

Game Night Snacks

_____
_____
_____
_____
_____
_____
_____

Good luck and have fun!
You deserve it for working so hard!

Base Camp

3

Geometry and Measurement

Are you ready for another fun climb up *SCORE!* Mountain? Let's get started! Good luck!

SCORE! MOUNTAIN TOP

BASE CAMP 5

BASE CAMP 4

BASE CAMP 3

BASE CAMP 2

BASE CAMP 1

1. David bought **14 gallons** of fruit punch for the class picnic. How many **quarts** of punch did he buy?

_____

Hint #1:

There are **4 quarts** in **1 gallon**.

Hint #2:

Use a proportion to solve the problem. Set up $\frac{quarts}{gallons} = \frac{quarts}{gallons}$.

Answer: David bought **56 quarts** of fruit punch.

Let the variable **n** represent the missing quarts and set up the proportion $\frac{quarts}{gallons} = \frac{quarts}{gallons}$ with the given information: $\frac{4}{1} = \frac{n}{14}$.

Cross multiply: **n** is **4 × 14 = 56**.

2. Antonio's father put up a fence around part of the backyard, as shown in the figure on the right, so that his dog can roam freely.

What is the **area** of the part of the backyard the dog gets to use?

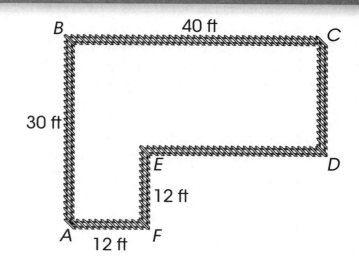

_____

Hint #1:

Divide the fenced in area into **two rectangles**, find the **area** of each, and then add the two areas.
The area of a rectangle is **base × height**.

Hint #2:

The length of **side EF** plus the length of **side CD** is equal to the length of **side AB**. Also, the length of **side AF** plus the length of **side ED** is equal to the length of **side BC**. Use these facts to find the lengths of the missing sides.

Answer: 864 square feet

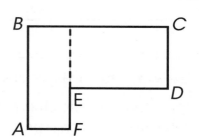

First, divide the area into **two rectangles**. One possible division is shown below:

The area of a rectangle is found using the formula **Area = base × height**. The rectangle on the left is **12 × 30 = 360 square feet**.

To find the area of the rectangle on the right, first find the **base length, ED**, and the **height length, CD**.

Side AF + side ED = side BC, so the length of **side ED** is **BC − AF**, or **40 − 12 = 28 feet**.

Likewise, the length of **side CD** is **AB − EF**, or **30 − 12 = 18 feet**.

The area of the rectangle on the right is **28 × 18 = 504 square feet**.

To find the total area, add the two areas, to get **360 + 504 = 864 square feet**.

© Kaplan Publishing, Inc.

3. The 2 triangles shown below are similar: $\triangle ABC \sim \triangle DEF$.
The measures of sides *AC*, *BC*, and *DF* are shown.
What is the measure of **side EF**?

_____

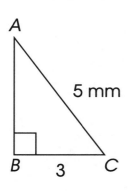

5 mm

A

B 3 *C*

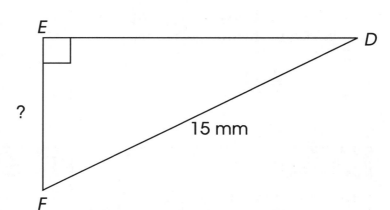

E

?

15 mm

F

D

Hint #1:

For **similar triangles**, the **corresponding sides** are in proportion to each other. Determine which side on the **big triangle** corresponds to which side on the **little triangle**.

Hint #2:

Set up a **proportion**, such as $\frac{big}{little} = \frac{big}{little}$ with the corresponding sides. Be sure to include **side EF**. Cross multiply to solve for **EF**.

Answer: The measure of side **EF = 9 millimeters**.

When triangles are **similar**, their corresponding sides are **in proportion**. Determine the corresponding sides by looking at the figures.

Side EF on the **big triangle** corresponds to **side BC** on the **little triangle**. They are the **shortest** sides of the triangles.

Side DF on the **big triangle** corresponds to side **AC** on the **little triangle**. They are the **longest** sides of the triangles.

One possible set up for the proportion is $\frac{big}{little} = \frac{big}{little}$, or $\frac{EF}{BC} = \frac{DF}{AC}$.

Use a variable, like *n*, to represent the measure of **side EF**: $\frac{n}{3} = \frac{15}{5}$.

Cross multiply to get **5n = 45**; divide both sides by 5 to get **n = 9 millimeters**.

© Kaplan Publishing, Inc.

4. What is the area of **parallelogram** *QRST* shown below?

_____

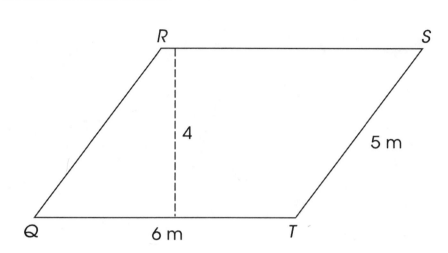

Hint #1:

The formula for the area of a parallelogram is
Area = base × height, or
A = bh.

Hint #2:

There are three measurements given. Determine which two are the **base** and the **height**. Use the formula to find the area.

Answer: The area of parallelogram *QRST* is **24 m²**.

The formula for the area of a parallelogram is **Area = base × height**, where the **base** is one of the sides, and the **height** is a segment perpendicular to the base.

In this figure, the base is **6 m** and the height is **4 m**.

Use the formula to find the area: **6 × 4 = 24 m²**.

5. In the given **circle O** shown below, identify a **central angle**.

_____

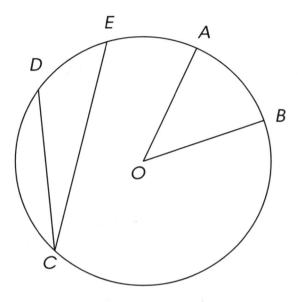

Hint #1:

A **central angle** has its **vertex** at the **center** of the circle.

Hint #2:

When naming an angle, the **vertex point** is the **middle letter** in the angle name.

Answer: ∠**AOB** or ∠**BOA**

A **central angle** is an angle whose **vertex** is at the **center of the circle**, in this case, **point O**. The only angle with a vertex at the center is ∠**AOB**, or alternately named, ∠**BOA**. When naming an angle, the **vertex point** is the **middle letter**.

6. On the chalkboard, Catherine drew a **circle** that has a **diameter of 16 inches**. What is the **area** of her circle?

_____

Hint #1:

The formula for the area of a circle is **Area = πr²**, where **r** represents the radius. **Pi (π)** is equal to **3.14** when rounded to the nearest hundredth.

Hint #2:

The **radius** of a circle is **one-half** the length of the **diameter**.

Answer: The area of Catherine's circle is **200.96 inches squared**.

The formula for the area of a circle is **_Area_ = πr²**, where **r** represents the **radius**. You are told that the **diameter** is **16 inches**, so the radius is one-half of this measure, or **8 inches**. Substituting the information into the area formula gives you **_A_ = π × 8²**, or **_A_ = π × 64**.

π ≈ **3.14**, so the area is **3.14 × 64 = 200.96 inches squared**.

7. In the circle below, ∠*ROS* has measure of **90°**. What is the **area** of the **shaded sector**? Leave your answer in terms of π.

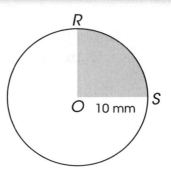

_____

Hint #1:

Remember that there are always **360° in a circle**. The area of the shaded sector is **90** of the **360** degrees, or $\frac{90}{360}$. Simplify the fraction to lowest terms. Then, set up a **proportion** with the ratios of $\frac{part}{whole}$, and cross multiply.

Hint #2:

Remember, the area of a circle is **Area = πr²**, where *r* represents the **radius**. In this circle, **segment OS** is the radius.

Answer: 25π mm²

A circle has a total of **360 degrees**. In this problem, the shaded sector is **90** of the **360 degrees**, or $\frac{90}{360}$. Note that this ratio of the **degrees of the sector** to the **degrees of the circle** is equal to the ratio of the area of the sector to the area of the circle.

Simplify the fractional ratio by dividing by the greatest common factor, which is **90**: $\frac{90 \div 90}{360 \div 90} = \frac{1}{4}$. Now, find the area of the whole circle. Use the formula for area, **A = πr²**, where *r* represents the **radius**.

In this circle, **segment OS** is the radius, whose measure is **10 millimeters(mm)**. The area of the circle is π × **10²**, or **100π**.

Next, let the variable *n* represent the area of the sector and set up a **proportion** using the ratios of $\frac{part}{whole}$, or $\frac{1}{4} = \frac{n}{100\pi}$.

Cross multiply to get **100π = 4n**.

Divide both sides of this equation by 4 to get **n = 25π mm²**.

8. Mr. Thomas designed his family's garden in the shape of a **trapezoid**. Find the **area** of the garden below:

_____

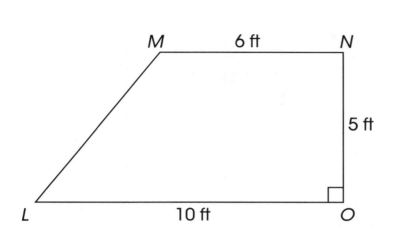

Hint #1:

The formula for the area of a trapezoid is $A = \frac{1}{2}(b_1 + b_2)h$, where b_1 and b_2 are the **bases** and h is the **height**.

Hint #2:

The **bases** are the **parallel sides**, and the **height** is **perpendicular** to the bases.

Answer: The area of Mr. Thomas's family garden is **40 ft²**.

The formula for the area of a trapezoid is $A = \frac{1}{2}(b_1 + b_2)h$, where b_1 and b_2 are the **bases** and h is the **height**. The bases are the **parallel sides**, labeled **MN** and **LO**. The values are $b_1 = 10$, and $b_2 = 6$.

The **height** is **perpendicular** to the bases. Because **angle O** is a **right angle**, **side NO** is **perpendicular** to the bases, and $h = 5$ **ft**. Substitute these values into the area formula: $A = \frac{1}{2} \times (10 + 6) \times 5$, which is $A = \frac{1}{2} \times (16) \times 5$.

Multiply from left to right to get $A = 8 \times 5$, or **40 ft²**.

Use the coordinate graph figure below to answer questions 9–12.

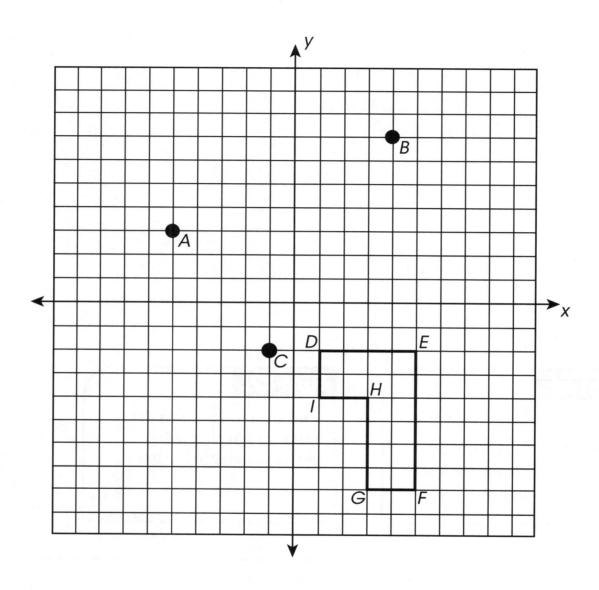

9. What are the **coordinates** of **point** A in the **coordinate graph**?

_____

Hint #1:

The **coordinates** of a point are the ordered pair (**x, y**). The **x-coordinate** is the number of spaces to the **right** or **left** of the **origin** (where the **x** and **y** axes meet). The **y-coordinate** is the number of spaces **up** or **down** from the origin.

Hint #2:

If the point is to the **left** of the origin, the **x-coordinate** is **negative**. If the point is **above** the origin, the **y-coordinate** is **positive**.

Answer: The coordinates of **point A** are (−5, 3).

The **origin** of the coordinate plane is where the **x** and **y axes meet**, and it is the ordered pair **(0, 0)**. An ordered pair is always written as (**x, y**).

Point A is **5 spaces** to the **left** of the origin, so the **x-coordinate** is −**5**. It is **3 spaces up** from the origin, so the **y-coordinate** is **3**.

The ordered pair of **point A** is (−**5, 3**).

10. In which **quadrant** is **point C** on the coordinate graph?

_____

Hint #1:

The coordinate plane is divided up into **four quadrants**, or areas, numbered with Roman numerals **I**, **II**, **III**, and **IV**. The four quadrants are divided by the **x** and **y axes**.

Hint #2:

The top right quadrant is named **quadrant I**. The other quadrants are named in a **counterclockwise** direction as **quadrants II**, **III**, and **IV**.

Answer: Point **C** is in **quadrant III**.

Point C is in the **bottom left quadrant**, or **quadrant III**.

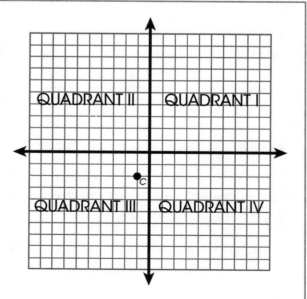

11. What are the **coordinates** of **point B** in the coordinate graph?

_____

Hint #1:

Remember, the *x-coordinate* is the number of spaces to the **right** or **left** of the origin, and the *y-coordinate* is the number of spaces **up** or **down** from the origin.

Hint #2:

If the point is to the **right** of the origin, the *x-coordinate* is **positive**. If the point is **above** the origin, the *y-coordinate* is positive.

Answer: The coordinates of **point B** are **(4, 7)**.

Point B is **4 spaces** to the **right** of the origin, so the *x-coordinate* is **4**. It is **7 spaces up** from the origin, so the *y-coordinate* is **7**.

The ordered pair of point B is **(4, 7)**.

© Kaplan Publishing, Inc.

12. Look again at the coordinate plane. What is the **perimeter** and **area** of the **polygon** in **quadrant IV**?

_____

Hint #1:

Remember, the **perimeter** is the distance around the polygon. Count the number of spaces that make up each side of the polygon and then add them together.

Hint #2:

The **area** is the number of square units it takes to cover a polygon. You can count the number of square units **inside** the figure.

Answer: The **perimeter** of the polygon is **20 units**; the **area** is **16 square units**.

The **perimeter** is the distance around the polygon. Count the number of spaces that make up each of the sides of the polygon and then add them together.

Side _DE_ is **4 spaces** in length; **side _EF_** is **6 spaces**; **side _FG_** is **2 spaces**; **side _GH_** is **4 spaces**; **side _HI_** is **2 spaces**; and side **_ID_** is **2 spaces**.

Add these together to get the **perimeter**:
4 + 6 + 2 + 4 + 2 + 2 = 20 units.

The **area** is the number of square units it takes to cover a polygon. There are **16 square units** inside the figure.

13. What is the **volume** of a **rectangular prism** with a length of
7 **meters**, a width of **3 meters**, and a height of **4 meters**?

_____

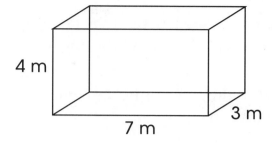

4 m

7 m

3 m

Hint #1:

The formula for the volume of
a rectangular prism is $V = lwh$,
where l is the **length**, w is the
width, and h is the **height**.

Hint #2:

Volume is measured in
cubic units.

Answer: The volume of the rectangular prism is **84 cubic meters**.

The formula for the volume of a rectangular prism is $V = lwh$,
where l is the **length**, w is the **width**, and h is the **height**.

Substitute the given dimensions into the formula: $V = 7 \times 3 \times 4 = 84$ **meters³**.

14. Nicole and Adam are planning to place a wallpaper border around the perimeter of their rectangular kitchen.

Nicole measures the length of the kitchen to be **6.4 meters**.
Adam measures the width of the kitchen to be **478 centimeters**.

How much wallpaper border, in **meters**, is needed to complete the job?

_____

Hint #1:

Notice that Nicole and Adam used different units for measuring. All units must be the same.

Hint #2:

The **perimeter** is the distance around the room. Because the kitchen is **rectangular**, there are two lengths and two widths.

Answer: 22.36 meters of wallpaper border is needed.

Nicole and Adam used **different units** for measuring. All units must be the same. The question asks for the length of the border in **meters**, so first **convert** the width of **478 centimeters** into **meters**. There are **100 centimeters in one meter**, so divide the amount of centimeters by 100 to find the width measured in meters.

478 ÷ 100 = 4.78 meters.

The **perimeter** is the distance around the room, and represents the amount of wallpaper border needed. Because the kitchen is rectangular, there are two lengths and two widths.

The total perimeter is **6.4 + 6.4 + 4.78 + 4.78 = 22.36 meters**.

15. What is the **circumference** of Amy's circular pizza if it has a **radius** of 3 centimeters? Round your answer to the **nearest tenth**.

_____

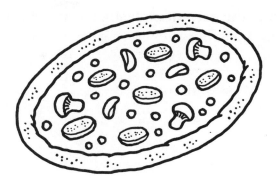

Hint #1:

Remember, **circumference** is the distance around a circle.

Hint #2:

The formula for circumference is **C = 2πr**. **Pi (π)** is equal to **3.14** when rounded to the nearest hundredth.

Answer: The circumference of Amy's circular pizza is **18.8 centimeters**.

Use the formula for circumference to determine the answer.

C = 2πr, so **C = 2 × 3.14 × 3 = 18.84**.

The circumference is **18.8 centimeters**, to the nearest tenth.

16. Natasha wears a **silver triangle charm** that has a **base** of 12 **millimeters** and a **height of 6 millimeters**.

What is the **area** of Natasha's silver charm?

_____

Hint #1:

The formula for the area of a triangle is $A = \frac{1}{2}bh$.

Hint #2:

Area is measured in **square units**.

Answer: The area of Natasha's silver charm is **36 millimeters²**.

The formula for the area of a triangle is $A = \frac{1}{2}bh$. Substitute in the values given for the base and height and simplify the expression to find the area.

The area is $A = \frac{1}{2} \times 12 \times 6$. Multiply left to right to get **6 × 6 = 36 millimeters²**.

17. A number cube has the dimensions of **1 inch × 1 inch × 1 inch**. How many of these number cubes would fit into a rectangular box with interior dimensions of **2 inches × 4 inches × 5 inches**?

_____

Hint #1:

Both the number cube and the box are **rectangular prisms**. The volume of a rectangular prism can be determined by the formula **$V = lwh$**, where **l** is the **length**, **w** is the **width**, and **h** is the **height**.

Hint #2:

Volume is the number of cubic units it takes to fill a 3-dimensional shape. The number cube has a volume of **1 cubic inch**.

Answer: **40 number cubes** would fit into the rectangular box.

Both the number cubes and the box are **rectangular prisms**. Because the number cubes are 1 × 1 × 1 inch, the number cube has a volume of **1 cubic inch**.

The figure below shows the bottom row of the rectangular box.

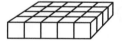

This represents an area of **5 × 4 = 20 cubes**.

The other dimension of the rectangular box, the **height**, is **2 inches**.

The figure below shows the cubes in the rectangular box.

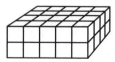

Multiply the **area** by the **height** of the rectangular box: **20 × 2 = 40**. Thus, **40 number cubes** can fit into the box.

18. The hospital has **80 pints** of blood in storage. How many **gallons** of blood is this?

_____

Hint #1:

First, convert the **pints** into **quarts**. There are **2 pints** in every **quart**.

Hint #2:

Next, convert the **quarts** into **gallons**.

Answer: The hospital has **10 gallons** of blood.

This problem can be solved with two steps. First, convert the **pints** into **quarts**. There are **2 pints** in a **quart**. So divide the number of pints by 2 to find the number of quarts: **80 ÷ 2 = 40 quarts**.

Next, convert the 40 quarts into **gallons**. There are **4 quarts** in every **gallon**. So divide the number of quarts by 4 to find the number of gallons: **40 ÷ 4 = 10 gallons**.

19. Find the **area** of the irregular figure below.

_____

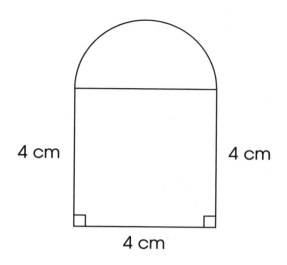

4 cm   4 cm

4 cm

Hint #1:

This irregular figure is made up of a **square** and a **half of a circle**. Find the area of each piece, and add the areas together to get the total.

Hint #2:

The **area of a square** is *Area* = s^2, where *s* represents the side length. The area of a circle is *Area* = πr^2, where *r* is the **radius**. Divide by **2** to get the area of the **half circle**.

Answer: The area of the irregular figure is **22.28 centimeters^2**.

The irregular figure is made up of a **square** and a **half of a circle**.

The **area of a square** is *Area* = s^2, where *s* represents the **side length**, **4 centimeters**. The area of the square is $4^2 = 4 \times 4 = 16$ **centimeters^2**.

The **area of a circle** is *Area* = πr^2, where *r* is the radius. The diameter is the same length as the side of the square, **4 centimeters**, so the radius is **4 ÷ 2 = 2 centimeters**, and the area of the circle is $3.14 \times 2^2 = 12.56$. Divide by 2 to get the area of the half circle: **6.28 centimeters^2**.

Add this to the area of the square: **16 + 6.28 = 22.28 centimeters^2**.

Challenge Activity

You're doing a great job so far!
Are you ready for a Challenge Activity?

Good luck!

Justin's dad is **70 inches tall** and casts a shadow that is **35 inches long**.
Next to him is a **tree**, with a shadow length of **105 inches**.

a) Draw a picture of the situation described in the problem.
Include all relevant measurements including the height of
Justin's dad, as well as his shadow length and the shadow
length of the tree.

b) Set up a proportion demonstrating the corresponding sides of
the figures created by Justin's dad, the tree, and
the shadows they cast.

c) How tall is the tree?

Hint #1:

Draw a picture of the situation.
The tree is taller than Justin's
dad. The dad and tree are
vertical, and the shadows
are **horizontal**. The objects
and their shadows meet at
the bottom and form a **right
angle**. Now, connect the top
of the object to the end of the
shadow to make **two similar
right triangles**.

Hint #2:

The corresponding sides
of similar triangles are **in
proportion** to each other.
Justin's dad and the tree are
corresponding vertical sides;
Dad's shadow and the tree's
shadow are **corresponding
horizontal sides**. Set up a
proportion, such as
$\frac{shadow}{real} = \frac{shadow}{real}$. Cross multiply
to solve for the height of the
tree.

Answers to Challenge Activity:

a) Draw a picture of the situation described in the problem. It is not necessary to be a great artist:

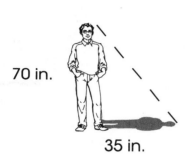

70 in.

35 in.

Justin's dad and his shadow

?

105 in.

The tree and its shadow

Make sure that your drawing shows that the tree is **taller** than Justin's dad. Justin's dad and the tree are **vertical**, and their shadows are **horizontal**. The objects and their shadows meet at the bottom and form **right angles**. The dotted lines connect the tops of the objects to the ends of the shadows to illustrate the two similar right triangles that are formed.

b) Set up a proportion demonstrating the corresponding sides of the similar right triangles, such as $\frac{shadow}{real} = \frac{shadow}{real}$.

Use the variable **n** to represent the height of the tree: $\frac{35}{70} = \frac{105}{n}$.

c) The height of the tree is **210 inches**.

Solve for **n** in the proportion set up in part **b**, $\frac{35}{70} = \frac{105}{n}$, to determine the height of the tree. Cross multiply: **70 × 105 = 35n**. Multiply on the left side to get **7350 = 35n**. Divide both sides of this equation by 35 to get **n = 210 inches**.

Let's take a quick test and see how much you've learned during this climb up *SCORE!* Mountain.

Good luck!

1. Victor drinks 3 cups of water every day. How many pints does he drink each week?

2. Find the volume of the rectangular prism below:

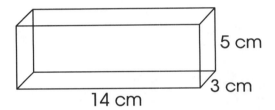

14 cm · 3 cm · 5 cm

3. What is the area of a circular fountain with a diameter of 3 feet? Round your answer to the nearest tenth of a foot.

4. The triangles below are similar; △**RST** ~ △**XYZ**. Find the length of **side RT**.

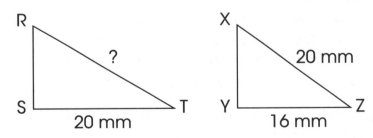

5. Find the area of the irregular figure below.

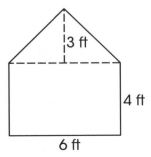

3 ft · 4 ft · 6 ft

Answers to test questions:

1. Victor drinks **10.5 pints** of water each week.

There are 7 days in a week. Victor drinks **3 × 7 = 21** cups of water each week. Now convert **21 cups** into **pints**. There are **2 cups in a pint**, so **divide** the number of cups by **2** to find the number of pints.

21 ÷ 2 = 10.5 pints

2. The volume of the rectangular prism is **210 centimeters³**.

The **length** of the prism is **14 centimeters**, the width is **3 centimeters**, and the **height** is **5 centimeters**. The volume of a rectangular prism is **$V = lwh$**, where l is the **length**, w is the **width**, and h is the **height**.

Substitute in the values to get **$V = 14 \times 3 \times 5 = 210$ centimeters³**.

3. The area of the circular fountain is **7.1 ft²**.

The area of a circle is found by the formula **$Area = \pi r^2$**. Divide the diameter, 3 feet, by 2 to get the radius of **1.5 feet**. Substitute into the formula to get **$A = \pi \times 1.5^2$**, or **7.065 ft²**, which is **7.1 ft²**, when rounded to the nearest tenth.

4. The length of side *RT* is **25 millimeters**.

Similar triangles have sides that are **in proportion** to each other.

Side ST on the big triangle corresponds to **side YZ** on the little triangle. **Side RT** on the big triangle corresponds to **side XZ** on the little triangle. One set up for the proportion is $\frac{big}{little} = \frac{big}{little}$, or $\frac{ST}{YZ} = \frac{RT}{XZ}$. Use a variable, like **n**, to represent the measure of **side RT**: $\frac{20}{16} = \frac{n}{20}$. Cross multiply to get **$16n = 400$**; divide both sides by 16 to get **$n = 25$ millimeters**.

5. The area of the irregular figure is **33 ft²**.

This figure is made up of a **rectangle** and a **triangle**. Find the area of each piece, and then add the areas together to find the total area. The **area of a rectangle** is **$Area = bh$**, where b is the **base length** and h is the **height length**. The area of the rectangle is **$6 \times 4 = 24$ ft²**. The **area of a triangle** is **$Area = \frac{1}{2}bh$** , where b is the **base length** and h is the **height length**. The base is the same length as the base of the rectangle, **6 ft**, and the height is **3 ft**, so determine the area: **$Area = \frac{1}{2} \times 6 \times 3 = 9$** . Add these two areas to get the total area: **$24 + 9 = 33$ ft²**.

Celebrate!

Let's take a fun break before we go to the next base camp. You've earned it!

Here's a fun idea:

Start a collection!

Have you ever thought about collecting something?

It's a fun activity, and a great way to learn about something new!

Congratulations!
You're halfway to the top of *SCORE!* Mountain.

Some ideas for things to collect are **coins**, **figurines**, **sports cards**, or **stickers**.

Another great idea is to collect **stamps**. The post office may have a starter kit to introduce you to stamp collecting. Or, just start collecting the stamps that come to your house in the mail on envelopes.

If you live near a beach, think about collecting **seashells**.

If you live near a lot of trees, think about collecting all the different types of **leaves** you can find. You can start a leaf scrapbook!

Maybe you live near a park or wooded area. Think about starting your own **rock collection**!

See if you can discover the history behind whatever items you decide to collect. There are books and websites devoted to all sorts of collection types!

You can even share your collection with your family and friends.

Maybe you can get them interested in collecting too!

Good luck and have fun!
You deserve it for working so hard!

Base Camp 4

Algebra

Wow! You're getting close to the top of *SCORE!* Mountain. Are you ready for another fun climb? Let's get started! Good luck!

1. What is the value of the expression $10a \div 2^3$, when $a = 4$?

_____

Hint #1:

Substitute **4** for the variable **a**. Also, remember that **10a** means "**ten times a**."

Hint #2:

Use the order of operations (**PEMDAS**) to find the answer. First, find the value of the exponent part of the expression.

Answer: 5

Substitute in the **4** for **a**, and the expression is now **10 × 4 ÷ 2³**. Using the order of operations, first find the value of **2³**, the exponent term of the expression: **2³ = 2 × 2 × 2 = 8**. The expression now reads **10 × 4 ÷ 8**.

Doing the multiplication and division from left to right gives you **40 ÷ 8 = 5**.

2. Solve the equation for n:

$$6n + 3 = 45$$

_____

Hint #1:

To solve an equation, get the **variable** alone on one side of the equation. Do this by using opposite operations. What would be the **opposite** operation to **addition**?

Hint #2:

First, do the opposite operation to addition, and subtract 3 from both sides of the equation. Then get the variable **n** alone by performing the opposite operation to multiplication.

Answer: $n = 7$

First, do the opposite operation to addition and subtract 3 from both sides of the equation: **6n + 3 − 3 = 45 − 3**. This simplifies to **6n = 42**. Now, do the opposite operation to multiplication, and divide both sides of the equation by 6: $\frac{6n}{6} = \frac{42}{6}$. The sixes on the left side cancel each other, and **42 ÷ 6 = 7**, so **n = 7**.

3. Which algebraic expression below means the same as "**a number divided by 5, plus 7**"?

- Ⓐ $5 \div n + 7$
- Ⓑ $5n + 7$
- Ⓒ $5 + n \div 7$
- Ⓓ $n \div 5 + 7$

Hint #1:

In this problem, words in a statement must be translated into an **algebraic expression**. Look for the key words and determine which numbers and symbols should be used in your expression. For example, replace the phrase "**a number**" with a variable, like **n**.

Hint #2:

What is the math symbol for the key words "**divided by**"? The number **5** is the divisor. What math symbol should be used for the word "**plus**"?

Answer: Choice **D** is correct.

Use a variable, like **n**, to represent the phrase "**a number**." The key words "**divided by**" gives the math symbol "÷." The number **5** is the divisor, so the first part of the expression is **n ÷ 5**. The word "**plus**" means addition, so the expression is **n ÷ 5 + 7**.

4. The music CDs that are available at an online store cost $8.00 for each CD, plus a one time charge of $5.00 for shipping any number of CDs ordered.

Create an **algebraic expression** that shows the total cost for any number of CDs ordered.

_____

Hint #1:

Let a variable, like **n**, represent the number of CDs purchased.

Hint #2:

Each CD costs **$8.00**, plus there is a **$5.00** shipping cost no matter how many CDs are ordered. It may help to make a table showing CD costs:

Number of CDs n	Cost
1	8 × 1 + 5
2	8 × 2 + 5

Answer: The total cost for any number of CDs is represented by the algebraic expression:
$C = 8 \times n + 5$ or $C = 8n + 5$

You are asked to find the **total cost** for any number of CDs ordered. Assign a variable, like **n**, to stand for this number of CDs. It may be helpful to make a **table** that shows how you calculate the cost of different number of CDs:

Number of CDs n	Cost
1	8 × 1 + 5
2	8 × 2 + 5
3	8 × 3 + 5
4	8 × 4 + 5
5	8 × 5 + 5
n	8 × n + 5

As you look at the table, observe that whatever the number of CDs is, you **multiply that number by 8**, and then **add in the shipping cost of 5**.

This leads to the formula to calculate the total cost as $C = 8 \times n + 5$ or $C = 8n + 5$.

5. The **ratio** of girls to boys in a chorus class is **3:2**. If there are **40 boys**, how many **girls** are in the chorus class?

_____

Hint #1:

A ratio can be written as a **fraction**. The ratio of girls to boys can be written as $\frac{girls}{boys} = \frac{3}{2}$.

Hint #2:

Use a variable, like **n**, to stand for the number of girls. Set up a proportion of $\frac{girls}{boys} = \frac{girls}{boys}$ and cross multiply to solve.

Answer: There are **60 girls** in the chorus class.

A ratio can be written as a **fraction**. The ratio of girls to boys can be written as $\frac{girls}{boys} = \frac{3}{2}$. Use a variable, like **n**, to stand for the number of girls. Set up a proportion of $\frac{girls}{boys} = \frac{girls}{boys}$. The proportion is $\frac{3}{2} = \frac{n}{40}$.

Cross multiply to get **3 × 40 = 2n**. Multiply on the left-hand side to get **120 = 2n**. Now, solve for **n** by dividing both sides of this equation by **2** to get **60 = n**, the number of girls in the chorus class.

6. The formula to convert from **Fahrenheit** to **Celsius** is $C = \frac{5}{9}(F - 32)$. Using the formula, what is the Celsius temperature equivalent to 68° **Fahrenheit**?

_____

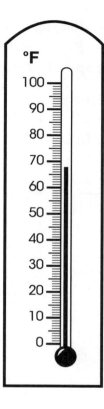

Hint #1:

In the formula, **C** represents the **Celsius temperature**, and **F** represents the **Fahrenheit temperature**.

Hint #2:

Substitute in the value for the Fahrenheit temperature and use the order of operations to find the Celsius temperature.

Answer: 20° Celsius

The formula is given as $C = \frac{5}{9}(F - 32)$. In the formula, **C** represents the **Celsius temperature**, and **F** represents the **Fahrenheit temperature**. Substitute in the value for the Fahrenheit temperature and use the order of operations to find the Celsius temperature.

The formula after substituting is $C = \frac{5}{9}(68 - 32)$. Using the order of operations, first subtract within the parentheses: $C = \frac{5}{9}(36)$.

Now, multiply $\frac{5}{9} \times \frac{36}{1} = \frac{180}{9} = 20$, so **68° Fahrenheit = 20° Celsius**.

7. The **distance** a car travels is found by using the **formula**
$D = R \times T$, where D stands for **the distance traveled**, R is
the speed of the car (the rate), and T is **the time in hours**.

How far will a car travel in **3 hours** at a speed of **60 miles per hour**?

_____

Hint #1:

First determine which numbers given in the problem go with which of the variables in the distance formula.

Hint #2:

Substitute the information into the formula and solve.

Answer: 180 miles

Determine which numbers go with which of the variables in the formula. The variable **R** is the **rate** at which the car is traveling, which is **60 miles per hour**. The variable **T**, the **time** in hours, is **3**. The variable **D**, **the distance**, is what we are solving for.

Substitute into the formula and calculate:

$D = 60 \times 3$, or $D = 180$ **miles**.

8. The figure below shows a **pattern** that is progressing over different stages.

Determine the number of **squares** and **triangles** that will be in **stage 9**.

Stage 1   Stage 2   Stage 3   Stage 4 . . . Stage 9

Number of **triangles** in stage 9: _____

Number of **squares** in stage 9: _____

Hint #1:

One way to solve this problem would be to extend the pattern out by drawing each stage up to stage 9.

Hint #2:

Another way to solve is to figure out the **pattern** in how the number of squares and triangles are progressing through each stage.

Answer: There will be **9 squares** and **1 triangle** in stage 9.

One way to solve this problem would be to extend the pattern out and draw each stage up to stage 9:

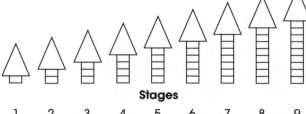

As the stages progress from 1 to 9, the number of triangles **remains constant at 1**, and the number of squares **is increasing by 1**.

So in stage 9, there will be a total of **9 squares** and **1 triangle**.

9. Evaluate the expression $10x^2 + 100 \div x$, when $x = 2$.

_____

Hint #1:

Substitute the number **2** for *x* in the expression, and then simplify. **10x^2** means **ten times *x* to the second power**.

Hint #2:

Remember to use the order of operations to evaluate the expression.

Answer: 90

Substitute the number **2** for *x* in the expression, and then simplify to get a numerical answer. **10x^2** means **ten times *x* to the second power**, so the expression becomes **10 × 2² + 100 ÷ 2**.

Now use the order of operations to evaluate the expression. Exponents are evaluated first, which gives **10 × 4 + 100 ÷ 2**.

Next, multiplication and division are done from left to right:

40 + 100 ÷ 2, and then **40 + 50 = 90**.

10. Look at the following figure sequence:

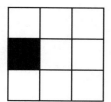 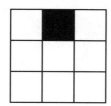 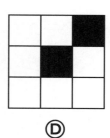

Which figure would come **next** in the sequence?

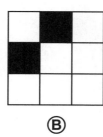 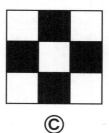 

Ⓐ   Ⓑ   Ⓒ   Ⓓ

Hint #1:

Look for a **pattern**.

Hint #2:

Study the movement of the colored square.

Answer: Choice **A** is correct.

Study the movement of the colored square, and look for a pattern. First, the colored square is in the **middle on the left**, then it is in the **middle on the top**, then it is in the **middle on the right**. The colored square is moving in a **clockwise direction**, and the next natural progression would be in the **middle on the bottom**, as shown in choice **A**.

11. Write an algebraic expression to represent the statement:

"Fifteen times a number, less six"

_____

Hint #1:

Use a variable, like *n*, to represent the phrase "**a number.**"

Hint #2:

The word "***times***" is a key word for **multiplication**. The word "***less***" is a key word for **subtraction**.

Answer: $15n - 6$ or $15 \times n - 6$

Use a variable, like *n*, to represent the phrase "**a number.**" The word "***times***" is a key word for **multiplication**. The phrase "**Fifteen times a number**" can be represented as **15*n***, or **15 × *n***. The word "***less***" is a key word for **subtraction**.

The algebraic expression is $15n - 6$ or $15 \times n - 6$.

12. Nancy was given the following equation to solve on the chalkboard:

$$\frac{n}{8} + 3 = 5$$

Can you help her solve it?

_____

Hint #1:

To solve this equation, get the variable **n** alone on one side of the equation. Do this by using **opposite operations**.

Hint #2:

First, do the opposite of addition and **subtract 3** from both sides of the equation. Continue until you get **n** alone on one side of the equation.

Answer: $n = 16$

To solve this equation, get the variable **n** alone on one side. Do this by using **opposite operations**. This is a two-step equation.

First, subtract **3** from both sides of the equation to get $\frac{n}{8} + 3 - 3 = 5 - 3$, which is $\frac{n}{8} = 2$. Next, undo the division by multiplying both sides by **8** to get $\frac{n}{8} \times \frac{8}{1} = 2 \times 8$, or **n = 16**.

13. Darren is trying to figure out the value of n in the equation $12n - 6 = 42$. Can you help him?

$12n - 6 = 42$

_____

Hint #1:

Get the variable **n** alone on one side of the equation by using opposite operations.

Hint #2:

First do the opposite of subtraction and **add 6** to both sides of the equation. Continue until you get **n** alone on one side of the equation.

Answer: $n = 4$

First, do the opposite of subtraction and **add 6** to both sides of the equation. The equation is now $12n - 6 + 6 = 42 + 6$. Simplify the equation to $12n = 48$.

Then, get **n** alone by dividing both sides by **12**: $\frac{12n}{12} = \frac{48}{12}$, or **n = 4**.

14. The formula for determining the **volume** of a rectangular prism is $V = l \times w \times h$.

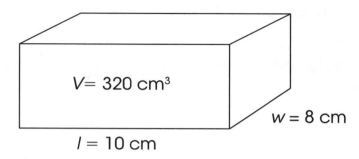

$V = 320 \text{ cm}^3$

$l = 10 \text{ cm}$

$w = 8 \text{ cm}$

If the **volume** of a prism is **320 cubic centimeters**, the **length** is **10 centimeters**, and the **width** is **8 centimeters**, what is the **height** of the prism?

_____

Hint #1:

You are given the formula for the volume of a rectangular prism. Decide how to substitute the given values into the formula.

Hint #2:

Substitute the given information into the formula, and then solve for the height.

Answer: The height of the prism is **4 centimeters**.

In the problem, you are told that the **volume** of the prism is **320 cubic centimeters**, the **length** is **10 centimeters**, and the **width** is **8 centimeters**.

Substitute the given information into the formula, and then solve for the height: **320 = 10 × 8 × h**. Multiply to get **320 = 80h**. Divide both sides of the equation by **80** to get $\frac{320}{80} = \frac{80h}{80}$ or **h = 4 centimeters**.

15. The formula for **simple interest** is $I = p \times r \times t$, where I is the **interest**, p is the **principal (original amount of investment)**, r is the **interest rate (written as a decimal)**, and t is the **time in years**.

What is the **interest** earned on **$100** for **2 years** at an **interest rate of 6%**?

_____

Hint #1:

Remember, the interest rate must be turned into a **decimal**.

Hint #2:

Six percent is $\frac{6}{100}$ or 0.06. Substitute the given values into the formula.

Answer: $12.00

Use the formula $I = p \times r \times t$ and substitute in the values for p, r, and t. $I = 100 \times 0.06 \times 2$.

Multiply the three numbers together to get I = **$12.00**.

16. Look at the sequence of arrows below.

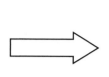  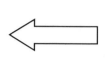

Which arrow comes **next** in the sequence?

Ⓐ   Ⓑ   Ⓒ   Ⓓ

Hint #1:

Look for a pattern.

Hint #2:

Look for a predictable movement from arrow to arrow.

Answer: Choice **B** is correct.

Notice that the arrows are moving in a predictable pattern. First the arrow is facing **right**, then the arrow is facing **up**, and then the arrow is facing **left**. The natural way for the next arrow to be facing is **down**, as shown in choice **B**.

17. The formula for the area of a circle is $A = \pi \times r^2$. Find the
area of a circle with a **radius** of **3 millimeters**.

_____

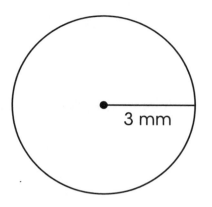

3 mm

Hint #1:

In the formula $A = \pi \times r^2$, **A** represents the **area**, **Pi** (π) is **3.14** when rounded to the nearest hundredth, and **r** is the **radius**.

Hint #2:

Substitute the values given in the problem into the area formula.

Answer: 28.26 millimeters

In the formula $A = \pi \times r^2$, **A** represents the area, **Pi** (π) is **3.14** when rounded to the nearest hundredth, and **r** is the **radius**. Substitute the values given in the problem into the area formula: $A = 3.14 \times 3^2$. Simplify to $A = 3.14 \times 9$, or $A = 28.26$ **millimeters**.

18. The **length** of a rectangle is **two times its width**. Write an **algebraic expression** to represent the **perimeter**.

_____

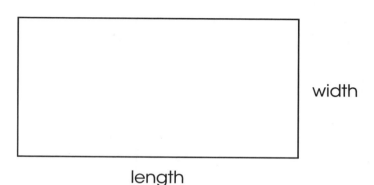

length

Hint #1:

Let **x** represent the **width**. What is the **length** in terms of **x**? It may help to draw a picture of the rectangle and label each side. Remember, the perimeter is the sum of the lengths of the sides.

Hint #2:

There are several possible correct equations for the answer.

Answer: **x + 2x + x + 2x** or **(2 × 2x) + (2 × x)** or **6x** or **other equivalent expression**.

The **length** is given as **two times the width**, so if we let **x** represent the **width**, the **length** is **2 × x**, or **2x**.

As stated in Hint #1, it may help to draw a picture of the rectangle and label each side:

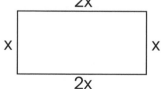

Perimeter is the sum of the length of the sides, so **P = x + 2x + x + 2x** or **6x**. Because opposite sides of a rectangle are the same measure, this can also be written as **(2 × 2x) + (2 × x)**.

19. Solve the equation $3x + 6 = 21$.

Hint #1:

Get the variable *x* alone on one side of the equation by using opposite operations.

Hint #2:

First do the opposite of addition and **subtract 6** from both sides of the equation.

© Kaplan Publishing, Inc.

Answer: *x* = 5

To solve this equation, get the variable *x* alone on one side of the equation. First subtract 6 from both sides of the equation: **3x + 6 − 6 = 21 − 6**, or **3x = 15**. Then **divide** both sides by **3** to get the answer. $\frac{3x}{3} = \frac{15}{3}$, or **x = 5**.

You're doing a great job so far!
Are you ready for a Challenge Activity?

Good luck!

Look carefully at the pattern below:

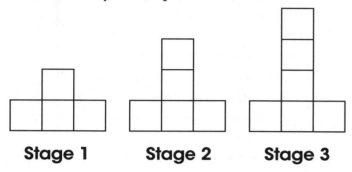

Stage 1   **Stage 2**   **Stage 3**

a) Draw what **stage** 4 in the pattern will look like.

b) How many **squares** will be in **stage 10**?

c) Write an **expression** to show the **number of squares** in stage *n*.

See hints and answers on following page.

Answers to Challenge Activity:

a) Your drawing for stage 4 in the pattern
should look something like this:

Notice that in each stage there are 3 squares that
make up the bottom row. This pattern will continue
through each stage. In each stage, the number of
squares atop the middle bottom square **equals** the
number of that stage. So **stage 4** has **three squares**
on the **bottom row** and **four squares** atop the **middle
bottom square**.

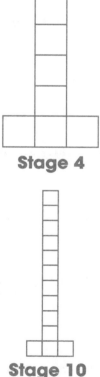

Stage 4

b) **13 squares**

Once you figure out the pattern, each stage
becomes easier to figure out. **Stage 10** will
have the **three squares** on the bottom,
plus **ten squares** atop the middle bottom
square for a total of **3 + 10 = 13 squares**.

c) *n* + 3 squares

Stage 10

To sum up, each stage has three squares on the bottom, plus a number
of squares atop the middle bottom square that always equals the stage
number. So if the stage number is *n*, the number of squares in that stage
is *n* + 3.

© Kaplan Publishing, Inc.

Let's take a quick test and see how much you've learned during this climb up *SCORE!* Mountain.

Good luck!

1. What is the value of the expression $(2x)^3 + 54 \div 9$, when $x = 2$?

_____

2. Solve the equation $6x - 8 = 40$.

_____

3. If a car traveled 440 miles at a constant speed of 55 miles per hour, how many hours did it travel?

_____

4. The skate park has a $10.00 membership fee, plus $2.00 admission for each visit. Show the price as an algebraic expression for any number of visits.

_____

5. The ratio of dogs to cats at an animal shelter is 3:5. If there are 21 dogs at the shelter, how many cats are there?

_____

See answers on following page.

© Kaplan Publishing, Inc.

Answers to test questions:

1. 70

Substitute in the value of 2 everywhere in the expression where there is an *x*. The expression is now **(2 × 2)³ + 54 ÷ 9**. Follow the order of operations, **PEMDAS**, or **P**arentheses, **E**xponents, **M**ultiplication and **D**ivision, then finally **A**ddition and **S**ubtraction. Evaluate the parentheses first to get **4³ + 54 ÷ 9**. Now, evaluate the exponent. **4³ = 4 × 4 × 4**, so the expression is now **64 + 54 ÷ 9**. Next, do the division to get **64 + 6 = 70**.

2. *x* = 8

To solve an equation, get the variable *x* alone on one side of the equation. First, **add 8** to both sides of the equation. The equation is now **6*x* − 8 + 8 = 40 + 8**, or **6*x* = 48**. Then **divide both sides by 6** to get the answer. $\frac{6x}{6} = \frac{48}{6}$, or *x* = **8**.

3. 8 hours

The **distance** a car travels is found by using the formula **D = r × t**, where *D* stands for **the distance traveled**, *r* is **the speed of the car (the rate)**, and *t* is **the time in hours**.

In the problem, the **rate**, or *r*, is given as **55 miles per hour**, the **distance**, or *D*, is **440 miles**. The variable *t* is what we are solving for. Substitute the given values into the formula and calculate: **440 = 55 × t**. To solve for *t*, **divide** both sides by 55 to get $\frac{440}{55} = \frac{55 \times t}{55}$, or *t* = **8 hours**.

4. 10 + 2 × *n*, or 10 + 2*n*

To show the price for any number of visits, assign a variable, like *n*, for the number of visits. There is a **one-time fee** of **$10.00**, and each visit costs **$2.00**. In this problem the word "**each**" tells you to use multiplication. The expression is **10 + 2 × *n***, or **10 + 2*n***.

5. 35 cats

A ratio can be written as a **fraction**. The ratio of dogs to cats can be written as $\frac{dogs}{cats} = \frac{3}{5}$. Set up a **proportion** of $\frac{dogs}{cats} = \frac{dogs}{cats}$.

Use a variable, like *n*, to stand for the number of cats.

The proportion is $\frac{3}{5} = \frac{21}{n}$. Cross-multiply to get **3 × *n* = 105**.

Divide both sides by **3** to get *n* = **35**, the number of cats.

Celebrate!

Let's take a fun break before we go to the next base camp. You've earned it!

Gather a couple of friends or family members and have fun writing a short play!

Congratulations! You're getting closer to the top of *SCORE!* Mountain.

© Kaplan Publishing, Inc.

Do you like **mysteries**, **comedies**, or **adventure stories**? Your play can be about anything you like!

Create fun **characters** for each person to play!

Look around your house for **costumes** you can use to help make your characters look the part!

Search around for **props** you can use to help make things seem even more convincing. These supplies can also help spark your creative ideas!

If you have a CD player with speakers, you can even add your favorite **music** to your play!

Perform your play for family and friends!

Good luck and have fun!
You deserve it for working so hard!

Base Camp

5

Probability and Statistics

Wow! You are getting close to the top of *SCORE!* Mountain. Great work! Let's keep going! Good luck!

1. The sixth grade students were **polled** about their favorite after-school snacks. Each student could only choose **one snack**. The results are shown in the **graph** on the right.

How many students were polled?

_____

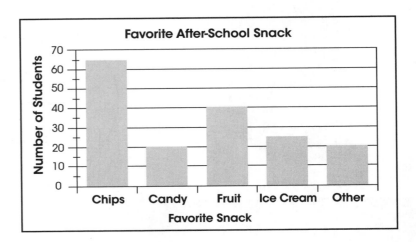

Hint #1:

Each **bar** in the graph shows the number of students who chose that snack. Look to the **left** of the bar on the **y-axis** to find the number of students selecting each snack type.

Hint #2:

Because each student could only choose one snack, add the numbers who selected each snack type to find the total number of students polled.

Answer: 170 students were polled.

Read the graph and find where the top of each bar meets the **y-axis**—this tells you the number of students that make up each bar.

The **chips** bar is halfway between 60 and 70, so the number of students who chose chips is **65**.

The number of students who chose **candy** is **20**, and the number who chose **fruit** is **40**.

The bar for **ice cream** is halfway between 20 and 30, so **25** students chose ice cream, and **20** students named some **other** snack.

The **total** number of students polled is **65 + 20 + 40 + 25 + 20 = 170 students**.

© Kaplan Publishing, Inc.

2. For lunch, the middle school students can choose **one item** in each category below:

Sandwich Choice	Fruit Choice	Beverage Choice
turkey	apple	milk
ham	orange	juice
peanut butter and jelly		

Based on the table, how many **different lunches** are available that includes **one sandwich**, **one fruit**, and **one beverage**?

_____

Hint #1:

It may help to make an **organized list** or **tree diagram**, or to use the **Fundamental Counting Principle**, which allows you to count the number of ways a task can occur given a series of events. To use the Fundamental Counting Principle to solve this problem, multiply the total number of choices in each food category to get the number of different possible lunches.

Hint #2:

Make sure your list or tree includes all the different lunch possibilities, and then count them.

See answer on following page.

Answer: 12 different lunches are available.

A **tree diagram**, shown below, is an effective way to show all the lunch possibilities available. You can also make an **organized list**, like the one shown to the right of the tree diagram, where **T** stands for **turkey, H** for **ham, P** for **peanut butter and jelly, A** stands for **apple, O** for **orange, M** for **milk**, and **J** for **juice**. Both approaches show that there are **12 different lunches available**.

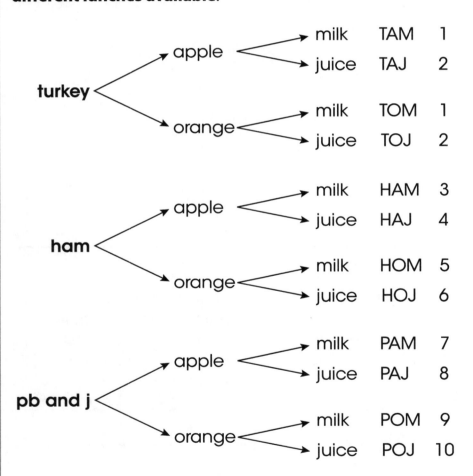

apple	milk	TAM	1
	juice	TAJ	2
orange	milk	TOM	1
	juice	TOJ	2
apple	milk	HAM	3
	juice	HAJ	4
orange	milk	HOM	5
	juice	HOJ	6
apple	milk	PAM	7
	juice	PAJ	8
orange	milk	POM	9
	juice	POJ	10

The other way to solve this problem is to use the **Fundamental Counting Principle**, and just **multiply** the total number of choices in each category to get the number of different lunches: **sandwich choices × fruit choices × beverage choices**, or **3 × 2 × 2 = 12 different lunches**.

3. In a middle school, **50 students** take a foreign language: either **Spanish** or **French**. Of these students, a total of **35 take Spanish** and **5 take both Spanish** and **French**.

How many students take **French only**?

_____

Hint #1:

Use a **Venn diagram** to solve the problem.

Hint #2:

Start the Venn diagram by placing the **5** in the area where the two circles **intersect**, and then fill in the number of students that take **Spanish only**. From there, determine how many take **French only**.

Answer: 15 students take French only.

Use a **Venn diagram** to solve the problem:

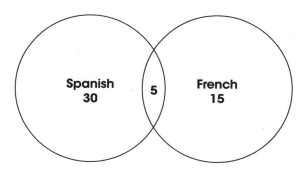

30 + 5 + 15 = 50 total students

The diagram will have **two circles** to represent the **two languages**. They will **overlap** because there are **5 students** who take both **languages**. Because the problem states that **35 students take Spanish**, there are **35 − 5 = 30 students** who take **Spanish only**. There are **50 total students** who take a language so there are **50 − 35 = 15 students** remaining who take **French only**.

© Kaplan Publishing, Inc.

4. Gary wants to determine how many middle school students think that The Pizza Parlor has the best pizza. Which of the following **sampling methods** should Gary use?

(A) poll all people as they leave The Pizza Parlor

(B) poll middle school students as they leave The Pizza parlor

(C) poll students in each homeroom of the middle school

(D) send questionnaires to all homes in Gary's neighborhood

Hint #1:

From what group of people is Gary seeking information?

Hint #2:

If Gary asks only people leaving The Pizza Parlor, he won't have a fair sample. Why?

Answer: Choice **C** is correct.

Gary is seeking information **about how many middle school students** think that The Pizza Parlor has the best pizza. So Gary should **poll or question middle school students only**. This **eliminates** choices **A** and **D**. If Gary polls middle school students leaving The Pizza Parlor, this group of students probably prefers the pizza there since they have chosen to eat there, so it isn't a fair sample. So you can **eliminate** choice **B**. Gary will get the best sample by **polling students in each homeroom of the middle school**.

5. Which type of graph would **best** show how Monica spends her babysitting money?

Ⓐ circle graph

Ⓑ line graph

Ⓒ bar graph

Ⓓ scatter plot

Hint #1:

The graph chosen will be one that clearly shows **parts** of a **whole**.

Hint #2:

Monica spends **percentages** of her money on different items.

Answer: Choice **A** is correct.

The graph chosen will be one that clearly shows **parts of a whole**. For Monica, the **whole** is her total babysitting money, and the **parts** are the different categories that she spends her money on. If you think of Monica as spending **different percentages** of her money on different items, the **circle graph** is the best choice.

6. Zoe scores the following points in each game of the basketball tournament:

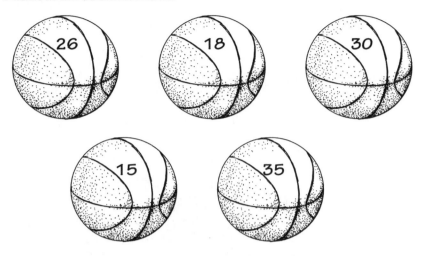

What is the **range** of her points?

_____

Hint #1:

Look for the **highest** and **lowest** values in the data set.

Hint #2:

The **range** is the **difference in the extremes** of her points.

Answer: The range is **20 points**.

The **range** is the **difference between the extremes**—the **highest** and the **lowest** values of the points in the data set.

The **highest** value is **35** and the **lowest** value is **15**. The word "**difference**" is a key word for **subtraction**.

The range is **35 − 15 = 20 points**.

7. Dylan's test scores in math class are shown below.

His overall score for the class will be the **mean** of the scores.

What is Dylan's overall score?

_____

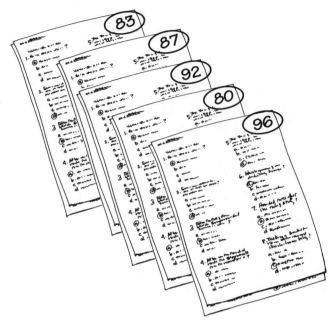

Hint #1:

Another word for the **mean** is the **average**. What is the average of his scores?

Hint #2:

How do you find the **average** of a set of numbers?

Answer: Dylan's grade is **87.6**.

Another word for **mean** is **average**. To find the mean, or average, add all of the scores and divide by the number of scores there are. **83 + 87 + 92 + 80 + 96 = 438**.

There are **5 scores**, so divide by 5: **438 ÷ 5 = 87.6**.

8. The sixth grade students are collecting canned goods for the needy for 6 days. The number of cans of food collected each day is shown below.

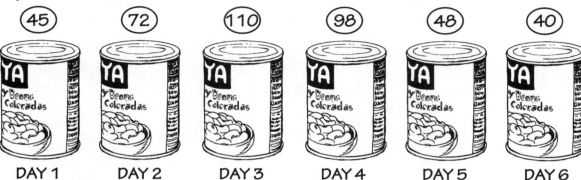

| DAY 1 | DAY 2 | DAY 3 | DAY 4 | DAY 5 | DAY 6 |

What is the **median** number of cans collected?

_____

Hint #1:

The **median** is the **middle data point** of the data when sorted.

Hint #2:

Order the data from **least** to **greatest**.

Answer: The median number is **60 cans**.

The sorted data, from least to greatest, are:

40   45   48   72   98   110

There are **six** pieces of data, so there is **no middle data point**. In this case, the **median** is the **average** of the two **middle** data points. Find the average of **48** and **72** to find the median.

48 + 72 = 120, and **120 ÷ 2 = 60 cans**.

9. The data on the right show the number of **absences** that the school secretary recorded over **10 days**.

What is the **mode** of the data?

_____

Total School Absences	
Day 1:	10
Day 2:	12
Day 3:	12
Day 4:	15
Day 5:	10
Day 6:	11
Day 7:	12
Day 8:	9
Day 9:	9
Day 10:	11

Hint #1:

The **mode** is the data value that occurs **most often**.

Hint #2:

Make a **tally chart** of each data value to see which occurs **most often**.

Answer: The mode of the data is **12**.

The **mode** is the data value that occurs **most often**. Make a **tally chart** of each data value to see which occurs most often:

Number of absences	Tally	Frequency
9		2
10		2
11		2
12		3
15		1

Notice on the chart that **12** occurs **three times**. It is the value that occurs **most often**, so **12** is the **mode** of the data set.

10. Celine wants to determine the **colors** of the blocks in a bin. She does not want to sort them all by color because she knows there are **1,000 blocks** in the bin. Instead, she will pick out a block, record its color, replace it, shake the bin, and repeat this procedure. All the blocks in the bin are **red, blue,** or **green**. The experimental results of her **sampling** are shown in the table on the right:

Color of Block	Frequency
Blue	35
Red	15
Green	20

There were **70 trials** in the experiment, meaning that Celine **chose** and **recorded** a block color **70 times**. Based on her experiment, what is the **total number** of **blue** blocks in the bin?

_____

Hint #1:

The **color distribution** shown should closely match the way the 1,000 blocks are distributed by color.

Hint #2:

Set up a proportion, showing $\frac{blue}{total} = \frac{blue}{total}$. Fill in the given values and solve the proportion.

Answer: There are **500 blue blocks** in the bin.

There were **70 trials** in the experiment. The **color distribution** shown should closely match the way the 1,000 blocks are distributed by color. You may notice that **35** out of the **70** blocks picked were **blue**. This is **one half** of the blocks chosen. One half of 1,000, the total number in the bin, is **500 blocks**.

You can also set up a proportion to solve this problem, showing $\frac{blue}{total} = \frac{blue}{total}$. Fill in the given values, using a variable, like **n**, to represent the number of blue blocks in the bin. $\frac{35}{70} = \frac{n}{1,000}$.

Solve the proportion by **cross multiplying**, which will give you **70n = 35,000**. **Divide** both sides by **70** to solve for **n**, to get **n = 500**.

11. If a penny is flipped and a standard number cube, numbered 1 through 6, is rolled, what is the **probability** that the coin will land on **heads** and the number cube will land on 4?

4

Hint #1:

Probability is the ratio of the number of favorable outcomes / the number of total outcomes .
First, find the probability of each event **separately**.

Hint #2:

The probability of one event **and** another event is found by **multiplying** the probabilities together. Remember to create **fractions** for each probability before you multiply.

Answer: The probability that the coin will land on heads **and** the number cube will land on 4 is $\frac{1}{12}$.

Probability is the ratio of $\frac{\text{the number of favorable outcomes}}{\text{the number of total outcomes}}$. First, find the probability of each event **separately**.

For the penny there are two possible outcomes: {**heads, tails**}.

The **probability** of the penny landing on **heads** is $\frac{1}{2}$.

For the number cube there are six total outcomes: {**1, 2, 3, 4, 5, 6**}.

The **probability** of the cube landing on 4 is $\frac{1}{6}$.

The **probability** of one event **and** another event is found by multiplying the probabilities together: $\frac{1}{2} \times \frac{1}{6} = \frac{1}{12}$.

12. The **circle graph** on the right shows the **percentage** of students at Gila Vista Middle School who chose various flavors of ice cream as their favorite.

Of the **400 students** polled, how many chose **vanilla**?

_____

Ice Cream Preference

Hint #1:

Percentages are shown in the circle graph. Find the percentage for **vanilla**.

Hint #2:

Remember, a percentage is a **ratio** comparing a value to 100.

Answer: 140 students chose vanilla.

Percentages are shown in the circle graph. Find the percentage for vanilla, which is **35%**. This means that for every 100 students, 35 chose vanilla.

If **400 students** are polled, then the number who prefer vanilla is **4 × 35 = 140 students**.

You can also solve this problem by setting up the proportion $\frac{35}{100} = \frac{n}{400}$.

Cross multiply and simplify to get **$n = 140$**.

13. Doug opens his dresser drawer and sees 2 **pairs of jeans, 5 shirts,** and **2 belts**. How many **different outfits** consisting of a pair of jeans, shirt, and belt can Doug make?

_____

Hint #1:

To solve this problem, you can make an **organized list** or use the **Fundamental Counting Principle**.

Hint #2:

Make sure your list includes all possibilities and then count them.

Answer: Doug can make **20 different outfits**.

Make an **organized list** that includes all outfit possibilities, as below, and then count them:

Doug's Possible Outfits

jean 1 – shirt 1 – belt 1	jean 2 – shirt 1 – belt 1
jean 1 – shirt 1 – belt 2	jean 2 – shirt 1 – belt 2
jean 1 – shirt 2 – belt 1	jean 2 – shirt 2 – belt 1
jean 1 – shirt 2 – belt 2	jean 2 – shirt 2 – belt 2
jean 1 – shirt 3 – belt 1	jean 2 – shirt 3 – belt 1
jean 1 – shirt 3 – belt 2	jean 2 – shirt 3 – belt 2
jean 1 – shirt 4 – belt 1	jean 2 – shirt 4 – belt 1
jean 1 – shirt 4 – belt 2	jean 2 – shirt 4 – belt 2
jean 1 – shirt 5 – belt 1	jean 2 – shirt 5 – belt 1
jean 1 – shirt 5 – belt 2	jean 2 – shirt 5 – belt 2

As shown here, there are **20 possible outfits**.

Another way to arrive at the answer is to use the **Fundamental Counting Principle**:

2 (jeans choices) × 5 (shirt choices) × 2 (belt choices) = 20 different outfits.

14. Courtney rolls a standard number cube, numbered from 1 to 6. What is the **probability** that the result is an **odd number**?

_____

Hint #1:

Remember that **probability** is the **ratio** $\dfrac{\text{the number of favorable outcomes}}{\text{the number of total outcomes}}$.

Hint #2:

The number of **favorable** outcomes is the number of cube sides that have **odd numbers**.

Answer: $\dfrac{3}{6}$ or $\dfrac{1}{2}$.

Probability is the ratio $\dfrac{\text{the number of favorable outcomes}}{\text{the number of total outcomes}}$. The total number of outcomes for a number cube is 6: **{1, 2, 3, 4, 5, 6}**.

From these 6 outcomes, there are **3 favorable outcomes**: **1**, **3**, and **5**.

The probability that Courtney rolls an odd number is $\dfrac{3}{6} = \dfrac{1}{2}$.

15. The **line graph** below shows Adam's savings account values. Between which two months is the **biggest difference** in values?

_____

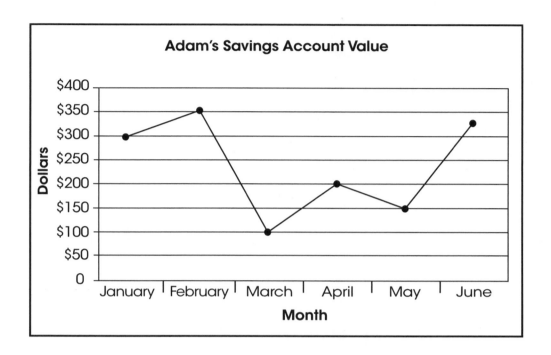

Adam's Savings Account Value

Hint #1:

To read the graph, follow each dot over to the **y-axis** on the **left** and find the **value** for each month.

Hint #2:

The problem is asking you to find the **biggest difference**, not the biggest value.

Answer: The biggest difference in values occurs between the months of **February** and **March**.

To read the graph, you can follow each dot over to the **y-axis** on the **left** and find the **value** for each month. The problem is asking you to find the **biggest difference**, not the biggest value, so look at the graph and choose the steepest line. This is between **February** and **March**. The difference here is **350 − 100 = $250**. The next biggest difference is between **May** and **June**, which is **325 − 150 = $175**.

16. The **Venn diagram** below shows the number of students on the varsity sports teams of **soccer** and **baseball**.

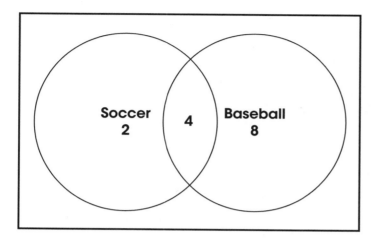

How many students are on **only the soccer team** or **only the baseball team**?

_____

Hint #1:

A Venn diagram shows **overlapping circles**. The overlap area represents the number of students on **both** the soccer and baseball teams. Should you count these students?

Hint #2:

The total number of students on these teams is shown in the circular areas of the diagram.

Answer: **28 students** are on only the soccer team or only the baseball team.

Look carefully at the numbers in the Venn Diagram.

According to the diagram, the number of students on either the soccer or baseball teams alone is **20 students + 8 students = 28 students**.

17. The **pictograph** below shows the number of movies attended last year for various people.

Number of Movies Attended Last Year

Juana	○ ○ ○ ○ ⟳
Alice	○ ○ ○
Jacob	○ ○
Sue	○ ○
Key: Each ○ stands for 4 movies	

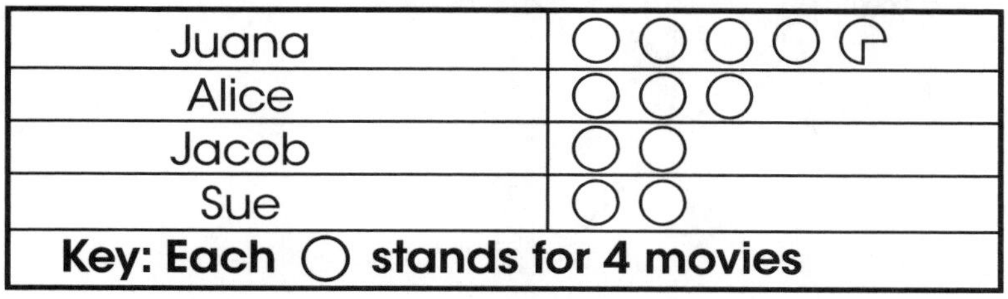

Juana attended how many more movies than **Sue**?

_____

Hint #1:

Compare the data for Juana and Sue. Make sure to review the key in order to correctly interpret the data.

Hint #2:

Are any of the pictures partial circles?

Answer: Juana attended **11** more movies than Sue.

Look at the entries for Juana and Sue, the **first** and **last** rows in the pictograph. Study the key to correctly interpret the data. Each circle represents **4 movies attended**.

Next to Juana's name, there are **4 whole circles**, and one **three-quarter circle**. This represents $4 \times 4\frac{3}{4}$ movies, or $4 \times \frac{19}{4} = $ **19 movies**.

Next to Sue's name there are two circles, which is **4 × 2 = 8 movies**.

To find out how many more movies Juana has attended, use subtraction: **19 − 8 = 11 movies**.

18. Kevin spun the spinners shown below.

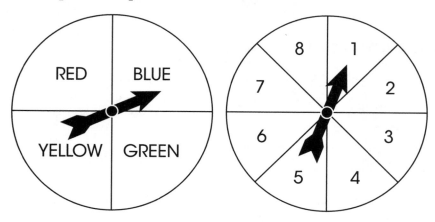

What is the **probability** that the spinners will land on **YELLOW** and **5**?

_____

Hint #1:

Remember, probability is the ratio $\frac{\text{the number of favorable outcomes}}{\text{the number of total outcomes}}$.

First, find the probability of each event, landing on the **YELLOW** and landing on **5**, separately.

Hint #2:

The probability of one event **and** another event is found by **multiplying** the probabilities together.

Answer: $\frac{1}{32}$

For the color spinner, there are **4** total outcomes: **RED, BLUE, YELLOW**, and **GREEN**. The probability of the spinner landing on **YELLOW** is $\frac{1}{4}$.

For the number spinner, there are **eight** total outcomes: **1, 2, 3, 4, 5, 6, 7,** and **8**. The **probability** of the spinner landing on 5 is $\frac{1}{8}$.

The probability of the spinners landing on **YELLOW** and **5** can be found by multiplying the probabilities together: $\frac{1}{4} \times \frac{1}{8} = \frac{1}{32}$.

19. Below is a **histogram** of heights for 50 people.

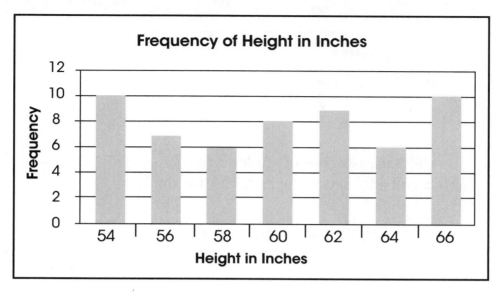

What is the **mode** of the data?

_____

Hint #1:

A **histogram** is a bar graph used to show frequencies of data.

Hint #2:

Remember that the **mode** is the data item that occurs most often.

Answer: The modes of the data are **54 inches** and **66 inches**.

A **histogram** is a bar graph used to show frequencies of data. Therefore, the bar that is the **highest** would be the **most frequent**. In this graph, there are **two highest bars**, so there are **two modes**.

The two highest bars are for the heights of **54 inches** and **66 inches**.

You're doing a great job so far!

Are you ready for a Challenge Activity?

Good luck!

Below are data that show the number of students participating in the Harriet Tubman Middle School Science Fair for the last 9 years:

<table>
<tr><td>52</td><td>24</td><td>33</td><td>60</td><td>38</td><td>38</td><td>42</td><td>48</td><td>43</td></tr>
</table>

a) Order the data set from **least** to **greatest**.

b) Find the **mean** and **median** of the data.

c) Find the **mode** of the data.

Hint #1:

Remember, the **mean** is the **average**. The **median** is the **middle number**.

Hint #2:

The **mode** is the value that occurs **most often**.

Answers to Challenge Activity:

a) The order of the data set from **least** to **greatest** is as follows:

    24   33   38   38   42   43   48   52   60

b) The **mean** is **42**. The **median** is **42**.

There are 9 values in the data set. The **median**, the exact middle, is the fifth element in this ordered list, or **42**. The **mean** is the average, found by adding all of the numbers and then dividing by the number of items:

24 + 33 + 38 + 38 + 42 + 43 + 48 + 52 + 60 = 378. 378 ÷ 9 = 42.

c) The **mode** is **38**. The **mode** is the value that occurs **most often**. In this data set, the value of 38 is the only value that occurs more than once, so **38** is the **mode**.

Let's take a quick test and see how much you've learned during this climb up *SCORE!* Mountain.

Good luck!

1. Listed below are shoe sizes for the basketball team.

8   10   10   9   8.5   7   8   8   7.5   9   10   10

What is the mean shoe size?

_____

2. Two standard number cubes, numbered from 1 to 6, are rolled. What is the probability that one cube lands on an even number and one cube lands on a number greater than 4?

_____

3. The pep rally T-shirts are available in green, gold, or white. You can choose long sleeved or short sleeved. Four sizes are available: small, medium, large, and extra-large.

How many different shirts are there to choose from?

_____

4. The graph below is a histogram of quiz scores.

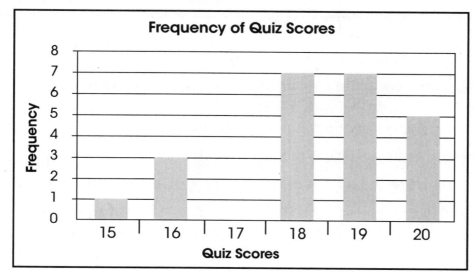

What is the range of the scores?

_____

5. One hundred people at a restaurant order salad or soup or both. Seventy-eight people order salad, and of these, 38 people order both soup and salad.

How many people order soup only?

_____

See answers on following page.

Answers to test questions:

1. The mean shoe size is **8.75**.

   The **mean** is the **average** shoe size. To find the average, add up all of the values and then divide this sum by the number of pieces of data. To add up the values, you can group them by the **frequency** of each.

   For example, there are **3** values of **8**, so you can multiply **3 × 8 = 24**.

   The sum is then **7 + 7.5 + (3 × 8) + 8.5 + (2 × 9) + (4 × 10)**.

   Do the multiplications to get **7 + 7.5 + 24 + 8.5 + 18 + 40**. Now add to get the sum of **105**. There are **12** pieces of data, so divide to get the mean.

   105 ÷ 12 = 8.75

2. The probability that one cube lands on an even number and one cube lands on a number greater than 4 is $\frac{1}{6}$.

   First, find the probability of each event separately. For each number cube, the total number of outcomes is 6: **{1, 2, 3, 4, 5, 6}**.

   The **probability** of the **first cube** landing on an **even number** is $\frac{3}{6} = \frac{1}{2}$.

   The **probability** of the **second cube** landing on a **number greater than 4** (**5** and **6** are the favorable outcomes) is $\frac{2}{6} = \frac{1}{3}$. The probability that one cube lands on an even number and one cube lands on a number greater than 4 can be found by multiplying the probabilities together. $\frac{1}{3} \times \frac{1}{2} = \frac{1}{6}$.

3. There are **24 different shirts** to choose from.

   You can make an **organized list** to show all the possibilities. Make 3 columns, one for **green shirts**, one for **gold shirts**, and one for **white shirts**.

green-short-small	gold-short-small	white-short-small
green-short-medium	gold-short-medium	white-short-medium
green-short-large	gold-short-large	white-short-large
green-short-extra large	gold-short-extra large	white-short-extra large
green-long-small	gold-long-small	white-long-small
green-long-medium	gold-long-medium	white-long-medium
green-long-large	gold-long-large	white-long-large
green-long-extra large	gold-long-extra large	white-long-extra large

Answers to test questions *continued*:

3 columns of **8** entries each is **24 different possibilities**.

You can also use the **Counting Principle** to find the answer. There are **3** color choices, **2** sleeve choices, and **4** size choices: **3 × 2 × 4 = 24**.

4. The range is **5**.

The **range** of data is the difference between the **largest** and **smallest** values. A histogram shows the data ordered from **least** to **greatest**. In this graph, the quiz grades range from **15** to **20**, so the range is **20 − 15 = 5**.

5. **22 people** order soup only.

Make a **Venn diagram**, like the one below, to solve this problem.

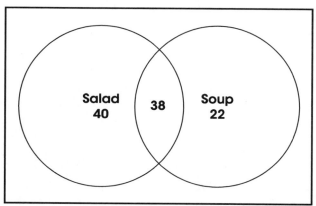

Make two circles, **one** for **soup**, **one** for **salad**, and have the circles **overlap**. Put the number who ordered **both** soup and salad in the overlap area. You are told that 78 people ordered salad, and also that of these, **38** of them also ordered soup. So there are **78 − 38 = 40 people** who ordered salad only.

100 − (40 + 38) = 100 − 78 = 22 people who ordered soup only.

Celebrate!

Let's take a fun break before we go to the next base camp. You've earned it!

Let's make a **creative paperweight** to hold down all of your important papers!

What you will need:

- a flat rock

- paint, such as tempera

Congratulations!

You're almost to the top of *SCORE!* Mountain.

Take a walk outside in the fresh air and find a good flat rock.

Choose some paint colors and use your imagination and creativity to decorate your new paperweight!

Here are some suggestions:

- Paint your name on your paperweight to personalize it, or paint someone else's name on it and give the paperweight as a gift!

- Paint your paperweight in your school colors or the colors of your favorite sports team!

- If you find a nice smooth flat rock, put a favorite photo on your paperweight! To do this, mix equal parts of powdered tempera paint and white glue together. Paint the rock with this mixture. Put the photo on the wet paint mixture, and carefully press it down.

After decorating your paperweight, allow it to dry completely. Enjoy your new paperweight!

Good luck and have fun!
You deserve it for working so hard!

Base Camp

6

Everyday Math

You've made it to the final base camp! Outstanding! Make it through and you'll be at the top of *SCORE!* Mountain. You can do it! Good luck!

1. The school play has 2 acts and a 20-minute intermission. If the whole production lasts $2\frac{1}{2}$ **hours**, how long is each act if they are equal in length?

_____

Hint #1:

First, convert the $2\frac{1}{2}$ **hours** into **minutes**.

Hint #2:

Next, **subtract** the 20-minute intermission. The remaining time is the length of **both** acts, and you are told in the problem that the acts are **equal** in length.

Answer: Each act is **65 minutes long**.

There are 60 minutes in an hour, so $2\frac{1}{2}$ hours is $(2 \times 60) + (\frac{1}{2} \times 60)$, which is **120 + 30 = 150** minutes. **Subtract** the 20-minute intermission, and the two acts together are **150 − 20 = 130 minutes long**. Because there are two acts, divide this time by **2**, and each act is **130 ÷ 2 = 65 minutes long**.

2. A rectangular television screen is **5 inches wider** than it is long. The **perimeter** of the screen is **78 inches**.

What are the **length** and **width** of this screen?

Hint #1:

Remember that the **perimeter** of a rectangle is two times the length plus two times the width.

Hint #2:

You can use the **guess and check method** of problem solving. Make a **chart**, showing length, width, and perimeter. Start your guess by picking a number for the **length**, and **adding 5** to this for the **width**. Then calculate the perimeter. Decide if this is **less than** or **greater than** the perimeter of **78**, and go from there.

Answer: The **length** is **17 inches** and the **width** is **22 inches**.
Make a chart as described in Hint #2:

length	width	2 x length	2 x width	perimeter
20	25	40	50	90

This guess has a perimeter that is **too big**. Try a **smaller value** for the length:

length	width	2 x length	2 x width	perimeter
18	23	36	46	82

This guess is still **too big**, but it is pretty close to the correct perimeter of 78. Try one less for the length:

length	width	2 x length	2 x width	perimeter
17	22	34	44	78

This third guess worked, so the **length** is **17 inches** and the **width** is **22**.

3. Some school lockers have **3 shelves** that are each $\frac{1}{2}$ inch thick. There is a **15-inch space** above and below each shelf.

How **tall** are these school lockers?

_____

Hint #1:

It may be helpful to draw a picture of the lockers described in the problem and label each part. There are 3 shelves, a floor, and a ceiling.

Hint #2:

To find the **height** of the locker, add together the **four** 15-inch spaces and the **three** one-half inch shelves.

Answer: The school lockers are **61.5 inches tall**.

Draw a picture and label each part, like below:

To find the height of the locker, **add** the four 15-inch spaces and the **three** one-half-inch shelves.
4 × 15 + 3 × 0.5 = 60 + 1.5 = 61.5 inches

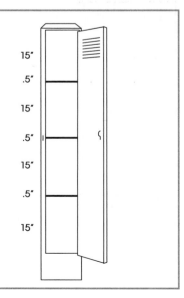

4. Ryan has **$40.00**. He wants to buy as many CDs as he can with his money. Each CD costs **$7.85**. Use **estimation** to determine how many CDs he can buy.

_____

Hint #1:

When using **estimation**, round up to **whole numbers**.

Hint #2:

Divide the rounded price into the money he has available in order to find out how many CDs he can buy.

Answer: Ryan can buy **5 CDs**.

When using **estimation**, round to **whole numbers**. Round **$7.85** to **$8.00**. Divide the rounded price into the money he has available. **40 ÷ 8 = 5**, so Ryan can buy **5 CDs**.

5. The Walsh family has **six children**.
Cindy is younger than **Sean** and **Patrick**.
Ann is older than **Thomas**, but younger than **Cindy**.
Thomas is older than **Joe**.

Who is the **fourth oldest child** in the family?

_____

Hint #1:

Use the **clues** given in the problem to determine the order of the children from **oldest** to **youngest**.

Hint #2:

Take the **clues** one by one to place them in order. It may be easier to use the first initial of each child's name when writing them out.

Answer: **Ann** is the fourth oldest child in the family.

Read the clues to determine the order of the children from oldest to youngest, using the first initial of each name to represent each child. Take the clues one by one to place them in order.

Because you are told that **Cindy** is **younger** than **Sean** and **Patrick**, the starting order is either **S, P, C** or **P, S, C**. Next, you are told that **Ann** is **older** than **Thomas** but **younger** than **Cindy**. So the order is either: **S, P, C, A, T** or **P, S, C, A, T** so far. The last clue says that **Thomas** is **older** than **Joe**. The final order is either: **S, P, C, A, T, J** or **P, S, C, A, T, J**. In either case, **Ann is the fourth oldest child**.

6. Miguel is selling raffle tickets.
He sells **one-half** of his tickets on **Monday**.
He sells **one-half** of what's left on **Tuesday**.
On **Wednesday**, he sells **one-half** of the
remaining tickets. He has **8 tickets left**.

How many **tickets** did Miguel **start** with?

_____

Hint #1:

It may help to work **backward** to solve this problem.

Hint #2:

Start with the **8 tickets** that Miguel has left. On **Wednesday**, he had sold **one-half** of his remaining tickets. So how many tickets did he have **before** selling on Wednesday? Continue with this method to find the right answer.

Answer: Miguel started with **64 tickets**.

Try working backward to solve this problem. Start with the **8 tickets** that Miguel has left. On **Wednesday**, he had sold **one-half** of his remaining tickets. So he had **8 × 2 = 16 tickets** before selling on **Wednesday**. Using the same reasoning, he had **16 × 2 = 32 tickets** before selling on **Tuesday**, and **32 × 2 = 64 tickets** before selling on **Monday**.

7. At the concession stand in a football stadium, **25 people** bought pizza. **17 people** bought **plain cheese** and **12 people** bought **pepperoni pizza**. How many bought **both** kinds of pizza?

_____

Hint #1:

The **17 people** who bought plain cheese pizza and the **12 people** who bought pepperoni pizza total **29 people**.

Hint #2:

29 people is **more** than the total number who bought pizza. What can that mean?

Answer: 4 people bought both kinds of pizza.

The **17 people** who bought plain cheese pizza and the **12 people** who bought pepperoni pizza total **29 people**. This is **more** than the **total** number who bought pizza. There were only **25 people** who bought pizza, so there must have been **29 − 25 = 4 people** who bought both kinds.

8. Alicia purchases athletic shorts and a jacket for **$26.00**. She then exchanged the shorts, which cost **$8.00**, for a different pair that cost **$10.50**.

What was Alicia's **final cost** for the shorts and jacket?

_____

Hint #1:

It is **not** necessary to know the cost of the jacket.

Hint #2:

You know the original cost. What is the **difference** after the exchange? Is this **more** or **less** than the original cost?

Answer: Alicia's final cost for the shorts and jacket is **$28.50**.

You know the original cost. The difference in price of the new shorts is **$2.50 more** than the original pair of shorts. Because this is more, **add** this cost to the original charge to get the final cost of **26.00 + 2.50 = $28.50**.

© Kaplan Publishing, Inc.

9. Samuel bought a computer, printer, and 2 software programs. The total charge was **$1,375.00**. If the computer cost **$825.00** and the printer cost **$200.00**, what is the cost of one software program if both software programs were the **same price**?

Hint #1:

First, **subtract** the cost of the computer and printer from the total charge.

Hint #2:

The remaining charge represents the cost of the 2 software programs.

Answer: The cost of one software program is **$175**.

First, subtract the cost of the computer. **$1,375 − $825 = $550**.
Now, subtract the cost of the printer to get **$550 − $200 = $350**.
This is the cost of the 2 software programs.
So one software program costs **$350 ÷ 2 = $175**.

10. Thea is planning to paint her bedroom. The bedroom consists of 4 rectangular walls. Two of the walls have dimensions of **6 feet by 8 feet**. The other two walls have dimensions of **8 feet by 10 feet**.

How many **square feet** of walls does she need to cover?

_____

Hint #1:

Square footage is calculated by finding the **area** of each wall.

Hint #2:

Find the **areas** of each wall, and then determine the **total square footage**.

Answer: Thea needs to cover **256 square feet**.

Square footage is calculated by finding the **area** of each wall. The walls are rectangular shaped, so the area is found by multiplying **base** times **height**.

Two of the walls have an area of **6 × 8 = 48 square feet**, and the other two walls have an area of **8 × 10 = 80 square feet**. Add these values to get the total square footage:

48 + 48 + 80 + 80 = 256 square feet.

11. Josh has set a goal to keep an **average** bowling score of at least **200**. His scores at yesterday's tournament were:

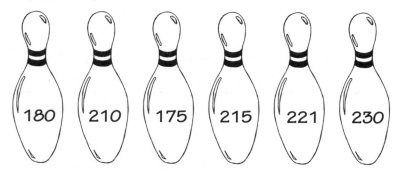

180 210 175 215 221 230

Did Josh reach his goal?

_____

Hint #1:

Find the **mean** of Josh's scores.

Hint #2:

Josh's goal is to have an average score of **at least 200**, but he can **exceed** his goal.

Answer: Yes, **Josh reached his goal.**

Find the **mean** of Josh's scores. Add all of his scores and divide by the number of scores: **180 + 210 + 175 + 215 + 221 + 230 = 1,231**.

There are **6 scores**, so divide **1,231 by 6 to get 205.17** (rounded to the nearest tenth). **205.17 > 200**, so Josh has **exceeded** his goal.

12. The **frequency table** below shows the number of weekend trips taken last summer by families in the neighborhood:

Number of Weekend Trips Taken Last Summer

Number of trips	Tally	Frequency
4	I I I I I	5
3	I I I I I I I I I I I I	12
2	I I I I	4
1	I I	2
0	I I I I	4

Look at the chart and answer the following questions:

How many families were surveyed?

_____

How many took 2 or more weekend trips?

_____

> **Hint #1:**
> Each family is accounted for **once** with a **tally mark**. The **frequency** is a **count** of the tallies.

> **Hint #2:**
> In this chart, "**2 or more**" means **2, 3,** or **4** weekend trips.

Answer: 27 total families were surveyed.
21 families took 2 or more weekend trips.
Each family in the frequency table is accounted for **once** with a **tally mark**. The frequency is just a count of the tallies. **Add** the frequency columns to get the number of families: **5 + 12 + 4 + 2 + 4 = 27 families**.

To find the number of families who took **2 or more** weekend trips, add the values from the frequency columns: **5 + 12 + 4 = 21 families**.

13. The cost to send a package is $0.39 for the **first ounce**, plus $0.24 for **each additional ounce**.

What is the price to send a **7-ounce package**?

_____

Hint #1:

Of the **7 ounces**, the **first ounce** is one price and the **other 6 ounces** are another price.

Hint #2:

The cost of the 6 additional ounces is **$0.24** per ounce. Use **multiplication** to find how much these 6 ounces costs.

Answer: It costs **$1.83** to send a 7-ounce package.

Of the 7 ounces, the first ounce is **$0.39** and the other 6 ounces are **$0.24 each**. Use **multiplication** to find this part of the cost.

The total cost is **0.39 + (6 × 0.24) = 0.39 + 1.44 = $1.83**.

14. You paid a total of **$8.80** for a **box of taffy** and **3 pounds of fudge**.

The taffy cost **$1.75**. What was the **unit price** per pound of fudge?

_____

Hint #1:

First, **subtract** the price of the taffy from the total. The remaining price is the price of 3 pounds of fudge.

Hint #2:

Unit price means the price for **one pound**.

Answer: The unit price per pound of fudge is **$2.35**.

First, subtract the price of the taffy: **$8.80 − $1.75 = $7.05**. The remaining price is the price of **3 pounds of fudge**. Unit price means the price for **one unit**, **here the unit is pound**.

Divide this remaining cost by 3: **7.05 ÷ 3 = $2.35**.

15. When Rachel returned from the amusement park, she had
$5.35 left in her pocket. She had spent **one-half** of her
original money on her admission ticket. Her other purchases
were **$5.25** for dinner, **$4.15** for lunch, and **$4.00** for games
of chance.

How much money did she start with?

_____

Hint #1:

Try working **backward** to find
the amount of money Rachel
had when she left for the
amusement park.

Hint #2:

First, add up all the expenses
that are given and be sure to
read the problem carefully.
Remember the amount of
money she had left in the end.

Answer: Rachel started with **$37.50**.

Try **working backward** to find the amount of money Rachel had to start
out with. The problem does **not** state the **price of admission**, so add up all
the other expenses to get **$5.25 + $4.15 + $4.00 = $13.40**.

Add in the **$5.35** that Rachel had remaining at the end of the day to
get **$13.40 + $5.35 = $18.75**. Half of her original money was spent on
admission; therefore, **$18.75** was the cost of admission to the amusement
park. Continue working backward to get her original amount of money:
$18.75 + $18.75 = $37.50.

16. At the All-Star game, **every 9th spectator** admitted received a **free baseball cap**. Every 15th **spectator** admitted received an **autographed baseball**.

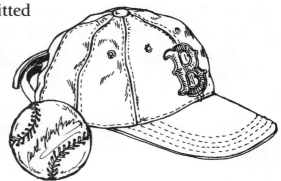

What is the number of the first spectator who received **both** a cap and an autographed baseball?

_____

Hint #1:

Try making an **organized list** to solve the problem.

Hint #2:

Think of the multiples of **9** and **15**.

Answer: The **45th customer** will receive both a cap and an autographed baseball.

Make an **organized list** of the spectators who will receive **each** of the free gifts. The **first number in common** will be the first customer to receive **both** gifts.

Baseball Cap: 9 18 27 36 ⟨45⟩ 54 63 72 81 90

Autographed Baseball: 15 30 ⟨45⟩ 60 75 90

17. An adult admission to the theater is $1.75 **more** than a child admission. The cost for **2 children** and **1 adult** is $19.00.

What are the prices of admission for an **adult** and a **child**?

_____

Hint #1:

First subtract out the difference between the adult cost and the child cost. Use this to find the **total** cost per child.

Hint #2:

Remember, an adult costs **$1.75 more** than a child.

Answer: The price of admission for a **child** is **$5.75**.

The price of admission for an **adult** is **$7.50**.

First subtract out the difference between the adult cost and the child cost. Since there is only one adult it is **19.00 − 1.75 = $17.25**. This is the cost for 3 children, so 1 child costs **17.25 ÷ 3 = $5.75**.

An adult costs **$1.75** more than a child, so the adult cost is **5.75 + 1.75 = $7.50**.

18. At the pancake house, you can choose from **buckwheat, buttermilk,** or **blueberry** pancakes. You can choose from **maple, strawberry,** or **cinnamon** syrup. Pancakes also come with a choice of **bacon** or **ham** on the side.

How many different meals are there to choose from, consisting of **one type of pancake, one type of syrup,** and **one type of meat?**

_____

Hint #1:

Try making an **organized list** to solve the problem.

Hint #2:

You can also use the **Fundamental Counting Principle**.

Answer: There are **18 different meals** to choose from.

Try making an organized list, like the one below, to solve the problem.

Meal Choices

BW – M – B	BU – M – B	BL – M – B
BW – M – H	BU – M – H	BL – M – H
BW – S – B	BU – S – B	BL – S – B
BW – S – H	BU – S – H	BL – S – H
BW – C – B	BU – C – B	BL – C – B
BW – C – H	BU – C – H	BL – C – H

Let **BW** stand for **buckwheat pancakes, BU** stand for **buttermilk pancakes,** and **BL** stand for **blueberry pancakes.**

Let **M** stand for **maple syrup, S** stand for **strawberry syrup,** and **C** stand for **cinnamon syrup.**

Let **B** stand for **bacon** and **H** stand for **ham.**

By counting up the number of meal choices in the list, you determine that there are **18 different meals** to choose from.

You could also use the **Fundamental Counting Principle** to solve this problem.

3 pancake choices × 3 syrup choices × 2 meat choices = 18 meals.

19. Bailey delivers newspapers in his neighborhood. He is saving to purchase a video game console for **$249.00**. Bailey delivers **40** papers each day, **7** days a week. He earns **$0.05** for every paper he delivers and gets **$20** each week in tips. He gets paid once a week, at the end of the week.

How many **weeks** will it take him to earn enough money for the video game console?

_____

Hint #1:

First determine how much Bailey earns **each day** for the 40 papers he delivers. Then figure out his weekly earnings.

Hint #2:

If you know Bailey's earnings per week, what **operation** will tell you how many weeks are needed for him to earn $249.00?

Answer: It will take Bailey **8 weeks** to earn enough money for the video game console.

First determine how much Bailey earns **each day** for the **40 papers** he delivers.

He earns **$0.05** for each of the **40 papers**, so that is **0.05 × 40 = $2.00 every day**, and **7 × 2 = $14.00** each week.

He earns **$20.00** in tips per week, so his weekly earnings are **$14 + $20 = $34.00**. At the end of each week, Bailey gets **$34.00**.

He wants to save up **$249.00**. **249 ÷ 34 = 7.32 weeks**, which means it will take him **8 weeks**, because he gets paid at the end of the week.

© Kaplan Publishing, Inc.

You're doing a great job so far!
Are you ready for a Challenge Activity?

Good luck!

Megan ordered a **30-inch submarine** sandwich for her birthday party. There will be **7 guests** and **herself** at the party. She will cut the sandwich into **equal** pieces.

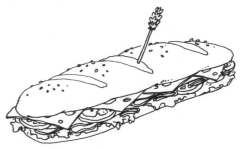

a) How **long** will each piece be?

b) How many cuts will she make in the submarine sandwich?

c) If the sandwich cost $28.00, what is the **cost per serving**?

Hint #1:

Use **division** to find the length of each piece and the cost per serving.

Hint #2:

It may be helpful to **draw a picture** in order to find out how many cuts Megan will make.

See answers on following page.

Answers to Challenge Activity:

a) Each piece will be **3.75 inches long**.

Megan is dividing the sandwich into **8 equal pieces**. Use **division** to find the size. **Divide** the total length of the submarine sandwich by the total number of people who will be attending the party: **30 ÷ 8 = 3.75 inches**.

b) Megan will make **7 cuts** in the submarine sandwich.

It may be helpful to **draw a picture**, like the one below, to find how many cuts Megan will make:

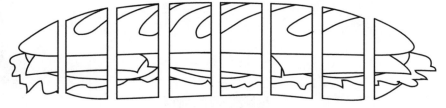

As you can see from the drawing, it takes **7 cuts** to make the 8 equal pieces that Megan needs.

c) **$3.50 per serving**

Use **division** to find the cost per serving. **Divide** the total sandwich cost by the **number of servings** that Megan needs to cut the sandwich into:

28 ÷ 8 = $3.50.

Let's take a quick test and see how much you've learned during this climb up *SCORE!* Mountain.

Good luck!

1. Kyle gives $\frac{1}{3}$ of his baseball cards to Tasha. With the remaining cards, he gives 10 cards to his little brother, Sam. He then gives $\frac{1}{2}$ of what is left to his friend Diego. He now has 15 cards remaining. How many cards did Kyle start out with?

_____

2. The truck rental company charges $50.00 per day, plus $0.25 for every mile driven. What is the charge for a 2-day rental, with a total mileage of 70 miles?

_____

3. Roxanna is making a quilt. Her quilt will have 6 squares of 8 inches each across the width. Between each square, and on the ends, there will be $1\frac{1}{2}$ inch wide strips. How wide will the quilt be?

_____

See answers on following page.

4. 50 people were at the lake.
20 people both swam and rented a boat.
38 people swam.
7 people did not swim or rent a boat.
How many people only rented a boat?

_____

5. At the local produce stand, corn sells for $2.25 for a half a dozen ears. Peaches are $1.49 per pound. Helena purchases 6 ears of corn and some peaches. If the bill was $5.23, how many pounds of peaches did she buy?

_____

Answers to test questions:

1. Kyle started out with **60 cards**.

Try working backwards to solve this problem. At the end of the problem, **Kyle** has **15 cards**. Since he had given **one-half** of what was left to **Diego**, Diego got **15 cards**, for a subtotal of **30 cards**.

Kyle had given his little brother, **Sam**, **10 cards**, so before he gave away those cards, **Kyle** had **40 cards**.

Tasha had received **one-third** of all of **Kyle's** cards. The **40 cards** make two-thirds of the original number. If **two-thirds** is **40**, then **one-third** is **20 cards**. The original number of cards is **40 + 20 = 60 cards**.

2. **$117.50**

There are key words in this problem that direct you to multiply: the words are "***per***" and "***for every***." There is a **$50.00** charge per day, and the truck was rented for **2 days**. This charge is **2 × 50 = $100.00**.

The additional charge is **$0.25** for every mile driven.

The mileage charge is **70 × 0.25 = $17.50**.

The **total** charge is **100 + 17.50 = $117.50**.

3. The quilt will be **58.5 inches wide**.

It would be helpful to make a picture, like the one below, to help you figure out the problem:

As you can see from the picture, there are **6 squares** and **7 strips**.

The total width will be **(6 × 8) + (7 × 1.5) = 48 + 10.5 = 58.5 inches wide**.

4. **5 people** only rented a boat.

Make a **Venn diagram**, like the one below, to help to solve this problem. Because 7 people **did not swim or boat**, the total number of people represented in the Venn diagram will be **43**:

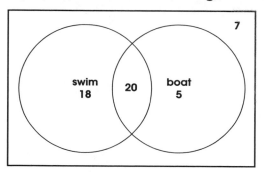

It's always easiest, when possible, to fill in the **overlapping area** of the Venn diagram **first**.

There were **20 people** that both swam and rented a boat. Because 38 total people swam, **38 − 20 = 18 people** that only swam.

Now **2** of the **3** areas of the diagram are labeled, and **18 + 20 = 38 people**. The total number of people represented in the circles is **43**, so **43 − 38 = 5 people that only rented a boat**.

5. Helena bought **2 pounds** of peaches.

Corn sells for **$2.25** for a **half dozen ears**.

A dozen is **12**, so a half dozen is **6 ears**, the amount that Helena bought. The total price was **$5.23**, so the peaches cost **5.23 − 2.25 = $2.98**.

Each pound of peaches costs **$1.49**, so **divide** to find the number of pounds of peaches Helena bought: **2.98 ÷ 1.49 = 2 pounds of peaches**.

Celebrate!

Let's have some fun and celebrate your success! You've earned it!

Now that you have tackled some math, how about learning a **new** skill?

Congratulations!
You've made it to the top of *SCORE!* Mountain.

You did a great job!

Think about something you've always wanted to learn about or try, and go for it!

Maybe you've always wanted to find out more about a certain sport, or sewing, writing poetry, or cooking.

Maybe you've always wanted to try sculpting or painting.

It's your choice!

Take some time to learn a fun new skill.

Take a class or join a club to meet other people who are interested in the same thing you are!

Maybe you can learn about the new skill by reading a book or doing research on the Internet.

Learning something new can be a fun, challenging, and rewarding experience!

Have fun learning your new skill and showing off your new abilities to your friends and family. They'll be impressed!

You should be really proud! I knew you could make it to the top!

Here are some helpful tools to guide you through each base camp!

Use these tools whenever you need a helping hand during your climb up *SCORE!* Mountain.

Place Value: Use the chart below to determine the place value of a given number:

Each X represents a single digit from

XXX,	XXX,	XXX,	XXX,	XXX
Trillions	Billions	Millions	Thousands	Units

Within each group of three XXX, the places are named hundreds, tens and one.

Order of Operations: To evaluate a numeric or algebraic expression, use the correct order of operations, which is:

Parentheses
Exponents
Multiplication and Division, left to right
Addition and Subtraction, left to right

Percent: Percent is a ratio that compares $\dfrac{part}{whole} = \dfrac{\%}{100}$

Proportion: A proportion is an equation that states that two ratios are equivalent. Proportions can be solved by cross-multiplication. If you are given a proportion such as $\frac{15}{100} = \frac{45}{n}$, cross multiply to get $15 \times n = 100 \times 45$. Then solve the equation for n, the variable term.

Perimeter: The perimeter of a figure is the sum of the lengths of the figure's sides. If the figure is on a coordinate plane, count the number of spaces to find each length.

Perimeter of a triangle: Perimeter = side + side + side

Perimeter of a rectangle or parallelogram:
Perimeter = 2 × length + 2 × width

Perimeter of a circle, which is called the **Circumference:**

Circumference = 2 × π × r, or **Circumference = π × d.** In these formulas, r represents the **radius** and d represents the **diameter. Diameter = 2 × radius.**

Similar Triangles: Similar triangles are triangles with the same shape, but different sizes. For similar triangles, the corresponding sides are in proportion.

Area: Area is the number of square units it takes to cover a figure. There are formulas to find the area of different figures:

Area of a parallelogram: Area = base × height

Area of a triangle: Area = $\frac{1}{2}$ base × height

Area of a circle: Area = π × r², where r represents the radius of the circle.

Area of a trapezoid: Area = $\frac{1}{2}$ (base$_1$ + base$_2$) × height, where **base$_1$** and **base$_2$** are the lengths of the parallel sides.

Area of an Irregular-Shaped Figure: To find the area of an irregular-shaped figure, break it up into more familiar figures. Then find the area of each piece and add the areas together.

Area of a Sector of a Circle: A sector of a circle is a piece of the circle, which is formed by two radii that form a central angle:

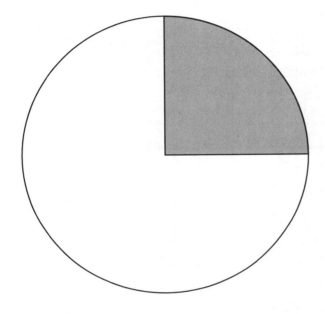

To find the area of the sector, set up a proportion reflecting $\frac{\text{part}}{\text{whole}} = \frac{\text{part}}{\text{whole}}$.

Compare the measure of the central angle to 360°, the measure of a circle. This ratio will equal the area of the sector, compared to the area of the whole circle.

Volume of a Rectangular Prism: The volume of a 3-dimensional solid is the number of cubic units it takes to fill the solid. The volume of the prism is found by using the formula:

Volume = length × width × height.

Coordinate Geometry: Points and figures can lie on a coordinate plane as shown below:

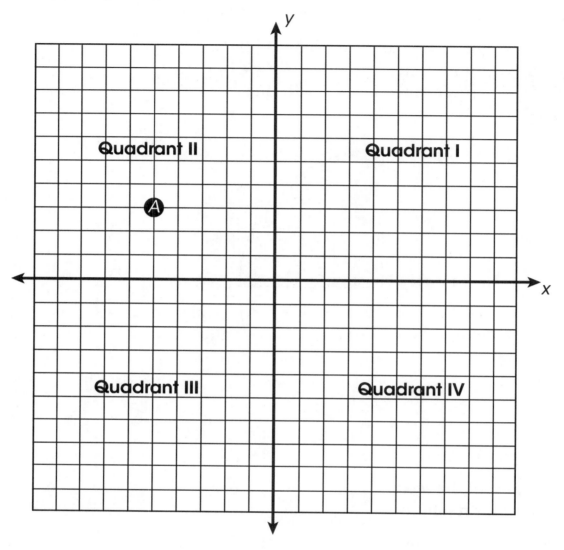

Notice that each quarter, or quadrant, is named with Roman numerals, in a counterclockwise direction. Points on a coordinate plane are located by using the form *(x,y)*.

The *x*-coordinate is the number of spaces to the left or right of the origin.

The *y*-coordinate is the number of spaces above or below the origin. If the point is to the **left** of the origin, the *x*-coordinate is **negative**, otherwise, the point is **positive** (to the right of the origin or at zero).

For the y-coordinate, if the point is **above** the origin, the y-coordinate is **positive**, otherwise it is negative (below the origin or at zero).

Point A in the figure above has coordinates **(-5,3)**.

Statistical Measures: There are four main measures used to describe a set of data:

Mean is the average value of the data set. To find the mean, find the sum of the list of data and divide by the total number of addends.

Median is the middle value in a data set. To find the median, sort the data from smallest to largest and then find the middle value. If there is an even amount of data, take the average of the middle two values.

Mode is the data value that occurs most often. To find the mode, you can make a tally chart and find the value that has the most tallies. There can be one mode, no mode, or several modes.

Range is the difference between the highest and lowest values in the data set. To calculate the range, subtract:
Range = highest − lowest.

Probability: The probability of an event happening is:
$$P(\text{event}) = \frac{\text{the number of ways the event can happen}}{\text{the total number of events}}.$$
The probability of one event and then another event is found by multiplying the probabilities together.

Problem-Solving Strategies: There are many different problem-solving strategies that can be used to solve problems. Here are some for you to consider when attempting to solve a problem:

1. Look for a pattern
2. Make an organized list
3. Make a table
4. Choose an operation
5. Draw a picture or diagram

6. Use estimation to find a reasonable answer
7. Work backward
8. Guess and check
9. Find the unit rate
10. Use a formula

Customary Measures:

Length
1 foot = 12 inches
1 yard = 3 feet

Weight
1 pound = 16 ounces

Capacity
1 cup = 8 fluid ounces
1 pint = 2 cups
1 quart = 2 pints

Length
1 foot = 12 inches
1 yard = 3 feet

Weight
1 pound = 16 ounces

Capacity
1 cup = 8 fluid ounces
1 pint = 2 cups
1 quart = 2 pints

You can do it!

Use these blank pages to work out the questions in your *SCORE! Mountain Challenge Workbook.*

You can do it!

You can do it!

You can do it!

You can do it!

You can do it!

You can do it!

You can do it!

You can do it!

You can do it!

You can do it!

You can do it!

You can do it!

You can do it!

You can do it!

You can do it!

You can do it!

You can do it!

You can do it!

ACADEMIC PROGRESS • CONFIDENCE • GOAL SETTING • MOTIVATION

Visit a center and see the *SCORE!* DIFFERENCE!

Research shows that when children study because they enjoy it, learning is deeper and lasts longer.

Fun learning. Seriously. Since 1992, *SCORE!* has helped more than 350,000 children, ages 4-14, develop a love of learning as they reach their academic potential in math, reading, writing and more. Step through our doors and you'll see the *SCORE!* difference: kids love to learn in our unique, vibrant environment.

While we know learning should be an enjoyable activity, we take a serious approach to academic progress. Our proven curriculum and individualized attention will help your child catch up, keep up or get ahead.

....

MENTION THIS AD AND RECEIVE A FREE ACADEMIC CONSULTATION!

....

1-800-49SCORE | scorelearning.com

SCORE! is a part of Kaplan, one of the world's leading providers of lifelong education. KAPLAN